LIVING OUTSIDE MENTAL ILLNESS

QUALITATIVE STUDIES IN PSYCHOLOGY

This series showcases the power and possibility of qualitative work in psychology. Books feature detailed and vivid accounts of qualitative psychology research using a variety of methods, including participant observation and fieldwork, discursive and textual analyses, and critical cultural history. They probe vital issues of theory, implementation, interpretation, representation, and ethics that qualitative workers confront. The series mission is to enlarge and refine the repertoire of qualitative approaches to psychology.

GENERAL EDITORS
Michelle Fine and Jeanne Marecek

Everyday Courage: The Lives and Stories of Urban Teenagers
Niobe Way

Negotiating Consent in Psychotherapy
Patrick O'Neill

Flirting with Danger: Young Women's Reflections on Sexuality
and Domination
Lynn M. Phillips

Voted Out: The Psychological Consequences of Anti-Gay Politics
Glenda M. Russell

Inner City Kids: Adolescents Confront Life and Violence
in an Urban Community
Alice McIntyre

From Subjects to Subjectivities: A Handbook of Interpretive and
Participatory Methods
Edited by Deborah L. Tolman and Mary Brydon-Miller

Growing Up Girl: Psychosocial Explorations of Gender and Class
Valerie Walkerdine, Helen Lucey, and June Melody

Voicing Chicana Feminisms: Young Women Speak Out on
Sexuality and Identity
Aída Hurtado

Situating Sadness: Women and Depression in Social Context
Edited by Janet M. Stoppard and Linda M. McMullen

Living Outside Mental Illness: Qualitative Studies of Recovery
in Schizophrenia
Larry Davidson

LIVING OUTSIDE MENTAL ILLNESS

Qualitative Studies of Recovery in Schizophrenia

LARRY DAVIDSON

Foreword by John S. Strauss

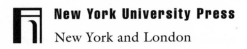

New York University Press

New York and London

NEW YORK UNIVERSITY PRESS
New York and London

Library of Congress Cataloging-in-Publication Data
Davidson, Larry.
Living outside mental illness : qualitative studies of recovery in
schizophrenia / Larry Davidson.
p.   cm. — (Qualitative studies in psychology)
Includes bibliographical references and index.
ISBN 0-8147-1942-2 (alk. paper)
ISBN 0-8147-1943-0 (pbk. : alk. paper)
1. Schizophrenia. 2. Qualitative research. 3. Phenomenology.
I. Title. II. Series.
RC514.D276 2003
616.89'82—dc21   2003007022

New York University Press books are printed on acid-free paper,
and their binding materials are chosen for strength and durability.

Manufactured in the United States of America

10 9 8 7 6 5 4 3 2

■   ■   ■   ■   ■   ■   ■   ■   ■

*To all those people who had
the generosity of spirit to
share their lives with us;
and to my wife, Maryanne,
whose love provides the
ground for me to stand on.*

Contents

■   ■   ■   ■

Foreword

John S. Strauss, M.D.
Professor Emeritus of Psychiatry, Yale University

Let's say you were living with a large group who, a couple of generations earlier, had made a very difficult journey west across a huge plain. They had had to develop from nothing the means of making that journey. Now, all of you are there at the edge of the mountains where they had settled. Some have made journeys into the mountain passes but never very far. You, on the other hand, want to go farther. But you have to develop means for crossing huge streams, for climbing steep rock faces, and you have gotten farther than anyone ever had. Now you have returned and are trying to describe what you had discovered to the people from the plain. You are surprised and saddened by many of the responses they make.

"You shouldn't have wasted your time. The real, the serious world is over here."

"You were just playing, instead of doing something really useful."

"We've seen mountains before. We see them every day. What could you be thinking? Just look there."

You try to explain that farther on it's different, that they really haven't understood that. They haven't seen the massive waterfalls, the huge rock slides, the way the trees grow up that protect the mountainsides. And there may be a huge ocean just farther west.

"But we see trees. See there is some water coming over those rocks. I don't know why you spent all that effort developing rafts, we have these fantastic plows. Nothing else is necessary. And I'll bet you didn't know, there were some academic types who tried to get into those mountains long before you. All they came back with was a bunch of long words and fancy theories. Nothing of any real use."

That's a bit how it is with pretty much anything new, for example, trying to understand from another perspective mental illness, psychiatric disorder, disability, whatever you want to call it. Try to find or develop a perspective from another point of view, such as that of the person struggling with the problems, from the point of view of the real detailed experiences of those who are having those problems, and all those same types of responses are very common:

> We know it already. We do it already. That's the art, but it has nothing to do with the science, the really serious important thing.

And mention phenomenology, and the history of that often arcane field makes real communication even more difficult.

Say you wanted to write a book to show people what you are finding, to show how important a contribution the perspective makes to understanding, studying, and working with mental illness and the people who experience it. What would you do to write such a book? To write a book where people might not stop reading just because they thought they "knew it already" or that it was cute or art but not real science, or that they stopped after one chapter thinking "Oh that's interesting. Now I understand all I need to know." How would you write such a book? This is such a book.

Acknowledgments

If writing this book has been gratifying, it is even more gratifying to be able to thank all those people without whom it would not have come to exist. First and foremost, of course, are the hundred plus people who have had first-hand experience of schizophrenia and who have been our teachers. Their courage and resilience in the face of adversity provide us with a constant source of inspiration and instill in us the resolve to ensure that their voices are heard above the din of stigma and indifference. We hope that we have made it possible for their stories, above all else, to be told and understood and for them to find a more welcoming reception when they dare to step outside of the shadow cast by their illness.

Second, we thank our students, from whom we continue to learn. They provide the reasons, and the rewards, for passing down the methods described in this book from one generation to the next. They also have collected a good deal of the data used in writing this book. Karl Haglund, Stacey Lambert, Peter Smith, Marge Allende, Joyce Shea, and Connie Nickou, in particular, have made valuable contributions to this book without taking, or getting, credit. We appreciate their energy, their openness, and their empathic sensitivity in conducting fine interviews. What we have been able to offer them they have given back in droves.

And then there are our colleagues, past and present. Most continue to be part of our program and thus share the byline, albeit in anonymity. David Stayner has been the stalwart and gifted copilot for most of the excursions described in what follows, always up for the journey. Richard Weingarten, Tom Styron, Jaak Rakfeldt, Michael Hoge, Ezra Griffith, and Will Sledge all have been collaborators on specific studies conducted over the last 12 years. Matt Chinman, Janis Tondora, Luis Añez, and Michael Rowe have also made significant contributions, if from a bit more of a distance. Dave Sells, Golan Shahar, and my father, Bernard Davidson, have read drafts of the manuscript and made valuable suggestions throughout. Martha Staeheli has not only read and reread drafts of the manuscript, ensuring our accurate use of such terms as *centrifugal* (as opposed, that is, to *centripetal*) but also has provided valuable suggestions, ongoing feedback, and a much needed counterbalance to the excesses of abstraction of which phenomenological philosophy is often guilty. And we thank our editors, who made useful and encouraging comments while waiting patiently for us to finish.

Finally, in a paragraph all his own, we thank John Strauss, my mentor and good friend, and the spiritual force behind our work and our program. John taught me both how to be rigorous and how to discard rigor when it gets in the way of spontaneity and connection. He showed all of us how "Wow!" can at times, and when said with sincere admiration, be a most effective way to encourage interview participants to continue on with their story, and how it is okay, even constructive, to tear up when they are relating particularly sad or tragic parts of their lives. Mostly, John has encouraged this work from the start and consistently throughout, believing firmly in its importance even more than we did. Like the caring person who believed in one of our participants, even when he no longer believed in himself, the steadfast conviction of a world-renowned scientist—who also happens to have a surprising amount of genuine humility—has gotten us through the difficult times of rejections, failed grant submissions, critical reviewers, and departmental skeptics. We owe much to the father of recovery and offer this book as a token of our appreciation.

■ ■ ■ ■ ■ ■ ■ ■ ■

Introduction

From a moral-practical standpoint, I am treating a human being as a
mere thing if I do not take him [*sic*] as a person. . . . Likewise, I am not
treating a human being as a subject of rights if I do not take him [*sic*] as
a member of a community founded on law, to which we both belong.
—Edmund Husserl, *Ideas II*

IF YOU HAVE PICKED UP THIS BOOK long enough to glance at this
page—and not because it has been assigned to you as required reading by
one of our friends—then it is most likely because you have an interest either in qualitative research or in schizophrenia. There may be a few of you
who approach this book with interests in both topics; if so, welcome to an
inviting, cozy, circle of your peers. It has been our experience that the area
of overlap between these two interests, that is, qualitative psychological research and serious mental illness, is relatively small and only sparsely inhabited by a few rare, but resilient, birds. Why this is the case may become
clear as we proceed; *that* this is the case, however, we have no doubt. And
thus one of the motivations for writing this book: we are seeking companionship. Consider this book a mating call.

There are a number of compelling reasons to approach the study of
schizophrenia with qualitative methods. We intend to enumerate these

below. There also are compelling reasons to view this devastating illness as providing a particularly good and timely opportunity to illustrate the unique contributions of a phenomenological approach to qualitative research in psychology. As we recognize that these topics are not linked intuitively in the minds of most readers, however, we would like to take a few pages before embarking on a qualitative exploration of life inside and outside of psychosis to make our case. For those with interests in qualitative research, we will begin by explaining why we have chosen schizophrenia as an area for qualitative study. For those with interests in schizophrenia, we next will explain why we have chosen a phenomenological approach for conducting qualitative studies of this phenomenon. Throughout, we will attempt to make technical philosophical or psychiatric terminology understandable for readers with little formal training in either discipline, so that someone being courageous enough to explore new territory will not lose his or her way among the brambles of professional jargon. Undoubtedly, we will not succeed fully in this effort.

As a heuristic, though, we are writing this book with our respective mothers looking over our shoulders. The interactive, somewhat informal, style that results may seem at first unusual for an academic text, but there are precedents. Plato, for example, had Socrates looking over his shoulder and acting as his interlocutor, as Socrates apparently had a daemon serving the same purpose for him. At some of his more understandable moments, Edmund Husserl, the founder of phenomenology about whom you will read later in this introduction, used the rhetorical strategy of raising questions that he expected would be on the minds of his readers, as did his contemporary Sigmund Freud. Appreciative of the effort we are making to render this text accessible to those who are not yet experts in the qualitative study of schizophrenia, and of the limited patience you, the reader, may have for this task, however, we must ask for your forbearance in advance. As suggested in the Foreword by John Strauss, we have found the path to qualitative findings about the nature of psychosis to entail a rocky and thorny climb through unfamiliar terrain. Rather than bringing you to the summit via helicopter—a trip that might take only a few pages—we have chosen to lead you along this same path. While it admittedly will take us longer to get there, we hope that by taking you along with us on this slow but steady journey you will pick up some of the tools needed to embark on future explorations of your own.

In order to prepare readers for this trek who may be less conversant with either schizophrenia or qualitative research, we offer the following, brief overview.

Schizophrenia is widely considered to be the most severe and disabling of the mental illnesses. It is characterized both by the more classic, so-called positive symptoms of auditory hallucinations (i.e., hearing voices), delusions (i.e., false but stubbornly held beliefs), and formal thought disorder (i.e., not making sense when you talk) and by the so-called negative symptoms of withdrawal, isolation, apathy, and a lack of energy, pleasure, or interest. Affecting one out of every one hundred people, schizophrenia is estimated to account for $66 billion annually in emergency room and criminal justice contacts and $273 billion annually in lost productivity in the United States alone. These figures do not include the billions of dollars spent on direct health care costs, not to mention the intangible amount of human suffering experienced by people who have the illness and their loved ones.

The term *phenomenology* has at least three different uses in current practice. Although furthest removed from the original meaning of the term, the definition of phenomenology perhaps most familiar to clinicians and clinical researchers is the form that allows for identification, categorization, and comparison of psychiatric conditions across people based on shared and readily observable features such as specific symptoms (e.g., hearing voices) and signs (e.g., loss of appetite) (Andreasen and Flaum, 1991). This form of phenomenology involves objective description of the signs and symptoms of illness utilized, for example, in the Third Edition of the *Diagnostic and Statistical Manual of Mental Disorders* published by the American Psychiatric Association (1980).

In its original meaning, phenomenology had referred both to an empirical, qualitative methodology for research in the social sciences and to the school of philosophical thought from which these methods were derived. As an empirical, qualitative method, phenomenology can be considered on a par with hermeneutics, grounded theory, and ethnography, as one approach among many that share an underlying theoretical framework. From both historical and philosophical points of view, however, it also could be argued that this underlying theoretical framework is itself derived from phenomenological philosophy. This is the case, we suggest, not only for empirical phenomenological methods but also for other qualitative approaches, even if this heritage is not always acknowledged.

The school of philosophical phenomenology was founded by the German mathematician and philosopher, Edmund Husserl, in the early part of the twentieth century. Its original meaning from the Greek can be defined as the study ("logos") of how things appear ("phainomena") in experience. Following Descartes and Kant, the basic tenet of Husserl's work was that knowledge is limited to what can be ascertained from how things appear to us in experience, given that our only access to objects, and to the world at large, is through experience itself. Restricting our attention therefore to the realm of experience, we develop our science based on what can be learned about the structures and components of experience itself—as opposed, that is, to what can be learned about the objects *of* experience.

Given that qualitative research similarly focuses on the structures and components of human experience, we argue in the chapters that follow that philosophical phenomenology provides a particularly appropriate and useful theoretical framework for qualitative research in psychology. We do so in the context of applying empirical phenomenological methods to studies of the lives of people with schizophrenia, describing both processes of illness and of improvement. We hope that this exercise will illustrate the value of employing qualitative research methods in psychology—and thus inspire others to embark on similar explorations of their own—while simultaneously demonstrating the value of exploring the role of the person in recovery from schizophrenia.

Why Phenomenology of *Schizophrenia*?

Perhaps there are also lunatic rejecters of the laws of thought: these will certainly also have to count as men [*sic*].

—Edmund Husserl (1970b, p. 158)

The decade between 1980 and 1990 was designated by the National Institute of Mental Health (NIMH) as the "Decade of the Brain." This designation was intended to capture the paradigm shift that was occurring in psychiatry at the time; a shift from what had been largely a psychological model of mental illness as caused by faulty parenting and other early childhood experiences to a neurobiological model that viewed mental illnesses as "brain diseases" (Torrey and Hafner, 1983). This shift, captured perhaps most eloquently in Nancy Andreasen's 1984 book aptly entitled *The Broken Brain*, promised to usher in a new, more enlightened, and more humane era in the treatment of mental illnesses and the people and families affected by them. Although this certainly was not the first time such promises had been made in the brief history of American psychiatry, the NIMH-sponsored shift to neurobiology—this particular version of the medicalization of mental illness—brought with it aspirations for substantive and long-term reforms of mental healthcare and of the ways in which people with mental illness are viewed by the broader culture.

To a large degree, we have now begun to see the fruits of these efforts. Recasting mental illness as a neurobiological brain disease potentially destigmatizes this most stigmatized of conditions and replaces a range of disorders that had been blamed on a variety of personal and familial sins and shortcomings for hundreds, if not thousands, of years by so-called no-fault diseases. This shift has been received with tremendous relief by the families of people afflicted with mental illness, as they are beginning to feel absolved of myriad ways in which they were blamed for contributing to their adult child's distress. Similarly, there is a growing sense that the person with the disorder need no longer be considered any more at fault for having a brain disease than if he or she had an endocrine or respiratory disorder.

As a result of this shift, a more hopeful and compassionate view of mental illness is being promoted within the broader community; a view reflected in recent legislative attempts, for example, to end discrimination in mental health coverage (for which arbitrary and overly restrictive caps on care exist in order to save money). If mental illnesses are illnesses like any other, then they should be treated as such by the insurance industry and other providers of healthcare coverage, bringing coverage for mental health into parity with the coverage offered for other medical disorders.

In addition to parity legislation, the promise of the shift to neurobiology is captured in the unprecedented 1999 *Mental Health: A Report of the Surgeon General* (U.S. Surgeon General, 1999). This report, highly recommended to anyone with further interests in mental illness per se, is unparalleled in its depiction of mental illness as a disease that affects *all of us,* either directly or indirectly, but for which most of us will neither seek nor receive appropriate care due to our misguided notions that mental illness happens only to *them* (whoever *they* are; cf. Davidson, 2001). The Surgeon General's basic message conveys the progress made during the Decade of the Brain: Mental illnesses are diseases like any other. If you think you or someone you love may be suffering from one, seek help from qualified professionals and have hope. Treatment is available and treatment works (U.S. Surgeon General, 1999).

This highly condensed history of contemporary psychiatry was perhaps a long way around to the question: Why conduct qualitative psychological research on schizophrenia, the most severe and debilitating form of mental illness? If we now know that schizophrenia, perhaps more than any other mental illness, is a neurobiological brain disease, of what interest could it be to psychologists looking to use meaning-oriented, narrative research methods? What could possibly be learned about a brain disease from the people who have it? We know, for example, that a common trait of many neurological diseases is "anosognosia," meaning a lack of awareness of one's own impairments. This trait has long been considered characteristic of schizophrenia as well (cf., e.g., Amador, 2000). Isn't a qualitative approach barking up the wrong tree? Wouldn't more be learned from psychology by conducting assessments to identify deficits in neurocognitive functioning? What light can people with schizophrenia shed on the nature of their disease or on its possible cure?

There certainly is much to be gained from neurocognitive assessments in schizophrenia. In fact, this approach represents an area of particular promise and growth not only in identifying deficits but also in developing promising strategies for their remediation (e.g., Bell et al., 2001; Green et al., 1992; Green, 1993; Jaeger and Douglas, 1992; Liberman and Green, 1992; Spring and Ravin, 1992). There also is much to be gained from qualitative research in schizophrenia, however, a lesson we hope to demonstrate in the remainder of this volume. What there is to be gained can be conceptualized broadly in two categories: (1) what can be learned about schizophrenia per se, and (2) what can be learned about the use of qualitative methods in psychology. We would like to suggest approaching the first question through the second. In other words, what we have to learn about schizophrenia—despite its putative nature as a brain disease—will become clear as we explore what studying schizophrenia tells us about qualitative psychological research.

This approach was suggested by an unexpected reaction to our first conference presentation of the findings of our first qualitative study of schizophrenia. The audience for the presentation was made up almost entirely of qualitative researchers affiliated with the phenomenological tradition, many of whom were also clinical psychologists. The presentation, on processes of recovery in schizophrenia, involved a description of ways in which people appear to pace themselves in their recovery efforts, determining how much energy and confidence they have available to take risks and try new things in relation both to managing their illness and to more general life tasks. This component of recovery we had come to refer to as "taking stock of the self" and to illustrate the point we had quoted from a qualitative interview with a young woman who we had called "Betty." Betty had described this process as follows:

> I have a good will. It just takes the right amount, the um, the kitchen has to be right, so to speak, before I . . . do the endeavors. The feeling . . . has to be right. [Like] everything has to be right before you can make a cake. . . . If you don't feel like buying the flour for six months . . . then you don't feel like it. Then you get your flour, and then you notice you don't have enough cinnamon, so you wait a while." (Davidson and Strauss, 1992)

Betty was similarly articulate in describing other aspects of the recovery process, as were other participants in this study. During the break following this presentation, an esteemed professor approached with the words: "That was great. I didn't know you could do that, talk with people who had schizophrenia. I would have thought that either they would be too disorganized to respond to an interview or, if they did respond, then what they would have told you wouldn't have made any sense. But those people didn't have any difficulties making sense. They were even eloquent."

What this story suggests is that schizophrenia—regardless of its causes, courses, or consequences—provides a good opportunity for challenging, and thereby demonstrating, the validity of qualitative research. There are many criticisms of qualitative research, but most of the substantial criticisms can be brought together in this one case. For example, some have complained that qualitative research only represents the perspective of articulate, intelligent, "well-socialized" (i.e., middle class?) adults and ignores or denies the experiences of more marginal, less vocal, groups. This is a parallel to the "YAVIS" argument leveled against much of psychotherapy research; that is, that psychotherapy was designed for, and only is effective for, young, attractive, verbal, intelligent, successful people (Schofield, 1964). A more basic criticism is that people will only tell you what they think you want to hear or will distort their experiences in order to make themselves "look good," as is well documented in impression management literature. Finally, an even more basic criticism underlying both of these is that people simply are not reliable or valid sources of information, not only about themselves but also about reality in general. Our experiences constitute such a tiny slice of the real, and even within that tiny slice the amount of information of which we may be consciously aware at any given time is an even tinier slice (cf. Dennett, 1991). Why use this miniscule window as a vehicle of entrée into the real? Isn't it a basic premise of science that we will gain more reliable and valid—and thereby credible—access to reality to the degree that we can minimize the contaminating role of subjectivity?

What better response to these criticisms could there be but to demonstrate the utility of qualitative research based on the self-reported descriptions of the experiences of people with schizophrenia? Psychosis continues to be understood, both by the lay public and by the mental health field at large, as involving a loss of touch with reality. Hallucinations, for example, are defined precisely as seeing or hearing things *that are not there,* delusions as believing things *that are not true,* etc. According to French philosopher and political historian, Michel Foucault, psychosis has been viewed in this way as representing the *not real* at least since the seventeenth century, when it was first conceptualized as a disease. Prior to the seventeenth century, "madness" was taken to represent the intrusions of an *alternative* reality, a window onto the spiritual or demonic realms. The reconceptualization of madness as a mental *illness* came at a time when interest in alternative realities was waning and when medical science was in the process of being born (Foucault, 1965).

Through the lens of the new clinical science, madness came to be redefined as "nothing more than a disease" (Foucault, 1965, p. 198). Psychosis was perceived to stand in such stark contrast to reality that, if it could no longer represent an alternative reality, it could represent only a *lack* of reality. What better way, then, to challenge the legitimacy of qualitative research than to take as our subject matter the self-reports of those who appear to have lost all touch with reality and who, in addition, typically stand in silence on the margins of society? If there still are useful things to learn—and we contend there are many—from conducting qualitative research with people presumed to be less articulate, less verbal, and less socialized than almost any other adults, then how much more robust qualitative research must be than its critics allege? For this reason alone, we would suggest that schizophrenia provides a particularly appealing and potentially quite useful area for qualitative research in psychology.

For the purpose of demonstrating the breadth and utility of qualitative research in psychology, it does not really matter, of course, whether or not these presumptions about schizophrenia are true. If these presumptions about schizophrenia are wrong—which we contend, for the most part, they are—then about whom, about what other group of people somewhat arbitrarily lumped together, would they be more true? Our opening quote for this section from Husserl, namely, that even "lunatics" still have to be considered people, suggests that such presumptions *may* not be true of anyone. So it is also, and more important, for this reason that we view schizophrenia as a particularly timely and valuable area of focus for qualitative research.

In order to elucidate this point further, we need to return to our brief history of contemporary psychiatry and ask again what we can learn about this brain disease from qualitative inquiry. For concurrent with the ascendancy of a neurobiological model of schizophrenia was the development of another, more descriptive, line of research that poses quite different questions about the nature of this disorder and its treatment. This line of research has challenged the legitimacy of the same presumptions about schizophrenia enumerated above and has helped to paint a more complicated and nuanced, but therefore also more accurate, picture of this multidimensional disorder. Finally, this same line of research has suggested that it is precisely the kind of information that can be generated through qualitative research that is needed to enable the field to take the next significant step or two forward in increasing our understanding, and enhancing our treatment, of schizophrenia.

For the most part, neurobiological models of schizophrenia, such as that found in Andreasen's 1984 book *The Broken Brain,* are based on

Emile Kraepelin's ([1904] 1987) original formulation of "*dementia prae-cox*" at the close of the nineteenth century. Kraepelin used this concept of "premature dementia" to distinguish schizophrenia from manic-depression; the difference between these two major forms of psychosis is in their course and outcome. While manic-depression was considered an episodic, cyclical disorder responsible for a moderate degree of impairment alternating with periods of intact functioning, schizophrenia was characterized by a chronic, unremitting course leading to progressive deterioration and early death. To the degree that there is any scientific basis to the presumptions about people with schizophrenia described above, it will be found in this legacy dating back to Kraepelin. A legacy based entirely on clinical observations of inpatients during the era of long-term institutional care, this view of schizophrenia considered it akin to a death sentence, condemning the person to a life of increasing incoherence, emptiness, and isolation, in which he or she inevitably would withdraw into his or her own world, cutting off all ties to family, friends, and constructive membership in society until death would come to put the tortured soul to rest.

Prior to the Decade of the Brain, however, evidence already had begun to mount from around the world suggesting that this view of schizophrenia was too simplistic, too pessimistic, and that—even if it had been somewhat accurate during the era of long-term institutional care—it no longer reflected the lives of people living outside of hospitals. Formally launched in 1967—only thirteen years after passage of the legislation launching deinstitutionalization in the United States—the International Pilot Study of Schizophrenia was initiated by the World Health Organization in 30 sites and 19 countries across the world (WHO, 1973). For this international study, investigators in each site conducted follow-along, longitudinal assessments of cohorts of people diagnosed with schizophrenia, using the same diagnostic criteria and research instruments in order to document the core characteristics, course, and outcome of the illness and to compare these findings across cultures (WHO, 1973).

As the findings from this international study began to appear, both schizophrenia experts and experienced clinicians were surprised to learn that schizophrenia was far from a death sentence. In fact, John Strauss, the lead American investigator for the WHO study and one of the first to begin to describe the longitudinal course of the disorder, reports that the first few papers he wrote with Will Carpenter, his close collaborator at the NIMH, were initially rejected by the field's top journals because reviewers insisted that their data simply could not be true. Those papers, eventually published in the early 1970s (in one of the field's leading journals after all), documented that already over a two-year period there was a wide discrepancy in course and outcome for people diagnosed with presumably the same disorder. Strauss and Carpenter's early papers (e.g., 1974, 1977) described a multidimensional disorder with both an unpredictable course and a far from certain outcome. Although some people did show a decline in functioning during this two-year period, many others showed improvements in functioning, while others remained relatively the same. In addition, declines or improvements in one area of functioning (e.g., employment) did not predict similar changes in other areas of functioning (e.g., social relationships), with each domain being relatively distinct and independent, even in relation to classic psychotic symptoms such as hallucinations and delusions (Strauss and Carpenter, 1977).

This groundbreaking line of research went so far as to suggest that even these symptoms—thought at the time to be characteristic of schizophrenia and of schizophrenia only—were actually on a continuum of functioning with so-called normal experiences and behavior, being differentiated only by a matter of degree (Strauss, 1969). In other words, some people have hallucinations who do not have schizophrenia, some people have schizophrenia without having hallucinations, and some people with schizophrenia go from having hallucinations to not having hallucinations and back again (or not) over time. Whether a particular experience is an accurate perception, an inaccurate perception, a distorted perception, a visual illusion, or a hallucination is simply a matter of degree: a quantitative, rather than qualitative, difference. With these findings, the line dividing sanity from insanity, normality from madness, became permeable. Schizophrenia no longer represented a lack of, or an alternative to, reality, becoming instead merely one state *of* reality; an extreme state perhaps, but a state in and out of which people can move over time, no longer trapped for the remainder of their lives in their own, separate world.

As we will see in chapter 1, Strauss and Carpenter's early work in the United States was soon replicated and extended by other investigators involved in the WHO International Pilot Study. These early findings on the short-term (2- and 5-year) course of symptoms and distinct domains of functioning also were extended to the longer-term (e.g., 11- and eventually 32-year) course and outcome of the illness as a whole. In stark contrast to the Kraepelinian legacy, these rigorous, large-sample, longitudinal studies at first suggested, and later confirmed, that there is a broad heterogeneity of course and outcome in schizophrenia (Carpenter and Kirkpatrick, 1988; Harding, Zubin, and Strauss, 1987). Rather than following a necessarily downward and deteriorating course leading inevitably to a poor outcome, many people with schizophrenia are able to recover to a significant degree over time, some recovering fully.

As a result of this research, Kraepelin's pessimistic and one-dimensional model of schizophrenia has since been replaced by more sophisticated and complex models that look to a dynamic interplay of genetic, biological, neurocognitive, psychological, and social factors to understand differences in onset, course, and outcome. With the chance of at least partial recovery hovering around 50 percent, people with schizophrenia can no longer be considered lost to the disorder, to their family and friends, or to the broader community.

These findings have important implications for research, clinical practice, and public policy, as well as for theoretical models of the disorder. For example, the presumptive loss of self and of touch with reality in schizophrenia, in which the individual becomes subsumed by the illness and withdraws into an "empty shell" of his or her former self (Andreasen, 1984), was consistent with certain aspects of institutional life. Once diagnosed and hospitalized, people often lost the opportunity, and eventually the ability, to make decisions and to speak and act on their own behalf. Having most of their day-to-day lives structured and dictated by others, people with schizophrenia—even when no longer in the hospital—became objects of the ministrations, deliberations, and actions (or neglect) of others, whether these others were family members, mental health providers, clinical investigators, or public policymakers. Such a situation may become necessary if the illness takes over the entirety of the person. It becomes problematic, however, as soon as there is a person remaining who, despite the disorder, wishes to act, speak, or make decisions on his or her own behalf. Recognition of the significantly enhanced possibilities of recovery, along with the reemergence of the person from behind the disorder, has made it necessary to make room within models of disorder, research, clinical practice, and public policy for this person to play an active and meaningful role.

The need for space within models of schizophrenia for the person to assume a role in coping with, compensating for, and perhaps recovering from the disorder has coincided with other pressures being exerted on psychiatry to be more respectful of people with mental illness. For example, it has now been over twenty years since the American Psychiatric Association (1980) changed the terminology in its *Diagnostic and Statistical Manual of Mental Disorders* from "schizophrenic" to "person with schizophrenia." From the National Alliance of the Mentally Ill, the NIMH, and the Surgeon General's attempts to destigmatize mental illness, to the growing Mental Health Consumer/Survivor Movement (about which we will have more to say in chapter 1), to the landmark legislation of the Americans with Disabilities Act of 1990 that prohibited discrimination against people with psychiatric disabilities in employment, education, and public affairs, public policy and attitudes have been slowly shifting over that time to a recognition of the common humanity—the personhood—that remains at the core of those with severe mental illnesses. For these political shifts to find their way into the scientific domain, approaches to research will have to be developed that go beyond the neurobiological reductionism of the "broken brain" to an appreciation, and investigation, of the role of the person in attempting to manage the disorder.

This conclusion was reinforced in a special issue of the NIMH's scientific journal devoted to schizophrenia research, the *Schizophrenia Bulletin,* published in 1989 as the Decade of the Brain was drawing to a close. Edited by John Strauss and Sue Estroff, a medical anthropologist who has played an important role in opening up and rigorously studying subjectivity in serious mental illness, the issue took as its theme "Subjective Experiences of Schizophrenia and Related Disorders." The editors' preface opened with the following introductory comment: "There is something seriously missing in a field of mental illness that does not attend closely and broadly to patients' subjective experiences and sense of self" (Strauss, 1989b, p. 177). In his own contribution to the issue, Strauss then went on to explain:

> The role of the person in mental disorder is not peripheral, merely as a passive victim of a disease to be fixed by medicine. . . . What we are dealing with

is not some rather stereotyped disease process stamped onto some shadowy "everyperson," but processes of disorder that interact with a very important and differentiated person—a person who is goal-directed, a person whose feelings and interpretations influence actions that in turn affect phases of disorder or recovery, and a person who uses regulatory mechanisms . . . as ways of making both continuity and change possible. (1989b, pp. 182, 185)

In order to explore processes of person-disorder interaction, Strauss and his colleagues had called in an earlier paper for new approaches to schizophrenia research:

The need for a more adequate model to reflect the evolution of a psychiatric disorder is especially glaring now that increasing evidence has been generated showing that even people with the most severe and chronic mental illness may experience major changes, often with partial or full recovery. . . . It is important in such an inquiry, as in any other scientific effort, to be faithful to the phenomena being studied, even though this may lead to shifts in research method. (Strauss et al., 1985, pp. 295–296)

The publication of the 1989 special issue of *Schizophrenia Bulletin* was the first such step toward shifting research methods. Both in and since that issue, Strauss and others have further articulated the need for these new methods to be oriented to the investigation of the subjective experiences of people with schizophrenia (e.g., Barham, 1984; Barham and Hayward, 1998a, 1998b; Corin, 1990; Corin and Lauzon, 1994; Estroff, 1989, 1994; Strauss, 1989a, 1989b, 1992, 1994, 1996).

For this task, qualitative research is extremely well suited. The longitudinal studies mentioned above, for example, have suggested a number of factors that facilitate the recovery process that appear to have more to do with the person struggling with the illness than with the illness itself. Factors such as hope, courage, and a sense of belonging, while difficult to integrate into neurobiological models of disorder, appear nonetheless to point to ways in which the person's activity may play a crucial role in the improvement process (Davidson and Strauss, 1995; Harding et al., 1987). Such findings call for qualitative study to identify those subjective factors that may mediate processes of illness and improvement and to shed light on how these processes of mediation may be facilitated or impeded (Strauss et al., 1985a, 1985b).

The need for new methods to address these new questions regarding the nature of schizophrenia is related to one final, although long-standing, reason for qualitative inquiry in this area. This reason is the very old attraction of the nature of psychotic experience. Psychosis has held a lure for qualitative investigators since the inception of qualitative methods, as it has since antiquity fascinated poets, storytellers, theologians, philosophers, and others interested in the structures and limits of human consciousness. One sign of the persistence of this lure even into the days of the height of the neurobiological paradigm in psychiatry is the fact that the NIMH has continued to publish a "First-Person Account" series in each issue of *Schizophrenia Bulletin*. More recently, the major publication of the American Psychiatric Association to deal with clinical research on severe mental illness, *Psychiatric Services*, has instituted a similar series. We know of no other illness that so regularly attracts attention to first-person accounts.

While this kind of aesthetic or intellectual curiosity is not alone enough to justify a book devoted to phenomenological studies of this topic, it does suggest that there still may be more to learn through systematic investigation of experiences of people with psychotic disorders. This may be true not only with respect to traditional interests in the ways in which psychotic experience differs from normal experience but also with respect to the less-appreciated ways in which people with psychosis remain like the rest of us (Davidson and Strauss, 1995). As we noted above, it is this latter task of investigating the ways in which people with schizophrenia remain people that is of more urgent scientific and political import at this time.

For these reasons, current understandings of schizophrenia call for the development and application of qualitative methods. If it is now time to come to grips with the ways in which even people who once were referred to as "lunatics" have also to be counted as people, then this provides a timely opportunity for demonstrating the utility of qualitative approaches to research in psychology. To our first question of "Why *schizophrenia?*" we thus can answer: Because it offers an area of pressing clinical concern that should be particularly intriguing to investigators interested in the development and application of qualitative approaches to psychological research.

Why *Phenomenology* of Schizophrenia?

Why don't you ever ask me what I do to help myself?
—Woman with schizophrenia talking to interviewer
(Quoted in Strauss, 1989b)

As noted above, madness has been a popular topic of literary, philosophical, and psychological reflection since antiquity, permeating the history of Western thought as perhaps no other human condition with the possible exception of love. There have been studies of aspects of the subjective experiences of people with schizophrenia from the perspective of grounded theory (e.g., Barker, Lavender, and Morant, 2001; McNally, 1997), hermeneutics (e.g., Corin, 1990, 1998), and ethnography (e.g., Cohen, 1992; Estroff, 1995; Wiley, 1989), and the following chapter will summarize some of the more salient findings from these studies. In addition, there has been substantial interest in schizophrenia throughout the history of the phenomenological tradition. Beginning with the pioneering work of Karl Jaspers (1964), there has been a consistent stream of phenomenological work on schizophrenia produced by Mayer-Gross (1924), Minkowski (1927, 1970), Wrysch (1940, 1942), Binswanger (1958, 1963), Boss (1963), Laing (1960, 1961), Macnab (1966), de Waelhens (1978), Borgna (1981), Van den Berg (1982), Kimura (1982), Sass (1987, 1988, 1990), Corin (1990, 1998), and Schwartz and Wiggins (1987), spanning the course of the last 85 years and emanating from Germany, France, Belgium, Switzerland, the Netherlands, Italy, England, Canada, Japan, and the United States.

On the one hand, this cursory review suggests that qualitative methods have been, and can be, brought to bear on the problem of schizophrenia. On the other hand, however, such a list may lead us to wonder if there is anything new to be learned from employing a phenomenological approach in this area. If so many people have already used the tools of phenomenology to explore these waters, and if they, taken together, have had such a modest impact on current understandings and treatment of schizophrenia, is this really a promising approach after all?

We intend to respond to this last question in what is to follow, allowing the proof of the pudding to be in the tasting. With respect to how phenomenological methods can be used to address the research agenda outlined above, however, we do have one rationale that we consider worth explaining ahead of time by way of further introduction. This rationale may be dismissed as groundless by adherents of grounded theory or be regarded as socially naïve by practicing ethnographers. Our point is not so much to compare phenomenology to other qualitative approaches, though, as to highlight that which makes empirical phenomenology particularly well suited to exploring schizophrenia and makes its other, less appealing, features worth tolerating.

The less-appealing features of phenomenology include the introduction and regular use of confusing and frequently obscurantist terminology (e.g., eidetic reduction, noema/noesis, the transcendental), an almost indiscriminant use of hyphens (e.g., "being-in-the-world," "being-with"), the framing of highly abstract concepts that border on being devoid of meaning, a potentially overly rigorous method that appears obsessed with achieving the very same standards it has renounced as irrelevant (e.g., interrater reliability), and a heavy emphasis on theory. It is this last feature of phenomenology, its explicit and self-conscious basis in theory, however, which also is one of its unique strengths when confronting such challenging phenomena as schizophrenia.

In what follows, we make every effort to avoid or clarify potentially confusing terminology, keep our use of hyphens to an absolute minimum, frame our concepts in the language and context of the practical everyday lives of the people with schizophrenia whom we have had the privilege to come to know, and refrain from accentuating the rigorous nature of our methods. We chose not to minimize the emphasis on theory, however, but rather embrace it. This is because, as reflective psychologists, we stand convinced that there is no such thing as an atheoretical position (as is claimed, for example, by the American Psychiatric Association's third edition of the *Diagnostic and Statistical Manual of Mental Disorders,* 1980). If it is not possible to hold a position that is not based on theory, then the least we can do is be aware of the theory we are using to ground our methodology. Experimental psychology proudly traces its origins back to Sir Francis Bacon and the rise of positivism. So, too, does qualitative research need to have an identifiable intellectual heritage that can be examined and questioned. We suggest that for qualitative inquiry phenomenology has played, and continues to play, this role.

All qualitative research is based on the premise that there is more than one kind of knowledge about more than one kind of subject matter. It is a given that methods of quantification and measurement based on the physical sciences have led to important discoveries and scientific advances across many fields, not the least of which is psychology. Were this all there is, however—were quantification and measurement enough to ground all of psychology—then there would be no need for qualitative inquiry. The development of qualitative methods is based on the premise that there is more to reality, more to experience, and more to psychology than can be captured through quantitative methods alone. But what is the nature of this more? What other kinds of knowledge are there, about what other kinds of subject matter?

Naturalistic inquiry purports to generate objective forms of knowledge about physical objects that appear to be embedded within the causal nexus of nature. In contrast, qualitative inquiry aims to generate subjective forms of knowledge about experiencing subjects who appear to be embedded within a network of meaningful relationships. Put simply, we do not experience ourselves solely as physical objects being buffeted about by other physical objects that cause our actions and behavior to take the forms that they do (this view may be referred to as the "billiard ball" model of psychology). Rather, we experience ourselves as social agents relating to others, making decisions, acting and behaving in accord with plans we have made (or not) based on *reasons*; based, that is, on motivations that involve our being directed toward goals (Davidson and Strauss, 1995).

It is not important for our present purposes whether or not we are explicitly aware of these reasons or motivations or to what degree they may be in conflict with each other. These issues are certain to be of interest to qualitative psychology, but at the moment we are interested only in establishing the possibility of developing an alternative approach to psychology grounded in motivational relationships of meaning as opposed to causality. Phenomenology, through its descriptive philosophical analyses of experience, provides the theoretical foundation for this possibility.

To justify this statement and explain its relevance for our present task, a brief return to philosophical phenomenology is in order. As the first and most crucial step in our approach to philosophical phenomenology, Husserl proposed to hold in abeyance or put in "brackets" (an idea derived from his training in mathematics) our usual conviction that there is a world "out there" independent of our experience in order to explore the structures and contents of experience itself. Having "reduced" (through what he called the "phenomenological reduction") our interest only to what we experience and only in precisely the manner in which we experience it, we are now free to see what is contained in that experience without being distracted by appeals to a world that exists, as it were, beyond our experiences of it. The relevance of phenomenology for our purposes comes not so much from what we have excluded from our science in this way but from what we are able to learn from what remains. Once we are restricted to the sphere of experience we begin to notice a number of important distinctions we otherwise might have missed. It is based on these distinctions that we are able to carve out the territory and approach of our qualitative science.

Husserl noticed, for example, that an object is experienced *as* a physical object (i.e., as having extension apart from my body) by virtue of the fact that there are an indefinite number of perspectives that can be taken on the object without exhausting the being of the object itself. What does this mean? Let's say that by now you are getting tired of reading all this theory, your concentration is starting to wane, and you figure that it is time to put the book down and go outside for a nice walk. It is autumn in New England, and you can't help but notice the beautiful foliage turning red, orange, and yellow all around you. You notice, in particular, your favorite tree, all ablaze in red, and approach the tree admiring its fall plumage. From each position you take in relation to the tree, you see a particular side of the tree, from a particular angle, and at a particular distance. You know, in addition, that were you to walk around the tree you would gain many different perspectives on the tree from many different angles. There would be, Husserl (1981) suggests, an indefinite number of "subjective appearances" of the tree, and yet in each case you would know the appearance in question to be an appearance of the very same tree that is given through the other appearances as well (p. 179). The tree retains its identity across these varied appearances.

Restricted as we are to the realm of experience, it only becomes possible to appreciate the tree as having an independent identity, however, against the background of the multiplicity of its appearances. In other words, your tree only comes to be experienced as an individually identical thing (i.e., as *a* tree) by virtue of its persistence through the varying subjective appearances of it. We come to realize that this thing is not contained in, not merely a part of, any one experience for it remains the same as its appearances vary. It may only be perceived through our experiences of it, but through these experiences it is experienced nonetheless as a thing that transcends these experiences themselves; as that which is other than our experiences of it (Husserl, 1981, p. 179). It is on the basis of this otherness, this transcendence, that the tree then comes to be perceived as being a physical object, as having its own existence in nature apart from its appearances in experience (Davidson, 1987).

But the tree doesn't remain the same over time, you say; it will be losing its red leaves soon as fall turns to winter. How can the identity of the tree persist through such changes if this identity is based on the tree remaining the same against a background of difference? This perfectly legitimate, perfectly reasonable, question provides the ground for natural scientific inquiry, for it is this question that led Husserl to conclude that physical objects are what they are only as a "union point of causalities" within the context of nature (1981, p. 179). We are able to experience a physical thing as the same over time despite such changes by virtue of the fact that the changes that do occur are ordered, predictable changes (e.g., the tree loses its leaves each fall) that abide by determinable (i.e., causal) laws. Only certain changes are possible if we are to continue to experience this thing as a tree; were it to take flight or begin to dance, it would no longer be a tree (except perhaps in a Disney movie). In the same vein, were it not to burn when exposed to sufficient heat, it would no longer be experienced as a tree. It can remain the same tree over time only because its interactions with its environment abide by the laws of possible changes that we identify as belonging to trees. As before, it retains its identity over time only against the background of a multiplicity of lawful changes. It is the nature of the laws by which changes occur that we conceptualize as causality. Husserl explains:

> Every thing itself is from the start apprehended as such a lasting individual which has its familiar style of causal behavior. . . . To know a thing means to foresee how it will behave causally, e.g., to have experienced, to know, a glass plate as such means always to regard and know it as something which will shatter if it is struck hard or thrown down. (1977, p. 77)

If any of you, upon returning from your walk, are beginning to feel that you are slipping into an autistic (i.e., self-contained) bubble of a world, in which everything is dependent on each person's unique experiences of it for its existence, be reassured that Husserl devoted the majority of his professional life to demonstrating in meticulous detail how experience is not individual in nature. Experience as the medium through which the world and all of its various objects are given to us must be intersubjective in nature, for it is only on this basis that the world can be experienced by us as a shared world that we inhabit alongside other experiencing subjects rather than as my world or your world alone. Further development of this dimension (the so-called transcendental dimension) of Husserl's thought will be taken up in chapter 3. Fortunately, however, we already have arrived at where we need to be for our present purposes in order to define the "more," and ground the alternative methods, of qualitative research. It is precisely the intersubjective nature of experience that we and, we suggest, qualitative researchers in general, take as our point of departure for exploring the realm of human experience. Let us see how this is so.

One of the more important contributions of phenomenological philosophy was to discover, and then to delineate, the ways in which experience cannot itself be understood as if it were an object *of* experience. Physical beings, as we said above, come to be experienced as individual objects by virtue of their persisting through, and standing out from, the multiplicity of subjective appearances through which they are experienced as "other" than these appearances themselves. This same thing cannot be said of psychical beings, however, since the realm of the psychic, the realm of experience, is precisely that in which physical things are experienced through multiple appearances. These appearances themselves, Husserl argues, "do not constitute a being which itself appears by means of appearances lying behind it" (1981, p. 179). To presume that appearances can only be experienced through additional appearances lying behind them would be to commit oneself to an infinite regress (a state of affairs considered unacceptable by most philosophers). Thus, appearances must be experienced differently than that which appears through them (Davidson, 1987).

How is it that appearances appear in experience? According to Husserl, experience is the same "flow of phenomena" we described above when following you on your autumnal stroll. At one moment you are reading this book, at the next moment you get tired of working your brain so hard that you decide to take a walk, the next moment you are outside admiring the beautiful colors of the New England fall, then you are approaching your favorite tree, and then, perhaps, you are beginning to think about what you will have for dinner. This "flow of phenomena," Husserl suggests, "comes and goes; it retains no enduring, identical being that would be objectively determinable as such" (1981, p. 180). Rather than being experienced as that which endures as identical over time and persists through change, the psychical is experienced as that which is constantly in flux, that which, like Heraclitus' river, is never the same twice. This ever-changing nature of the psychic has been described perhaps nowhere better than in J. D. Salinger's novel *The Catcher in the Rye* (1951). When Holden, the novel's protagonist, recalls his many childhood visits to the Museum of Natural History in New York City, he underscores the contrast between physical and psychical being we have been trying to draw. Salinger writes:

> The best thing, though, in that museum was that everything always stayed right where it was. Nobody'd move. You could go there a hundred thousand times, and that Eskimo would still be just finishing catching those two fish, the birds would still be on their way south, the deer would still be drinking out of that water hole, with their pretty antlers and their pretty, skinny legs, and that squaw with the naked bosom would still be weaving that same blanket. Nobody'd be different. The only thing that would be different would be you. Not that you'd be so much older or anything. It wouldn't be that, exactly. You'd just be different, that's all. You'd have an overcoat on this time. Or the kid that was your partner in line the last time had got scarlet fever and you'd have a new partner. Or you'd heard your mother and father having a terrible fight in the bathroom. Or you'd just passed by one of those puddles in the street with gasoline rainbows in them. I mean you'd be different in some way. (pp. 121–122)

How, then, to pursue knowledge of a kind of being that is constantly in flux? What different kinds of methods can be used to obtain what different kinds of knowledge about this different kind of subject matter? If experiences are not things, and therefore are not related to each other causally, then what is the nature of the relationship between them? What determines the flow of experience? Husserl suggested that, rather than being connected through external relations of causality, experiences are connected to each other immanently through the flow of time itself. In other words, each experience belongs to the same flow of experiences to which the experience that has just passed away also belonged and to which the experience about to come belongs as well (Davidson, 1987). You are, right now, aware of the words on the page you are reading. You are aware of your reading these words both as coming just after you read the words on the page before and as coming just before you put the book down to take another walk outside. There is a unity to this flow that does not have to be explained based on factors external to the experiences themselves. The experiences carry within them their own intrinsic continuity; a continuity which unfolds over time through relationships of meaning.

There are three important implications to this view for our development of a qualitative psychology. First, it is evident from this analysis how qualitative psychology has come to be regarded as particularly well suited to investigating the role of the person with schizophrenia and the nature of person-disorder interactions over time. Husserl's analysis of the differences between physical and psychical being allows us to establish new methods appropriate to this newly delimited realm of the psychic; methods suited to studying the subjects of experience rather than its objects. Qualitative methods are in this way experience-based, and take as their aim the description and understanding of a person's subjective experiences as they unfold immanently over time and as they relate to one another through motivational relationships of meaning. It is within this conceptual framework that we then can return to our interest in the person's crucial role in the recovery process.

Second, it is evident from this analysis that in attempting to understand the role of the person as a subject of experience, no single experience can stand on its own. Just as your favorite tree can retain its identity only by interacting with its environment in causally determined ways over time, each experience is what it is only as one moment of a synthetic temporal flow, arising out of a particular past and leading into a particular future. This observation suggests that, along with experience per se, temporality should be a key dimension of any qualitative approach to psychology, viewing experiences within the temporal context in which they occur rather than as discrete entities that exist on their own (e.g., as "a delusion" or "a hallucination").

Third, the observation that experiences are intentional and connected to one another immanently through relations of meaning suggests that any qualitative approach to psychology will be concerned also with motivation. Motivation in the sense being used here is not necessarily a reflective or conscious sense of motivation; of knowing why we are doing what we are doing at any given point in time. Rather, motivation is used as a parallel to causality to describe the nature of the relationship between experiences, regardless of whether or not we are aware of these relationships. Husserl argued that one task of phenomenology is to uncover the "laws" of motivation that operate implicitly in determining the flow of experience. Ordinarily, these laws operate without our awareness, leading from one experience to the next in meaningful and interrelated ways.

How, then, do we uncover the laws of motivation operating in the temporal flow of experiences? By studying the meaning of the experiences themselves in their relationships to each other. Having set up our base camp inside the realm of subjectivity, the challenge of our scientific explorations "is to take conscious life, completely without prejudice, just as what it quite immediately gives itself, as itself, to be" (Husserl, 1970a, p. 233). We need not look anywhere other than to experience to generate knowledge about the nature, structures, and laws of experience. It is on this basis that we can ground the development of a qualitative psychology that takes as its subject matter the "more" of the meaning and motivations of our subjective life.

Before moving on from this exegesis of the Husserliana, we should return to the issue of intersubjectivity introduced above and explain how the study of our subjective life requires the development of different methods for psychology. Like most philosophers, Husserl reflected primarily on his own experiences and drew inferences about the nature of subjectivity from what quantitative psychologists would consider an N of 1. Although in principle it would be possible to base a psychology similarly on reflection on one's own experiences, there would be obvious limitations to the ability of such a psychology to explore and understand mental illnesses like schizophrenia. Not that people with schizophrenia would not, or could not, be interested in reflecting on their own experiences. There are, after all, several outstanding examples both of psychologists (e.g., Pat Deegan, 1988, 1992; Fred Frese, 2000) and of psychiatrists (e.g., Dan Fisher, 1984; Carol North, 1987) who have had, and may continue to have, schizophrenia and whose work is informed by their own experiences. We would not want to suggest, however, that psychologists can understand only those things they have experienced directly themselves. This would place overly restrictive limits on qualitative research in psychology and on approaches to clinical practice based on it.

It is here where the intersubjective nature of experience becomes crucial in providing the ground needed for developing qualitative methods that can tap the experiences of others. Thus far, we have described how physical objects appear to experience and how experience appears to itself; the question remaining for psychology is how *others* appear to me in my experiences of them. Do I experience another person as a physical object, as another immanent flow of experiences, or as something else altogether? To the degree that I experience the other person as embodied, I perceive him or her as a physical object (i.e., his or her body) susceptible to, and governed by, the causal laws of nature. To the degree that I experience this body as being occupied, so to speak, by another person, however, I also experience him or her as an experiencing subject with his or her own immanent flow of experiences parallel to, but separate from, my own. In the kind of meticulous, if enlightening, detail that would serve as the impetus for many long walks through New England foliage, Husserl devoted the entirety of the second volume of his *Ideen* (Ideas) series (1989) to describing the differences between the ways in which inanimate nature, animate nature, and human nature appear in experience. In what is perhaps an unsurprising but still useful distinction, Husserl suggests that naturalistic approaches to psychology are best suited to investigating the nature of the human body, while phenomenological approaches are best suited to investigating the nature of human subjectivity.

How could phenomenological methods be used to investigate the experiences of others rather than of myself? What access do we have to other people's experiences, and how should we go about trying to understand those experiences? Chapter 2 will begin to address these questions in detail, as we lay out the various steps of the empirical phenomenological method we have used in investigating experiences of people with schizophrenia. We should note, however, that these are the kinds of questions that are rarely asked by other qualitative approaches such as grounded theory. The question of how we gain access to the subjective, experiential life of others is one of those thorny theoretical questions that will need to be addressed in grounding and justifying any qualitative approach to psychology. It also happens to be one of the theoretical questions to which phenomenology has offered a response.

If the fundamental law of subjective life is motivation, then we can imagine that investigating the experiences of other people will involve identifying and coming to understand their motivations. As Husserl explains:

> The question is how they, as persons, comport themselves in action and passion—how they are motivated to their specifically personal acts of perception, of remembering, of thinking, of valuing, of making plans, of being frightened and automatically starting, of defending themselves, of attacking, etc. (1970a, p. 317)

But how do we, as psychologists, gain access to this kind of subjective information immanent to another person? "I can have a 'direct' experience of myself," writes Husserl, but I cannot have such a "direct" experience of others. "For that I need the mediation of empathy," he continues; "I can experience others, but only through empathy" (1989, p. 210). Similar to the active and disciplined listening required in the practice of most forms of psychotherapy, phenomenological psychologists will need to be able to relate empathically to each participant in their study, immersing themselves enough in the participant's experiences to begin to have a sense of what it would be like to be having such experiences themselves. As Husserl suggests:

> A first step is explicitly to be vitally at one with the other person in the intuitive understanding of his experiencing, his life situation, his activity, etc. (1970a, p. 328)

In qualitative research, as in clinical practice, there are no tricks, short cuts, or recipes for the cultivation of such intuitive understanding. Empathic listening requires practice, skill, and at least a bit of talent, grace, and good luck. As when an actor is learning to assume the role of a new character, however, there are a few strategies that can be used by qualitative researchers to construct empathic bridges between their own experiences and the experiences of their subjects. We will illustrate some of these strategies beginning in chapter 3. We only note here that in the case of schizo-phrenia, building empathic bridges to the lives of people with severe and persistent psychiatric disorders may pose particular challenges.

In our view, however, the particular challenges it poses to qualitative in-vestigators are yet additional arguments for the value of schizophrenia as an illustrative focus for qualitative study. If empathic bridges can be built to experiences of psychosis—and we intend to demonstrate in what follows that, and how, they can—then psychologists presumably need not fear that their understanding of subjectivity will be limited to what they themselves have experienced directly. In the interim, we can return to our initial ques-tion of "Why *phenomenology*?" to which we now can answer: Because it provides rigorous methods for psychological research, well grounded in an explicit theory of human subjectivity, and therefore particularly well suited to describing the role of the person in recovery from psychosis.

So, How Do You *Do* a Phenomenology of Schizophrenia?

We describe and illustrate each step of the phenomenological method we have used in our empirical studies of schizophrenia beginning in chapter 2. There is one last issue, however, that we would like to discuss as we bring this Introduction to a close. This issue pertains to a key method-ological decision made in the development of any empirical phenomeno-logical approach to qualitative psychological research regardless of the phenomenon being studied. As described above, the data for phenome-nological inquiry is provided by first person accounts of subjective experi-ence of the phenomenon in question. To date, there have been three basic routes to generating such data, either through autobiographical narratives, intensive case studies that include self-description, or intensive, open-ended interviews. We close this chapter by explaining why we have chosen the third route.

It is evident from a brief review of the phenomenological literature in psychiatry and psychology that the first two of these options have been the clear preferences of investigators to date. Early phenomenologically ori-ented clinicians, following Kraepelin as much as Husserl, employed inten-sive case studies of one or a few patients as the data for their structural analyses of psychopathology. Minkowski, for example, offered his insights into schizophrenia based on the case of one patient whom he happened, by "happy circumstance," to spend "night and day" with for an extended period of time (1970), while Binswanger (1963) based the bulk of his theory of schizophrenia on five intensive case studies, which met his only precondition of having adequate case material and self-description available for analysis and interpretation. Karl Jaspers was the first to suggest the use of autobiographical accounts, preferring "good self-descriptions" to accounts offered by patients in response to direct questions (1968). This approach has been used most recently by Louis Sass (1987, 1988, 1990), who has reinterpreted descriptions of psychotic experiences drawn from Marguerite Sechehaye's patient "Renee" in her *Autobiography of a Schizophrenic Girl* (1951) and from Daniel Paul Schreber's *Memoirs of My Nervous Illness* (1955), employing theoretical concepts from Heidegger, Wittgenstein, and Foucault. While there is much to be said for the richness of the data derived from these sources, there are several reasons why we decided to pursue the least traveled route of open-ended, qualitative interviews with people with schizophrenia.

First, the vast majority of people with schizophrenia, just like the vast majority of people in general, do not provide us with autobiographical accounts of their life experiences. It therefore seems fair to assume that those few people with schizophrenia who do write their autobiographies, while providing a real service, nonetheless do not represent the majority of people so afflicted. In order to avoid even the potential for there being any substance to the "YAVIS" critique of qualitative research—that is, that it only taps the experiences of young, attractive, verbal, intelligent, successful adults—this should not be our first choice for a source of data about the lived experiences of people with schizophrenia.

There are similar concerns about the choice of intensive case studies, in that these too comprise a very limited, and fairly restrictive, sample. People who are able to benefit from intensive relationships with clinicians over extended periods of time most likely have the independent financial means and residential stability required to do so, as well as typically have higher levels of premorbid functioning than the average person with schizophrenia. In addition, intensive case studies, due to their nature as clinical examples, are more vulnerable to being (or at least being criticized for being) a showcase for a particular clinician's own theoretical framework or formulation. It is difficult in reviewing a case study to

know what material was generated spontaneously by the client, what material was generated primarily in response to the clinician's implicit conceptualizations and expectations, and what material was generated by the clinician him- or herself. Lastly, and most important, case studies are written from the perspective of the clinician rather than from the perspective of the client; the latter being a core requirement for phenomenological study. One need only glance at the differences between Freud's case study of the Wolfman and the Wolfman's own account of his relationship with Freud to appreciate the magnitude of such differences in perspective (cf. Gardner, 1971).

In addition to these reasons to avoid autobiographies and intensive case studies, there are a few advantages to basing phenomenological studies of schizophrenia on narrative, open-ended interviews with people living with the condition. First, such an approach is most consistent with Husserl's admonition: "To the things themselves" (1983). This principle, which has since become something of a motto of phenomenology, is meant to direct our attention to how the phenomena of interest present themselves to us in "originary" (first-person) experience as opposed to through the filters of our often implicit and unacknowledged assumptions and preconceived notions about what those phenomena are. Given the long and unfortunate history of schizophrenia as a magnet for misconceptions, this approach offers a particularly good opportunity to begin afresh with what people who have the condition actually report about their experiences.

In a related vein, the choice of open-ended interviews as the method for data collection helps to bring phenomenology out of the ivory tower of academia and puts it quite literally onto the streets. As mentioned above, phenomenology has a checkered history of appearing overly abstract and overly theoretical at the expense of being accessible or faithful to the concrete and practical nature of everyday language and experience. Conducting qualitative interviews with people who are homeless and actively psychotic in the back of a social service agency's van, as some of our interviews have been, has a way of bringing otherwise theoretically inclined people down to earth. For qualitative research to be most useful in informing the development of interventions to assist such people in reclaiming their lives, studies need to be based on the actual experiences of the people living with the conditions of interest, and as much from their own perspective and in their own terms as possible.

Finally, interviewing people who are currently experiencing schizophrenia affords us an opportunity to incorporate a degree of rigor often recommended, but rarely pursued, in psychological research. This added degree of rigor has been referred to in a number of different ways in the qualitative tradition, including "adversary hearing" (Tebes and Kraemer, 1991), "member checking" (Allende, 2000), and participant feedback (Davidson, Stayner, Lambert, et al., 1997). All of these techniques involve having interview participants review the researchers' attempts to describe and interpret the significance of what they have said in their interviews and to integrate their feedback into the final version of the findings. These techniques serve at least two purposes.

First, they enhance the credibility of qualitative research by offering another check on the investigator's own biases. In ways that authors of autobiographies and objects of intensive case studies are rarely able to, interview participants can let investigators know when they have missed something important, distorted the meaning of a person's experience, or imposed their own ideas onto another person's description. Second, these techniques operate at a more basic level in inviting the participant to be a collaborator in the research process. Rather than trying to turn the participant into a fellow psychologist, these techniques respect the participant as an active agent in his or her own right who has his or her own expertise to contribute to the research process; this expertise consists of first person experiences of the phenomena being investigated.

Although we did not begin our own research efforts with this conviction, we have come to appreciate over the last decade that viewing the person as playing an active role in her or his own recovery necessarily requires viewing the person as playing an active, collaborative role in the research enterprise as well. Just how this is so, and how an approach of "participatory research" enriches the enterprise of qualitative investigation in psychology, we hope to demonstrate in what follows.

1

■　■　■　■　■　■　■　■　■

Is There an Outside to Mental Illness?

(With Maria O'Connell, David Sells, and Martha Staeheli)

What is needed is not the insistence that one see with his [*sic*] own eyes; rather it is that he [*sic*] not explain away under the pressure of prejudice what has been seen.

—Edmund Husserl, *Philosophy as Rigorous Science*

HOW, THEN, TO BEGIN? By articulating what it is that we are interested in learning more about through our investigation. We may have framed our primary research question already, albeit implicitly, but it will be useful in guiding our efforts to make this question both focused and explicit. It is:

How does the person who has schizophrenia affect the course and outcome of the illness?

With our focus being on processes of improvement, in particular, we may frame this question more specifically as:

How do the person's experiences and activities affect processes of recovery in schizophrenia?

Once these questions are made explicit, it is customary in the conduct of research to review the relevant scholarly literature in order first to discover what answers have been proposed to these questions in the past, based on what evidence. The review of the literature also is intended to identify gaps in what is currently known about the topic, and what next few steps could be taken to advance current knowledge. Despite being a well-established, almost rudimentary, step in conducting research, this fairly straightforward step has been the matter of some dispute within the qualitative research community. We will begin our discussion of methodology here, by exploring this dispute.

Presuppositions, Preconceived Notions, and Other Forms of Unintended Prejudice, and What We Can Do about Them

Why would qualitative researchers question the appropriateness of reviewing the existing literature on their topic of interest prior to initiating a new investigation? The issue at stake here has to do with the status of all the preconceived notions and presuppositions about the nature of the phenomena in question that investigators inevitably bring to their research, and the question of what to do about them. Are we able to investigate experience "completely without prejudice," as phenomenology encourages us to do? If so, then how are we to accomplish this? If not, then what must we do instead?

Husserl was himself a keen idealist in pursuit of an approach to research that was without presuppositions. It was his belief for most of his career that all such prejudices could be bracketed in the phenomenological reduction, enabling the phenomenologist simply to describe experience as it appears. In other words, each of us already sees reality in and through originary experience; the challenge, as captured in the quote above, is not to "explain away" what we *see* based on our theories about what *is*.

Following Husserl's lead, a school of qualitative research has emerged that suggests that investigators approach their subject matter with as pure and untarnished a lens as possible. As a first step in clearing the path to a description of originary experience, these investigators attempt to purge themselves of all prejudices and preconceptions about the nature of the phenomena they are to examine. Within this school of thought, it therefore makes no sense to review the existing literature on one's topic prior to undertaking phenomenological inquiry. Such a review would only add to the assumptions and prejudices of which one is trying to rid oneself. Reviewing what we think is known is actually moving in the wrong direction, so this line of thought contends, as we then have to place such knowledge in brackets in order to describe our experiences precisely as they are experienced (rather than as they are thought to unfold).

According to this perspective, the less one knows about a topic prior to investigation, the better able one will be to arrive at a pure description of how it is experienced. Being familiar with this perspective, we were not too surprised, for example, when we discovered that some of our best qualitative interviews were conducted by a second-year medical student who knew very little about schizophrenia. Having no prior experience working with people with psychosis, there was not much that this young man needed to put in brackets in order to approach his subjects with a fresh and unbiased eye (Davidson, Haglund, et al., 2001).

Despite our delight in discovering in this medical student a natural phenomenologist, we have yet to achieve or to witness the achievement of such a state of pure presuppositionless. In this we certainly are not alone, as most experienced qualitative investigators likewise have reached the conclusion that it is not possible to purge oneself entirely of all preconceptions (e.g., Merleau-Ponty, 1962). Late in his career, Husserl too finally gave up striving for pure presuppositionless, focusing instead on the fact that all experience necessarily unfolds over time. If experience is temporal in nature, then what sense does it make to strive for a static state of presuppositionless? We should instead view ourselves as immersed in a historical process. We are products of our individual and collective history, building on what has come before us and creating the building blocks for what is yet to come. We cannot escape the social, cultural, and historical evolution of which we are ourselves a part in order to stand, as it were, outside of it or to reflect on it from a distance. As a result, purification is no longer the best metaphor for how qualitative researchers prepare themselves for their work.

What else, then, can we do about our nagging and inevitable prejudices? And what implications will this have for our review of the literature as an initial step in our investigation? Following the later Husserl (e.g., 1970a), we opt for the less ambitious aim of bringing these nagging preconceptions to explicit awareness. In this view, assumptions are detrimental to the research enterprise only to the degree that they operate implicitly and out of our thematic awareness; to the degree, that is, that we do not know that they are influencing us. To the extent that we can bring these ideas to awareness, we can then examine them and play with them in our imagination in order to see how they might be influencing, and limiting, our perceptions and understanding.

We describe the phenomenological technique of "imaginary variation" in the next chapter when we set about the empirical enterprise of doing research. For now, we will simply conclude that reviewing the existing literature on our topic is not only a useful, but also a crucial, step in preparing ourselves for our phenomenological journey. It is through this review that we will be able to make explicit the most salient assumptions governing our current understanding of schizophrenia and influencing us in our approach to this topic. This review helps us to identify the predominant notions that both delimit (i.e., constitute) and limit our understanding of psychosis, giving us a springboard from which to leap into the experiential waters described by participants in our studies. In this task we aspire not so much for the naiveté of our medical student immersing himself in the immediacy of these experiences but to achieve the disciplined naiveté of an "immediacy *beyond* reflection" (Kierkegaard, 1983). Let us turn, then, to reviewing the existing literature on recovery in schizophrenia.

Kraepelin's Legacy

Given the focus of this volume, we will not attempt to review the thousands of pages of books, monographs, journal articles, and other publications that have been devoted to research on, and theories of, the cause, course, treatment, and outcomes of schizophrenia. As a context for understanding the last 40 or so years of work on recovery in schizophrenia, however, some historical background is useful. In order to keep our review of this background brief, we necessarily will have to truncate our treatment of over one hundred years of psychiatric research and practice, relying on simplistic distinctions between complicated theories in order to summarize this history in a few paragraphs. Readers who are unfamiliar with this history, and who are interested in a more detailed review, are referred to

Strauss and Carpenter's seminal 1981 book *Schizophrenia* and to Carpenter's more recent review (Carpenter and Buchanan, 1994).

The illness, or family of illnesses, we currently consider to be schizophrenia was first identified by Emile Kraepelin just prior to the end of the nineteenth century. As we noted in our Introduction, Kraepelin (1904) originally labeled this condition *"dementia praecox,"* or premature dementia, in order to capture the inevitable downward and deteriorating course he considered to be the hallmark of this illness. According to his clinical observations—which, again, occurred within the context of long-term hospitalization—schizophrenia was characterized by an unremitting course leading to progressive deterioration and early death. It was assumed to be an organic disorder that attacked the person's brain, leaving those afflicted with little hope for a life beyond neurological degeneration and irreversible dementia (Kraepelin, [1904] 1987).

This understanding of schizophrenia as a neurobiological disorder has formed the basis for a number of approaches to the illness over the last century, ranging from involuntary frontal lobotomies and insulin shock treatments earlier in the twentieth century to the new generation of more effective medications developed within the last decade. Proponents of this model do not necessarily believe that schizophrenia is caused solely by genetic or biological factors. The stress-vulnerability version of the model views schizophrenia as caused by a complex interaction of genetic predisposition, subtle neurological impairments, stressful life events, and inadequate resources for coping with these events. Although this model acknowledges the role that social environment and coping play in schizophrenia, it typically has failed to address the question of how people come to be more or less successful in managing the illness. In addition, and more important, these models do not allow for the possibility that people can ever recover fully, or even partially, from the disorder. The most one can hope for is containment of the damage caused by the illness and a degree of mastery over one's continuing symptoms. The illness and its underlying vulnerability will persist for the remainder of the person's life, it is believed, requiring active treatment and rehabilitation for the person to preserve any remaining areas of independent functioning (Davidson and Strauss, 1995).

This Kraepelinian model has not only formed the foundation for various treatments of schizophrenia over the last century but also has informed social policy and community attitudes toward people with mental illness. Although not responsible for the two hundred years of segregation that preceded it, it has perpetuated the stigma of mental illness and justified the continued exclusion of "the mentally ill" from social debates about their fate (Davidson, 1997). The legislation, policies, and programming that dictate the locus of care and the practices of mental health professionals have been decided with little to no input from the people most directly affected by these decisions: the patients themselves. Based on the perception that the person is lost to the illness, others have stepped in to make decisions and speak *for* the person.

Such an exclusion of the person would be less surprising were we concerned with the technical evolution of surgical procedures that typically have developed independent of the wishes or preferences of prospective patients (e.g., earlier use of mastectomy). Psychiatry has differed from most other parts of medicine, however, in extending its authority to include most aspects of patients' lives, including where they live, with whom they associate, what they eat, when they bathe, and what they do with their time. While this psychiatric hegemony was more obvious in the context of the large state mental hospitals in which hundreds of thousands of people lived the majority of their adult lives, these same institutional structures and attitudes can been found operating at a more implicit, but yet powerful, level in the impoverished lives of the hundreds of thousands of individuals now living in the community (Davidson, Hoge, et al., 1995; Estroff, 1995).

The degree of social control exerted by psychiatry over the lives of people with psychiatric disabilities usually is found only with conditions that render the person entirely incapable of taking care of him- or herself, such as severe developmental disabilities and autism, or with communicable diseases that threaten the lives of the broader public, such as tuberculosis. It was for this reason that Foucault (1965) did not consider it to be simply a coincidence that the first insane asylums were instituted in depopulated and refurbished leper colonies. The majority of people with severe psychiatric disabilities do not pose any particular public health or societal risk that would justify this degree of segregation and control by others, however (Monahan, 1992; Monahan and Arnold, 1996; Mulvey, 1994). In addition, and as we will see below, most people with severe psychiatric disabilities do not require the long-term custodial care or supervision that may be required by some individuals with irremediably devastating conditions (e.g., Harding, Zubin, and Strauss, 1987). The fact that such was the fate of hundreds of thousands of people over at least one hundred years of our history, and that a less overt but still intrusive degree of supervision continues to be provided in some community settings into the present day, reflects the pessimism and hopelessness of the Kraepelinian model.

This despairing picture remained relatively unchallenged for the first half of the twentieth century until two related developments began to converge on an alternative view of serious mental illness. These two developments were the emergence of the contemporary Mental Health Consumer/Survivor Movement and a body of rigorous outcome research conducted by clinical investigators skeptical of Kraepelin's certainty about the inevitability of a chronic course and poor outcome for schizophrenia.

"Nothing about Us without Us!"

Not everyone with a severe psychiatric disorder becomes the passive victim of an intrusive and controlling mental health system. Many people, as we noted in our Introduction, do not come into contact with the mental health system at all and therefore never receive any treatment for their condition. In other cases, people have rejected the services offered them, either picking and choosing what they find helpful and can tolerate or attempting to go it alone. In still other cases, people who have been recipients, or objects, of psychiatric treatment have spoken out about what they consider to be its less-helpful aspects and its abuses and have worked to change the conditions that allow for this kind of treatment to continue. These individuals have come to call themselves self-advocates or members of the Mental Health Consumer/Survivor Movement; survivor referring to the fact that they "survived" psychiatric treatment (most often involuntary hospitalization) and are now trying to change the psychiatric system so that future generations will not have to face what they endured.

There have, of course, been isolated individuals who have been discharged from psychiatric hospitals and who have spoken out about their mistreatment for as long as there have been such institutions. What distinguishes the contemporary Consumer/Survivor Movement from its predecessors is that it has become a collective political force that has effectively joined societal debates about the future of mental health services for people with psychiatric disabilities. Their motto in doing so, adopted from the broader Disability Rights Movement, is the phrase: "Nothing about us without us" (Charlton, 1998).

This motto is meant to express the sentiment among people with psychiatric disabilities that they fully intend to remain in control of their own lives. Whether this requires wresting control back from the mental health system or not ceding control to the system in the first place, the Consumer/Survivor Movement is based on the shared conviction of people with psychiatric disorders that they do not need other people to make decisions or to speak on their behalf; that, despite their disabilities, they are capable of doing so for themselves. In arguing for self-determination, consumer/survivors have taken issue with the Kraepelinian model and the intrusive social policies associated with it. In a representative statement, this approach has been described as "highly paternalistic . . . emphasizing illness over health, weaknesses rather than strengths, limitations rather than potential for growth." As a result, advocates have come to view the Kraepelinian model "as stamping out hope by implying that biology is destiny and emphasizing an external locus of control" (Munetz, Geller, and Frese, 2001, p. 36).

As an alternative, the Consumer/Survivor Movement has, over the last 25 years, endorsed a more optimistic and personally (and politically) "empowering" model under the rubric of what they have termed "recovery." We place recovery in quotes because recovery from psychiatric disorder may look quite different, and take on different meanings, from the typical use of the term in relation to physical conditions. At its most basic level, the recovery model argues that psychiatric disability is only one aspect of the whole person (Corrigan and Penn, 1998) and that recovery from psychiatric disorder does not require remission of symptoms or other deficits. In other words, and unlike in most physical illnesses, people may consider themselves to be "in recovery" from a psychiatric disorder while continuing to have, and be affected by, the disorder. What recovery seems to entail is that people overcome the effects of being a mental patient—including rejection from society, poverty, substandard housing, social isolation, unemployment, loss of valued social roles and identity, and loss of sense of self and purpose in life—in order to retain, or resume, some degree of control over their own lives (Anthony, 1993; Deegan, 1996a, 1996b).

Is Recovery Possible?

But are these psychiatric consumers/survivors credible? Is there any validity to the model that they are proposing as an alternative to the Kraepelinian view? Should people who have psychotic disorders be *allowed* to retain, or to take back, control of their own lives? Just because they demand to be included in policy debates does not necessarily mean that they are right or that they *have* the right to self-determination if their impaired judgment puts the larger society at risk. If their own definitions of recovery include continued disorder and disability, why should we listen to people who appear to admit that they are at least, in part, "insane"?

Critics of the Consumer/Survivor Movement argue that the leaders of this movement do not represent the majority of people with serious mental illnesses. These effective and eloquent advocates appear to be less disabled by their conditions than most of their peers. They either have milder conditions (e.g., dysphoria as opposed to major depression) or, these critics argue, they were misdiagnosed and do not suffer from a psychiatric disorder at all. Kraepelin's legacy has been so deeply entrenched in psychiatry that some experts have claimed that anyone who does, in fact, recover *must* have been misdiagnosed because what they had could not have been schizophrenia in the first place. In elegant but circular reasoning, this position is based on the tautology that people who have schizophrenia cannot recover, therefore, if people do recover they could not have had schizophrenia. They must have had something else.

The counterevidence to these criticisms is provided by a growing body of research involving longitudinal outcome studies of people diagnosed with schizophrenia according to established criteria. As we noted in our Introduction, since the late 1960s a highly consistent picture has emerged around the world, across countries and individuals, and over time consisting of a broad heterogeneity in outcome for individuals with schizophrenia regardless of setting. Each study conducted documented a full range in outcome, from severe and continuous incapacity to full recovery, with a significant portion of each sample falling into each category along this spectrum. Most differences across these studies were attributed to methodological artifacts such as differing sample characteristics, with one noteworthy exception. Participants were more likely to have a favorable outcome if they lived in the developing, as opposed to developed, world

(Ciompi, 1980; Davidson and McGlashan, 1997; Lin and Kleinman, 1988; McGlashan, 1988; McGlashan, Carpenter, and Bartko, 1988).

Since 1988, when a special issue of *Schizophrenia Bulletin* was devoted to this topic, there have been at least another 10 studies on long-term outcome appearing in the literature along with several studies exploring in more detail differences across domains of functioning within people and over time as well as across individuals. In our own review of these studies, we concluded that the last 30 years of research consistently had found between "21% to 57% of subjects achieving a good outcome ranging from mild impairment to recovery" (Davidson and McGlashan, 1997, p. 37). Consistent with earlier findings, but for reasons that are not yet entirely clear, the top end of this range is increased to 67 percent when one takes into account cross-cultural studies that continue to find people in the developing world having better outcomes than their peers in the developed world. More specific information on the course of the illness has accumulated over this period of time as well, suggesting even more revisions to Kraepelin's original view of the nature of the disorder. Our summary continues:

> It appears that the broad prognostic heterogeneity that was initially discovered through long-term follow-up studies may already be present at the time of the first episode. It also appears that the most significant amount of deterioration in functioning that will occur for many individuals with schizophrenia has already occurred by the time of the first episode, if not by the prodromal phase. Negative symptoms and the deficit syndrome continue to represent an important component of the . . . disorder, being relatively stable over time and associated with cognitive impairments and incapacity in social and work domains. (Davidson and McGlashan, 1997, p. 37)

The Kraepelinian view of schizophrenia, in which severity of the illness increased over time, being relatively mild at the time of the first episode and becoming increasingly disabling with each exacerbation of symptoms, has persisted into the present day, with clinicians, family members, and policymakers assuming, for example, that hospitalizations are necessarily destructive events. What this recent research suggests, instead, is that the primary damage to be done to the person by the illness may already have taken place by the end of the first episode. In fact, some preliminary research has started to suggest that much of this damage may even take place prior to onset. A plateau in functioning then typically is reached following the first episode. This plateau may be at the same depressed level as the person reached prior to the first episode but typically will be above that level. In some cases, people may actually function better after their first episode of schizophrenia than they did just prior to, or during the build up to, this episode. Their level of functioning rarely will be restored immediately to where it was prior to the initial decline that led up to this episode, but it will show improvement as the episode resolves.

The possibility that the person can then go in almost any direction from the plateau they often reach following the first episode is what accounts for the broad heterogeneity in outcome. This heterogeneity is not only found in the long-term outcome of schizophrenia (e.g., 32–35 years after onset), but we also now know that it already can be found at the end of the first episode. If the prodromal period and the first episode are characterized by prominent cognitive impairments and/or negative symptoms, the person is more likely to have a poor outcome. More than positive symptoms, these negative components appear to contribute to the plateau in functioning reached following the first episode. People who have prominent positive symptoms without cognitive impairments or negative symptoms are more likely to regain the level of functioning they had prior to an acute exacerbation. Cognitive impairments and negative symptoms appear to be more stable over time and thus may limit the degree to which people can regain functioning following acute episodes. Regardless of these preliminary prognostic indicators, however, the important lesson from this line of research is that a full range of outcomes is possible following a first episode of psychosis. Recovery is possible for many people who have schizophrenia, and—although it may be for some people—it is not necessarily a long-term process for all.

So What Do We Know about Recovery?

Long-term, longitudinal and short-term follow-up studies offer evidence that people can and do recover from schizophrenia. Other than the possible roles of cognitive impairments and negative symptoms as indicators of poor outcome, and the presence of depression and later, more abrupt onset as indicators of better outcome, we know very little about the processes of recovery from this illness, however. Part of the reason we know so little may be due to the fact that, until fairly recently, we did not know that people recovered and therefore did not know to ask. Another reason may be that even if we do know to ask about recovery, we may not yet know *how* to ask in order to arrive at the right data. In other words, the processes involved in recovery may not lend themselves to discovery through our usual methods of clinical research. As Estroff suggests, we may be limited by our inherited models of disorder in our choices of ways of investigating them. She writes:

> The challenge for researchers . . . is to develop methods and principles that reflect accurately the experiences, meanings, and needs of people with severe, persistent, mental illnesses. The challenge is not to reduce the complexity of the task, but to make it understandable. The reconstitution of lives is a complex process, much of which we fail to find in our outcome research not necessarily because of the bleak course of schizophrenia, but because of conceptual and methodological shortcomings. (1995, p. 87)

Attempting to move beyond the conceptual and methodological shortcomings Estroff refers to, the growing body of recovery literature relies primarily on the self-reports of individuals who either have recovered from schizophrenia—in one of the several senses of the term we will describe below—or are "in recovery," with recovery in this case understood as an on-going process. Much of this literature has been autobiographical and therefore limited to the experiences of a particular person. To a lesser degree, however, there also are an increasing number of qualitative studies of recovery to which we hope to contribute this present volume. These studies are based on narratives of people with schizophrenia, ranging in number of participants from a few to many. Following our review of these literatures, we will point out some of their limitations, and, in closing, outline their implications for our investigation as useful background for the empirical work beginning in chapter 4.

People in Recovery Speak about Recovery

Like advocacy, first-person accounts of illness and recovery have been written for centuries by people with serious mental illness. Among those of historical interest, for example, are Daniel Paul Schreber's *Memoirs of My Nervous Illness* (1955) and Clifford Beers's *A Mind That Found Itself* (1935). Most first-person accounts in recent literature, however, have come from people who affiliate themselves more or less with the Mental Health Consumer/Survivor Movement described above. In addition to speaking out against system abuses and advocating for change, consumer/survivors began writing about their experiences in the form of personal narratives at the beginning of the movement in the 1970s. More recently, their stories have begun to appear in well-respected scientific journals. This growing literature may shed light, both conceptually and experientially, on aspects of the recovery process, as we describe below.

First, and in contrast to the rigorous definition of recovery utilized in outcome studies, there is little consensus in the consumer/survivor literature about the definition of recovery. What recovery involves appears to depend on whom you ask. Despite this lack of a uniform conceptualization, however, most definitions of recovery involve some component of acceptance of illness, having a sense of hope about the future, and finding a renewed sense of self. For example, two of the more often-cited definitions of recovery offered in this literature are:

> "Recovery refers to the lived or real life experience of persons as they accept and overcome the challenge of the disability." (Deegan, 1988, p. 15)

> "Recovery is a process by which people with psychiatric disabilities rebuild and further develop important personal, social, environmental, and spiritual connections, and confront the devastating effects of discrimination through . . . empowerment." (Anthony, quoted in Spaniol and Koehler, 1994, p. 1)

Such definitions obviously differ from those employed in clinical psychiatric research, in which recovery involves alleviation of the symptoms that cause a person distress or ill health and/or a return to his or her premorbid level of functioning. Recovery, from this more conventional perspective, is an absence of something undesired, such as symptoms, illness, alcohol, or other drugs, or the removal of something that was not part of a person's life prior to the illness, such as medications or hospitalization (White, 2000; Whitwell, 2001). While this model of recovery also may include more positive, objective indicators of improvement such as employment, housing, and relationships, the focus remains nonetheless on removing the obstacles to an otherwise normal or healthy state. From the perspective of consumer/survivors, however, recovery is not understood as an ideal or static "end product or result." It is neither synonymous with being cured nor does it simply involve a return to a premorbid state. Rather, it is a life-long process that involves an indefinite number of incremental steps. As a result, many people view the process of recovery as something that almost defies definition. It is often described as more of an attitude, a way of life, a feeling, a vision, or an experience than a return to normalcy or health.

One reason that consumer/survivors do not typically view recovery as a return to a previous state is that they view the experiences of disability, treatment, hospitalization, stigma, and discrimination associated with their psychiatric disorder as having changed their lives irrevocably. An analogy to this view of mental illness would be survivors of concentration camps or prisoners of war, who similarly can never simply return to their lives prior to their experiences of imprisonment, torture, and near death. In its more severe forms, schizophrenia appears to be experienced in a similar fashion as a life-threatening and life-altering condition. For example, Walsh describes how mental illness had such a profound effect on him that it was impossible for him to return to his life as it was before the illness: "I agree that we can never go back to our 'premorbid' selves. The experience of disability and stigma attached to it, changes us forever" (1996, p. 87). Some people, in addition, would not want to go back to their lives prior to their illness because that would in effect deny an important part of their existence (Corrigan and Penn, 1998) and/or negate gains they have made in the process of recovery.

Many people indicate that one of the more essential gains made in the process of recovery was accepting their illness and incorporating it into a newly defined sense of self. In this sense, recovery entails learning to live with a disability while still striving to achieve life goals and/or attempting to achieve these goals despite remaining disabled. Because this sense of recovery does not entail cure or a return to a healthy state, some have argued that "recovery" may not be the best term to capture the essence of the concept. For example, Jacobson and Greenley (2001) propose the notion of "healing" as more precisely capturing such a process of transformation. Part of healing, they suggest, involves having control and defining a self apart from illness (Jacobson and Greenley, 2001). Other authors refer to recovery as health-related psychological and social well-being irrespective of disability. The goal of recovery in this sense is not necessarily to become part of mainstream society. It is for each individual to experience an enhanced sense of self and to achieve whatever goals or aspirations she or he set for him- or herself (Deegan, 1988).

Because, from this perspective, the process of recovery may be different for different people, it is difficult to come up with one set of "essential" ingredients that will be true for everyone. Our review of these personal accounts reveals several common aspects of the journey of recovery, however. In addition to redefining self and accepting illness, these include overcoming stigma; renewing a sense of hope and commitment; resuming control over and responsibility for one's life; exercising one's citizenship; managing symptoms; being supported by others; and being involved in meaningful activities and expanded social roles. These areas provide examples of many of the ways in which people achieve what is perhaps the essence of recovery: a renewed sense of self as a whole person, despite or incorporating one's illness, along with a redefinition of one's illness as only one aspect of a multidimensional self.

Redefining Self. The redefinition of one's self as a person of whom mental illness is simply one part is probably the most overarching aspect of recovery. Psychiatric disorder has been described as a disease of the "self" (Estroff, 1989). Not only does a person experience psychological and emotional symptoms, social consequences, and stigma, but also he or she may be socialized into assuming the role and identity of a "mental patient." This role is reinforced by a system that has historically valued and rewarded compliance and passivity and been skeptical (at best) of signs of autonomy and independence.

Accepting Illness. Acceptance of illness is often described as the first step in recovery. This is not to say that one must accept a particular framework or conceptual model of illness (e.g., a narrow biomedical view of schizophrenia) in order to recover. Accepting one's illness also does not mean accepting the identity of a "mentally ill person." Accepting one's illness has instead to do with redefining how a person understands this particular one of life's challenges. There may appear to be a somewhat paradoxical quality to this form of acceptance, as Deegan (1988, p. 15) describes, "that in accepting what we cannot do or be, we begin to discover who we can be and what we can do."

Overcoming Stigma. Recovery involves more than overcoming the devastation of one's mental illness; it involves recovering from the social consequences and devastation of the stigma of mental illness as well (Ridgway, 2001). Societal stigma is viewed as one of the major barriers to recovery (Perlick, 2001). People do not live in isolation (no matter how much one may try) but within a social context. This context exerts tremendous influence on a person's sense of self and identity. As a result of the impact of stigma, some people internalize their community's notions of serious mental illness and withdraw into a "mental patient" role and identity. Recovery, on the other hand, requires developing resilience to stigma and/or actively fighting against it.

Renewing Hope and Commitment. The importance of having hope and believing in the possibility of a renewed sense of self and purpose is an essential component of recovery. For hope to be channeled into effective efforts toward improvement of one's condition and situation, it must be translated into a desire and commitment to recover.

Resuming Control and Responsibility. People must assume primary responsibility for their transformation from a mental patient or a disabled person to a person in recovery. Taking control of, and responsibility for, one's life helps the person to "shed the role of the victim" and increases the person's sense of efficacy in his or her life. In order for the person to take control of, and responsibility for, his or her life and regain a sense of agency and efficacy, however, she or he must be afforded opportunities to make choices and must have options to choose from. People in recovery need to be actively involved in all aspects of service planning, development, and implementation, as well as in other aspects of their lives outside of treatment and rehabilitation. Only this kind of substantial involvement can lead to a sense of empowerment, or to a sense of mastery and control over one's environment and self, which also are considered critical aspects of recovery.

Exercising Citizenship. While people have the right to be different, they also have the right to be treated the same. This means that people with disabilities are entitled to the same rights and responsibilities as other members of society. Part of recovery is therefore participating as full, contributing, and responsible members of society. Resuming the role of citizen may require advocacy as well as activity, however, as there are numerous legislative, attitudinal, and material barriers to full participation in civic life for people with disabilities (Rowe, 1999).

Managing Symptoms. Although complete symptom remission is not necessary for recovery to occur, people do indicate that being able to manage symptoms in some way is essential for them to be able to take an active role in their own recovery (Fisher, 1994; Ridgway, 2001). The methods by which people manage symptoms may differ substantially from one person to the next—whether it be through medication, therapy, or alternative methods of healing—and the methods themselves are not as important as the freedom and latitude the person regains by bringing the symptoms under some degree of control. Recovery in this sense is about *using* treatment, services, medication, or coping skills in a different way by becoming an active *participant* in treatment rather than simply a recipient of services and a beneficiary of the efforts of others (Deegan, 1996b; Ridgway, 2001).

Being Supported by Others. This is not to say that other people are not also important. Recovery, after all, is not a solitary, but a social, process (Jacobson and Greenley, 2001). People often describe the importance of having someone believe in them when they could not believe in themselves, having someone else stand by them, even when they felt they had had to abandon themselves to their illness. Having supportive others, whether they be family members or friends, professionals, community members, or peers, to provide encouragement through the difficult times and to help celebrate the good is critical to recovery. People in recovery speak also of the importance of having another person in recovery as a mentor or role model as they go through their own journey. Such role models can give people a sense of what recovery may entail and require of them and also may give them ideas about what to hope and strive for.

Being Involved in Meaningful Activities and Expanded Social Roles. A final, but important, aspect of recovery is involvement in meaningful activities and the development or expansion of valued social roles (Ridgway, 2001; Young and Ensing, 1999). Here again it is not so important what activities or roles people choose to become involved in or to pursue as much as it is important for them to participate in personally meaningful and gratifying activities that also afford them a sense of making worthwhile contributions to their community. This kind of participation also affords the person a sense of purpose and direction in his or her life. In addition to a person's own particular interests, education, employment, and spirituality are some of the primary and socially sanctioned ways in which people can acquire more meaning and purpose in their lives (Rogers, 1995; Sullivan, 1994). Many people in recovery emphasize the importance of their believing in something or of having faith when everything else was at its bleakest; this faith is often viewed as spiritual in nature (Sullivan, 1994).

Is There a Role for Treatment and Rehabilitation? Thus far, we have discussed primarily the role that people with the illness play in their own recovery, with some room left for others to be supportive by believing in, or standing by, the person. Does this mean that there is no role in recovery for the elements of psychiatric treatment and rehabilitation? The answer to this question, as we might expect by now, is a complicated one. There are ways in which treatment, rehabilitation, and other kinds of support facilitate recovery, but there also are ways in which these same practices may impede it. Let us see how this is so.

On the positive side, there are more recent approaches to the provision of mental health services such as psychosocial or psychiatric rehabilitation, in vivo skills training, cognitive behavioral treatments for psychosis, and assertive community treatment that share common values and goals with the recovery model. Even in these cases, however, an important distinction exists between rehabilitation and recovery-oriented services on the one hand and recovery on the other. Rehabilitation and other mental health services are what service providers and mental health programs do, whereas recovery clearly is the task of the individual (U.S. Surgeon General, 1999; White, 2000). Most proponents of the recovery model view the recovery process as distinct and parallel, at best, with the services provided by a mental health system. That said, some groups view treatment as providing the necessary path *to* recovery or at least as one of its most essential tools (e.g., the National Alliance for the Mentally Ill), while others believe recovery-oriented services may help to support people in their recovery, but that the services themselves are neither necessary nor sufficient for this "deeply personal" journey (Deegan, 1996a).

Unfortunately, just as common are negative perceptions of the mental health system and the treatment it provides. From their very first contact with mental health professionals up to their eventual "graduation" from the treatment system, consumer/survivors have identified multiple ways in which mental health services impede their recovery. Early in the course of their illness, for example, people report being told to relinquish their dreams, to expect a chronic and/or recurrent course of illness and dysfunction, and to anticipate a lifetime of mental health treatment, medication, and disability. Deegan describes the destructive impact of these messages and of her experiences of being hospitalized, being diagnosed with schizophrenia, and bearing the side effects of her medications as follows:

> And then, at a time when we most needed to be near the ones we loved, we were taken away to far off places. At the age of 14 or 17 or 22 we were told that we had a disease that had no cure. We were told to take medications that made us slur and shake, that robbed our youthful bodies of energy and made us walk stiff like zombies. We were told that if we stayed on these medications for the rest of our lives we could perhaps maintain some semblance of a life. They kept telling us that these medications were good for us and yet we could feel the high dose neuroleptics transforming us into empty vessels. We felt like will-less souls or the walking dead as the numbing indifference and drug induced apathy took hold. (1996a, p. 3)

Many of the stories told by consumer/survivors suggest that these kinds of early messages of hopelessness and despair have a destructive impact far beyond the initial shock, disbelief, or discouragement they elicit. Pessimistic pronouncements and the offer of poor prognoses, along with societal stigma and other social consequences of the illness, appear to compound the loss of self brought about by aspects of the illness (Davidson and Strauss, 1992; Estroff, 1989). This loss of self is exacerbated further by a system that reinforces passivity and compliance over autonomy and independence. Consumer/survivor narratives are replete with examples of how the structures and attitudes of the mental health system undermined, blocked, or discouraged their own efforts toward recovery. Indeed, the very term "survivor" is meant to signify surviving the mental health system as much as surviving the illness per se.

So, is everyone with schizophrenia able to recover? From the perspective of conventional clinical psychiatry, in which recovery is defined as the alleviation of symptoms and distress, not everyone may be capable of recovery. From the consumer/survivor perspective on recovery, which involves a restoration of life, the pursuit of goals, and the *addition* of meaning, social roles, personal empowerment, and citizenship *despite* residual disability, however, everyone is considered capable of recovery, although perhaps not to the same extent. This is because from this perspective, recovery does not mean that the person no longer requires supports (Munetz, Geller, and Frese, 2000). Rather, as with other disabilities, different types of support may be needed at different stages of recovery (Frese et al., 2001; Munetz, Geller, and Frese, 2000).

In the end, however, Deegan (1996b) reminds us that our job is not to "judge who will and who will not recover. Our job is to establish strong, supportive relationships with those we work with" in order to maximize everyone's chances for recovery. At this point, we only know that each person has a 50/50 chance of partial to full recovery, even as defined by clinical psychiatry, and we cannot yet predict who will and who will not achieve this degree of recovery. Therefore, from the consumer/provider point of view—and particularly given the field's history of overly bleak, pessimistic pronouncements—the risk is considered too great *not* to believe in the potential of every person for recovery, regardless of severity, symptoms, or functioning (Jacobson and Greenley, 2001).

Qualitative Research on Recovery

Qualitative research on recovery in schizophrenia represents a small but dense literature. The size may be accounted for, in part, by the field's historical reluctance to conceive of narrative data as offering a viable foundation for science, and correspondingly, to collect and analyze such data. The density speaks to the richness of the information comprising existing studies. In this review, we focus on the work of Barham (1984, 1992), Barham and Hayward (1998a, 1998b), Corin (1990, 1998), Corin and Lauzon

(1992, 1994), Estroff (1989), and Lovell (1997). We organize the work of these investigators across the two successive themes of strategies of existence and mechanisms of recovery.

Strategies of Existence

This heading is borrowed from Corin and Lauzon's 1994 report describing findings from a project that investigated experiences of community living among Canadian men afflicted with schizophrenia. This work emerged as one of the sturdiest planks within the literature in terms of method and findings, and we will rely on it heavily both in terms of its substantive content and as an organizing framework for our review.

As the basis for her investigation, Corin (1990, 1998; Corin and Lauzon, 1992, 1994) conducted open-ended qualitative interviews with 45 male participants (25 to 50 years old) who had previously been diagnosed with schizophrenia. The resulting narratives were grouped and analyzed according to participants' rates of rehospitalization (essentially high, medium, or low) rigorously employing discourse and structural analyses. The investigators assumed that lower rates of rehospitalization were consistent with the notion of recovery and therefore focused, in particular, on the results obtained by the participants who were rehospitalized least often. Their organizing interest was to identify those aspects of the experiences of these participants that appeared to be positively associated with their enhanced community tenure and, thereby indirectly, their recovery.

Public Space. Several of the participants who had the lowest rates of rehospitalization were found to frequent particular types of public locations, some according to regular schedules. Although the locations varied from person to person, all of the spaces had in common an impersonal character. They were spaces people typically come and go from within a narrow timeframe and with only superficial social contact. Examples included fast food restaurants, shopping malls, and outdoor squares. Corin noted that visiting such places appears to be very meaningful for men with schizophrenia and may be construed as "a kind of metaphor of a relationship with the environment" (1990, p. 176).

This finding was confirmed and expanded by Lovell (1997) in her qualitative research on schizophrenia and homelessness in New York City.

Lovell described a complex process through which homeless people with schizophrenia projected "home spatially" over an entire city (p. 363), as a way of constituting a sense of home distinct from places such as the shelters that are imposed on them. This sense of home also promotes a sense of movement to and from things; a sense of movement, argued Lovell (1997), that evokes in individuals a sense of transformation, of change, even of development. Corin's participants may have experienced a similar sense of progression through the social sphere, insofar as frequenting impersonal public spaces could be viewed as an attempt to move toward others within a context that feels both safe yet meaningful. We will elaborate on this idea below in our discussion of mechanisms of recovery.

Spirituality. Another characteristic of participants who had low rates of rehospitalization was an active religious life. For example, Corin and Lauzon (1992) described a participant who they called "Mr. A," who constructively applied his beliefs in God to various life goals. One goal, in particular, was Mr. A's desire to become a calmer person through increasing his self-confidence, noting that "it is not an ideal society for giving a sense of security to the person who is sick" (Corin and Lauzon, 1992, p. 267). Mr. A's references to God were constructive in this manner in shifting his attention toward internal values. At the same time, his religious interests provided a social context for rewarding interactions with those who shared his interests in a religious meditation group. Other participants with low rates of hospitalization also emphasized the importance of spirituality and religion in their narratives.

In a British study, Barham and Hayward (1998b) found that in order for spiritual life to have maximum benefit for people with schizophrenia, it must be disentangled from their illness. This is, of course, not such a straightforward task. It is a task that may differ, Barham and Hayward suggest, depending on how the afflicted individual conceives of schizophrenia; broadly speaking, in either an existentialist or materialist framework. Espousing an existentialist viewpoint could lead one to think of the illness as a spiritual vehicle, a religious tool. As Ben, a participant in this study, stated:

> Some of my fantasies and ideas were as a result of my illness really. You
> see, my illness questions things about truth and knowledge and existence,

because it's such a shattering experience, and I find it a bit religious. (1998b, p. 167)

Ben's statement highlights the tension that exists between the existentialist ("I find it religious") and materialist ("my illness") views of schizophrenia. Barham and Hayward suggest that existentialist conceptions of schizophrenia tend to blur the distinction between illness and spirituality, rendering the latter just as difficult to reconcile to one's life as the former. In this case, spirituality may become intricately linked to schizophrenia. A materialist conception, however, helps to delineate boundaries between the two. Thinking of schizophrenia as "some kind of chemical reaction in the brain," for example, places it in the domain of illness (I have) rather than existence (I am) (Barham and Hayward, 1998b, p. 167). Based on Ben's ideas and course of illness, Barham and Hayward proposed that a materialist view of schizophrenia is optimal, as it need not undermine the integrity of the person's spirituality, which can facilitate recovery.

Linguistic Tactics. Men with low rates of rehospitalization in Corin and Lauzon's (1994) work also demonstrated a propensity to rework language when expressing themselves, comprising a linguistic style that the authors described as "reopening language from inside" (p. 27). This style refers to the way in which the participants used words, particularly with respect to self-definition. For example, one man described himself as "simple," explaining its meaning as: "I make things simple. I don't make a big fuss over unimportant things. I am a peacemaker. I am able to stop verbal arguments" (1994, p. 28). According to Corin and Lauzon, what this participant has done is to transform a static, perhaps pejorative, quality into an active, positive attribute.

Other tactics employed by participants with low rates of rehospitalization extended beyond restructuring the qualities of words to introducing entirely new meanings. One participant, for example, described the phrase "a lazy person" as not "tak[ing] life too seriously, you relax better" (1994, p. 29). Again, such tactics appear to take language that is typically demeaning and turn it to constructive ends. As Corin and Lauzon (1994) note, this behavior goes beyond a means of coping to representing a useful approach to cognitive restructuring.

Mechanisms of Recovery

Positive Withdrawal. Corin and Lauzon (1992) suggested that the strategies employed by the participants described above have in common a stance that distances them from, and yet simultaneously fosters participation across, various social spheres. We know, for example, that the public locations frequented by those with the lowest rates of rehospitalization are busy though impersonal spaces, in which one can be in the company of others without the social demands of intimate interaction. We know additionally that what seems useful about these persons' spiritual outlooks is that they provide a way of using a socially sanctioned tool to justify distance from common indicators of success such as money, prestige, power, etc. Finally, we recognize that these people tailor one of the most defining characteristics of human social behavior—that is, language—in manners that infuse it with highly personal meanings. All of these strategies come together in what Corin and Lauzon (1992) conceptualized as a stance of "positive withdrawal." Involving simultaneously being inside and outside of the consensual social world, this stance is suggested as an overarching mechanism for recovery in schizophrenia.

We appreciate that one of the common functions of this mechanism is to negotiate a necessary personal space through which the person with schizophrenia can approach the world, his or her self, and, perhaps, his or her illness. As the term "withdrawal" suggests, however, this strategy involves a degree of social marginalization. But to what ends? That is, people afflicted with schizophrenia have likely already been socially marginalized due to their illness and the stigma associated with it. Surely, we are not suggesting that this kind of extrusion has been found to promote recovery. Rather, according to Corin and Lauzon, it is only an *intentional* form of marginalization, a form of social distancing actively pursued by the individual, that can affect favorable change. We have only alluded to these strategies in our discussion of what those with schizophrenia do, but it will now be useful to summarize more succinctly *how* (via positive withdrawal) these strategies can promote recovery. That is, how does positive withdrawal mediate the relationship between strategies of existence and recovery?

Larger Life Frames. In their analysis of their participants' narratives, Corin and Lauzon (1994) outlined three potential outcomes of positive withdrawal—what they referred to as "larger life frames" (pp. 35–41)—which might be understood in terms of how the strategies of existence considered above promote recovery. These include the person's (a) reworking his or her personal history and sense of temporality; (b) constructing an intersubjective field; and (c) elaborating a personal position within the world. Each of these is described briefly below.

Reworking one's personal history and sense of temporality might be understood as recasting one's past into a positive relation to the present, in which it becomes possible to reconcile past and current problems, both personal and social. Given the substantial and unexpected problems introduced by schizophrenia, it may be a significant challenge to find ways in which one's present situation can be viewed in favorable terms and connected in a meaningful, contiguous way to one's past.

Corin and Lauzon (1994) illustrated such a process through their example of Mr. A, whose Catholic upbringing was punctuated by a desire to become a priest, a notion to which his mother was opposed. In adulthood, in spite of his illness, Mr. A was able to create his own personal religion to which he attracted a fair number of adherents. This achievement connected his present to his past goals and likely also served as a way for him to exert a sense of autonomy and free himself from others' restrictive opinions of him and his life. This, in turn, appeared to provide a sense of agency, which may have made it possible for him to sever ties with his immediate family more formally. Far from sharing his family's perception of him as the alienated "black sheep," his historical perspective on himself and his choices helped him to recast his present identity into an autonomous, self-reliant framework. In this example, Corin and Lauzon (1994) illustrated the role of Mr. A's intentional withdrawal from his family and the organized religion of his childhood in recovering and reconstructing a more robust sense of self.

Construction of an intersubjective field can be thought of as nurturing psychological space for one's personal interests and associated self-perceptions, wherein there is room to define the self in favorable ways. Again, in the case of the person suffering from schizophrenia, the cultivation of an adequately durable personal space, via engagement of one's interests, may pose a considerable challenge in the face of the barrage of overt and covert negative perceptions and messages conveyed by the broader social context. To illustrate this process, Corin and Lauzon (1994) provide the example of Mr. C, a man ostracized by his family who also had treated him as an invalid. Mr. C's engagement in a Christian charismatic group that was unaware of his illness provided him the opportunity to redefine himself as something other than an invalid and provided the space within which he could consider himself as a worthwhile and effective person. Additionally, his religious education afforded him a sense of direction that was a reflection of a more favorable personal identity than that afforded by his family.

In this example we again observe the tension inherent in the experience of schizophrenia articulated above by Barham and Hayward: the tension between the "I am" (as conveyed to Mr. C by his family), and the "I have" (as discovered when he joined this religious group). Estroff (1989) considered this distinction at length in her ethnographic work on people with schizophrenia, suggesting that how one thinks of her or his illness is, in part, a function of interpersonal processes and one's interpersonal context. Conceptions of illness and identity are based, in part, on the social roles the person is afforded by his or her social environment, which then can facilitate or impede an exploration of larger frames within which to live. Therefore, with regard to positive withdrawal, the valence of "positive" is contingent on what it is from which one withdraws. In Mr. C's case, it was his family and the restrictive nature of his relationship with them.

Elaboration of a personal position within the world refers to discovering ways in which one can approach and engage in some involvement in the broader social context. In the case of coping with schizophrenic illness, the challenge is one of identifying those avenues to reengagement in the world that remain open and available to the person and accessing these avenues in ways that foster, rather than threaten, a positive sense of self. By way of illustration, Corin and Lauzon (1994) describe another participant, Mr. E, who, like others in the study, found himself systematically alienated from his family. Mr. E, however, tended to idealize the notion of strong family bonds he never actually knew or experienced. His routine of frequenting different public spaces afforded him a sense of connection to the world and, over time, allowed him to develop a new network of friends in the community that included his neighbors, as well as other people in recovery. It required Mr. E's withdrawal from the perpetual disappointment of familial rejection for him to be able to seek out others with whom he then could establish intimate bonds and experience a sense of affiliation.

Stepping Outside. Given this cursory review of qualitative findings, it appears—perhaps surprisingly—that many of the goals and means for attaining them, employed by people with schizophrenia, are the same as, or at least similar to, those employed by those of us who do not have schizophrenia. In other words, much of what we have discovered to pertain to recovery in schizophrenia would appear to apply equally well to other life situations, in which people seek personal space, meaningful connections, and a positive sense of identity.

Most of us untouched by schizophrenic illness negotiate some "personal space" within which we engage the world. Most of us use that space, in part, for the purpose of pursuing our interests, which, to some degree, come to define who we are. Most of us attempt to make sense of our histories, as a way of understanding our actions, thoughts, and selves in the present. Although such activities may be complicated by schizophrenia, they apparently are not ravaged by it. If we define an "outside" to schizophrenia in this way—by the persistence of basic human qualities and capacities that endure beyond the illness—then we recognize that there is, in fact, an outside to schizophrenia. It is here, on the outside of the disorder, that processes of recovery appear to be initiated and to unfold.

Summary and Implications for Research

What have we learned from this review, and what implications do these lessons hold for our investigation of experiences of recovery in schizophrenia?

From the consumer/survivor literature we have been told that recovery from schizophrenia does not require remission of symptoms or of any other deficits brought about by the disorder. Rather, recovery appears to involve minimizing, managing, or overcoming the effects of being a mental patient, including, but not limited to, rejection from family, peers, and society as a whole; poverty, unemployment, and substandard housing; loss of valued social roles and identity; loss of sense of self as an effective social agent and of the sense of purpose and direction associated with it; and loss of control over, and responsibility for, one's major life decisions. In addition, most authorities in the U.S. consumer/survivor community appear to agree that recovery involves some degree or form of acceptance of one's illness within the context of a sense of hopefulness about the future, in general, and, more specifically, about one's ability to rebuild a positive sense of self and social identity.

Rather than leading the person back to a preexisting state of health, the processes by which people with schizophrenia are to achieve these components of recovery are considered to be on-going or lifelong in nature. Finally, given the traumatic nature of being a mental patient, people should not expect to return to the lives they led prior to the onset of their illness. Like other trauma, these experiences change the person's life forever. The best that can be hoped for is a multidimensional sense of self and a personally meaningful and rewarding life of which the illness becomes a smaller and smaller part over time. Whether or not such a view of recovery can be reconciled with the approach of clinical psychopathology remains to be determined.

To these elements of recovery, the qualitative studies that have been completed to date add a focus on the processes by which people with schizophrenia attempt to achieve or establish these foundations for improvement. These studies suggest that adaptation to schizophrenia, at least in ways that promote community tenure, involves a process of distancing oneself voluntarily from the mainstream community and its normative social expectations. In the psychological and social distance opened up in the process, the person then has adequate room and opportunity to carve out his or her own niche, based more on idiosyncratic meanings and indirect or less intimate ways of connecting to others. Whether or not this process characterizes everyone with schizophrenia who shows improvement, and whether or not it may be equally characteristic of people who do not have schizophrenia, also remain to be determined.

In summary, the consumer/survivor literature has made us aware of issues of acceptance of illness, hope, self-definition, loss, stigma, agency, control, and involvement in meaningful activities. Previous qualitative studies suggest in addition that achievement of these elements of recovery may require an intentional withdrawal from mainstream society in order to open up the social space needed for the person to reestablish a personally meaningful and gratifying life that is reconnected to others in a safe but distant manner and places few social demands on them. We shall keep these issues in the back of our minds as we analyze our narratives of recovery in schizophrenia.

In closing it is important to note, however, that these literatures shed little light on our original research question:

How do the person's experiences and activities affect processes of recovery in schizophrenia?

The consumer/survivor literature identified a number of components that people who have had a serious mental illness have found important in reclaiming their lives *despite* remaining disabled. As useful and important as this literature may be both personally and politically, its relevance to processes of improvement is limited to the extent that this approach differs substantially from the definitions of partial to full recovery utilized in the psychiatric outcome literature. The psychiatric research that demonstrated a heterogeneity in outcome for people with schizophrenia had a much more narrow definition of recovery that explicitly *included* remission of symptoms and remediation of deficits; both of which were explicitly *excluded* from the consumer/survivor literature. Insofar as we are interested in understanding the processes that lead to remission in symptoms and remediation of deficits, that is, to the more narrow definition of improvement, the consumer/survivor literature will therefore be limited in its applicability. For example, such issues as acceptance of illness and stigma would not necessarily be of concern to someone who was no longer ill. Similarly, milder forms of the illness, from which people might recover more rapidly, would most likely not require wholesale redefinitions of self and one's relation to the world.

With respect to previous qualitative studies, we again find investigators identifying the ways in which people with serious mental illnesses attempt to restore their lives irrespective of whether or not they are simultaneously improving their health. For example, Corin and Lauzon's construct of "positive withdrawal" speaks to a constructive coping strategy that people with schizophrenia may use as long as they continue to have schizophrenia. Were these people to recover in the narrow sense utilized in outcome research, they presumably would no longer need to utilize such a strategy in adapting to community living. We pointed out that processes utilized by people who have schizophrenia may be utilized just as much by people who do not have it. To the degree that this is the case, to the degree that people who do not have schizophrenia also employ strategies of positive withdrawal, we can no longer consider this strategy to be characteristic of recovery in schizophrenia. On the other hand, to the degree that such strategies are characteristic of serious mental illness only and not ordinary human experience, they no longer characterize the lives of people who have recovered.

These may appear to the sympathetic reader to be unfair criticisms of the consumer/survivor and qualitative literatures. It might appear, for instance, that this last criticism amounts to a kind of "catch-22" situation, in which research on illness cannot be considered relevant to people who have regained their health because they are no longer ill, while research on regaining health cannot be considered relevant to people who are ill because they are not yet healthy. We will argue that there is a way out of this dilemma when we turn to exploring narratives of recovery. It is not possible for us to argue this case, however, until we have a firm grasp on the fundamental elements of phenomenological methodology, as it is the framework offered by phenomenology that we suggest allows us an escape from this trap. It is thus to this topic that we now turn.

2

■　　■　　■　　■　　■　　■　　■　　■　　■

Eliciting Narratives

Suppose a mountain has gold
and no one is allowed to mine it anymore;
the water will bring it to light, the water
which reaches into the silence of stone,
it does the wanting.

　　　　　　　—Rainer Maria Rilke, *Das Stundenbuch*

WE WANT TO LEARN MORE about the ways in which people with schizophrenia may influence the course and outcome of the disorder and decided to do so by interviewing people who are currently living with the disorder (as opposed, e.g., to reading autobiographical accounts). Now what? Don't we simply identify a number of people diagnosed with schizophrenia and ask them: "In what ways do you influence the course and outcome of your disorder?" No, we do not. The reasons we do not ask this type of question are manifold, and we will explore several of them in this chapter. We will begin, however, with the most important reason, which also perhaps is the source of many common misunderstandings of qualitative and phenomenological methods.

Is the Person a Psychologist or a Storyteller?

The primary reason we do not ask such a question is because the role of the participant in our research is not to be a fellow psychologist but to be precisely what she or he is: a person experiencing life with schizophrenia. Contrary to the constructivist views of Piaget and Kelley, we do not view people as going about their everyday lives as if they were untrained but naturally intuitive scientists: collecting data, testing hypotheses, and drawing inferences based on experience. Nor do we view people as lay phenomenologists, reflecting on and trying to determine the structural elements of their own experiences. Husserl undertook such reflection in his formal role as a philosopher, not in his role as a lay member of German society in the early twentieth century. Kierkegaard, the Danish theologian we alluded to in the previous chapter, similarly may have functioned as a "proto-phenomenologist" in the sense that he reflected on his own experiences in ways very similar to those later proposed by Husserl, even though he predated Husserl by half a century. He did so, however, in his role as a theologian and not as part of his everyday life as a citizen of Copenhagen.

Regardless of their training or occupation, people go about their everyday lives precisely as people: becoming hungry and eating; having other needs and desires for such things as love, friendship, meaningful activity, leisure, and sex; setting and pursuing personal goals; admiring art and the beauty of a pretty face; encountering obstacles and becoming annoyed or frustrated; going for walks in the autumn foliage; relishing a child's smile as she opens presents on Christmas morning, etc. Again, this may seem obvious, but these are the experiences that provide the grist for phenomenological reflection. We do not get to these experiences by asking the person to become a psychologist.

How, then, do we gain access to these experiences? We want to include the person with schizophrenia as a partner in the research enterprise. We do so not by including this person as a fellow scientist but rather by including him or her as *the* expert on the domain of his or her everyday life. We remember that we are interested in the original, first-person experiences that are prior to, and provide the basis for, theoretical and scientific conceptions. This is true not only when we reflect on our own experiences but also when we reflect on the experiences of others. We are not so much interested in the conceptions they have derived from their experiences as we are in the experiences themselves. As a result, we have no need of arguing with those critics of qualitative research who point out that most people are not aware most of the time why they make most of the decisions they make or behave or act in many of the ways they do. We readily agree with this point but simultaneously insist that it is irrelevant to our quest as phenomenologists. We are not asking people to explain their experiences or actions to us, to account for why they do what they do, or to identify factors influencing their experiences. If any of these issues are at all relevant to qualitative approaches, it will be our job as psychologists to address them, not the job of our participants.

So what is the job of a participant in a phenomenological study? How can a participant as an expert on his or her everyday life provide us with access to the domain of his or her original experience? Simply *and only* by describing his or her experiences to us as closely and faithfully as possible to the ways in which they were originally experienced. In other words, rather than asking a person to explain his or her experiences *to* us, we are asking him or her to share his or her experiences *with us*: to tell us stories about his or her life as he or she lived it. The role of a participant in a phenomenological study is therefore that of autobiographical storyteller. We are interested in narratives that capture the flow of experience over time in the lives of each person. As a result of this interest in narrative, we are more likely to find useful concepts derived from literature and drama, such as plot and role, than we are to find concepts derived from the physical sciences such as causality (Davidson and Cosgrove, 1991).

Phenomenological interviews are robust to the degree that they provide rich narrative and descriptive detail. The art of storytelling, after all, is not so much in plot or character development as it is in the sensuous rendering of descriptive detail. Stories cannot be told in the abstract, only in the particular. And it is through the particular, through the specific, intimate details of each person's concrete everyday life, that we are able to approach the universal. The meaning and application of this important principle for phenomenological inquiry will become clear as we proceed through the use of illustrative examples. For now, we accept that participants in our study will play the role of storyteller as opposed to that of scientist. Our next challenge is to figure out how to engage them in this process.

Why Not Just Ask?

If we want people to tell us stories about their lives, why don't we just ask them? Why do we frame this as a challenge? We listen to stories practically from the time we are born. We are raised on stories. Some investigators have gone so far as to suggest that narrative is an inherent structure of human cognition (Bruner, 1986; Schank, 1982, 1990). What could possibly be challenging about eliciting stories from people? In other words, do you have to be trained to do phenomenological interviews? Is there, in fact, a science and an art to doing qualitative research such that both rigor and experience enable a person to become better at conducting narrative interviews?

This, unfortunately, is one of the several areas in which qualitative researchers have done themselves and their craft a disservice. It has long been accepted in quantitative research that one's data can be no better than the tools used to collect it. It is for this reason that an entire industry has grown up around the development, testing, and validation of quantitative instruments. We have no reason to believe that this principle is any less relevant for qualitative research. Most qualitative investigators, however, mention little about how they developed the questions they employed, the interview style or techniques they used, or the criteria by which they judge one interview to be better than another. In fact, most qualitative studies are presented as if no thought at all had been given to what kinds of questions were to be asked and how, as if this were a simple and straightforward affair that required no specific expertise or explanation.

Anyone who has been involved in conducting qualitative research or, for that matter, has watched talk show hosts on television or listened to them on the radio, however, has observed that people exhibit varying degrees of competence in conducting interviews. To conduct rigorous and high quality research, qualitative investigators need to devote no less time and energy to the development and administration of their narrative interviews than quantitative researchers do to the development and standardization of their instruments. This is both a little appreciated and relatively undeveloped area of qualitative expertise.

Some of the challenges inherent to the task of eliciting stories become obvious the minute we imagine asking a person with schizophrenia the simple and straightforward question: "Can you please tell me what it has been like to have schizophrenia?" In the first place, and as we noted in the Introduction, there is a common perception within psychiatry that many people diagnosed with schizophrenia have little to no insight into, or are in denial of, their condition. In this case, a common response to the above question might be a simple "Who me?" or "What's that?" or, in the case of more verbally inclined individuals: "I don't know what you're talking about. I don't have schizophrenia." Putting this issue aside for the moment, however—as it is not characteristic of most qualitative research topics—there still are many challenges to succeeding in having people respond to this kind of question by telling stories of their experiences of life with schizophrenia.

Imagine for a moment that the topic were different and you were approached by someone armed with a tape recorder, a blank consent form, and the seemingly simple and straightforward question: "Can you please tell me what it has been like to be in graduate school?" or to study psychology, or to read this book? How might you respond? How would you respond if this person were to ask you what it has been like to have cancer, diabetes, or asthma? Would you launch spontaneously into an autobiographical narrative rich with descriptive detail? If they were not worried about the potential repercussions of their responses to people who represent the mental health system—including qualitative psychologists—but felt free to be honest and blunt in their answers, many people with schizophrenia would most likely respond to the above seemingly simple and straightforward question with the simple and straightforward reply: "It sucks."

As important as these issues may be, we are not referring here primarily to the issues of trust, rapport, or impression management explored and acknowledged in the clinical and social psychology literatures. These interpersonal issues will impact on the conduct of qualitative interviews, just as they impact on clinical interviews, job interviews, etc. But that is not our current focus. Our current focus is on how to frame questions so that they elicit detailed narratives. What we are looking for most in narratives, as we said above, are rich, descriptive details about a person's subjective experiences in the context of his or her everyday life. We are unlikely to elicit this kind of detail by asking vague or general questions such as the one above. Vague questions typically elicit vague responses. To elicit specific, detailed responses, then, we most likely need to ask specific, detailed questions

(Edelson, 1993; Strauss, 1996). We don't necessarily want to ask someone explicitly to tell us a story—as in "Can you please tell me a story about what it has been like to have schizophrenia?"—as this remains a vague and general question. Rather, we want to encourage our participants to return to their own experiences and simply and spontaneously describe to us what happened in the ways they remember it happening.

Is it in fact possible, however, to ask specific, detailed questions while at the same time leaving these questions open-ended so as to elicit a narrative? Isn't this a contradiction? A specific and detailed question, for example, would be: "Did you watch the New York Yankees play in the World Series (again)?"; its psychiatric equivalent being: "Did you hear voices over the last week/month/six months, etc., when no one else was around?" Such a question, however, is likely to elicit only a yes or no answer instead of a story. Similarly, the question: "What did you have for dinner last night?" is typically answered by one or a few words (e.g., pot roast, vegetarian lasagna and salad) and is unlikely to generate a story of the interviewee's dining experience. A parallel question regarding schizophrenia, for example, "What kinds of things did these voices say to you over the last week/month/six months?" is likely to generate parallel answers such as "That I was a mental patient" or "That I was a rock star about to hit it big with my next song." Although this begins to get us a bit closer to experiences of hallucinating, we still are a long way from an intimate, personal account of the participant's unique experiences of life with the disorder.

It has been our experience that finding the right questions to ask and learning how to frame them in the right ways pose considerable, if unacknowledged, challenges to qualitative researchers. A significant amount of effort is required early on in the development of a new study in order for us to familiarize ourselves with the phenomena in question enough to begin to get a sense of what to ask about and how. Extensive, informal, and unstructured discussions with members of the prospective target population and/or other key stakeholders, review of areas of inquiry and potential phrasings of questions with these same parties, as well as conducting pilot interviews to test sample questions, are all essential steps in the process of formulating an interview protocol.

We will explore some of these steps in what follows. Prior to introducing principles for conducting qualitative interviews, however, an example may be useful in persuading the reader that this kind of attention is, in fact, warranted. It is possible, after all, that you may be skeptical of the emphasis we are placing on how qualitative investigators develop and frame their questions. Just in case you harbor such doubts, allow us to illustrate the point in the following story.

One of our graduate students chose to focus her doctoral dissertation on how people with serious mental illnesses experience outpatient psychiatric treatment and rehabilitation in order to identify those aspects of the current mental health system that are perceived as useful, as well as those aspects that are perceived as harmful. After reviewing relevant literature, talking with a number of her clients, and engaging her advisors in several discussions of possible ways to frame the first, open-ended question of her interview protocol, the student decided on the question: "What have your experiences of psychiatric treatment been like?" After completing three pilot interviews that began with this question, the student was quite surprised to note that all three participants had described their experiences of being hospitalized only, apparently viewing treatment as what happens while they are in the hospital. Not one of her participants spontaneously offered an account of an experience in outpatient treatment, and, when the student tried to encourage them to do so, they did not seem to understand the notion of "outpatient treatment" per se. If treatment is indeed what happens in the hospital, then the notion of outpatient treatment becomes an oxymoron.

It took the student several more discussions with advisors, presentations to classmates, and additional pilot interviews to identify a way of framing her first question, which elicited the kinds of stories she was looking for; stories of how people related to, and were treated by, their outpatient mental health providers in ways that were both helpful and not. As it turned out, the question had to focus initially on these relationships with providers rather than on the treatment or rehabilitation process, as participants did not view what transpired in various outpatient settings as either treatment or rehabilitation. In fact, the only element of their experience that they appeared to perceive as active treatment outside of the hospital was their medication. All the other elements involved were experienced as part and parcel of their relationships with the people who were their clinicians, case managers, or rehab therapists. As a result, the final version of her first question focused on these relationships as the entrée into the broader outpatient domain.

How to Ask

In addition to the kind of groundwork this student had to lay prior to conducting her interviews, there are a few principles of qualitative interviewing worth mentioning. Before enumerating them, however, it is important to include the disclaimer that—despite their areas of technical overlap—qualitative interviews are not to be confused with psychotherapy, as there are several crucial differences between the two.

Psychotherapy involves an explicit contractual relationship entered into on the part of the client with a goal of addressing an area of personal distress or as a vehicle for personal change for which the client and/or his or her healthcare insurer reimburses the therapist for his or her time and expertise. Qualitative interviewing, while also involving an explicit contract (i.e., informed consent), is oriented neither toward changing nor ameliorating the distress of the participant and (typically) involves reimbursing the participant for his or her time and willingness to share his or her experience. While it is possible that some people find being interviewed to be cathartic or healing in some way, participants agree to share their experiences solely for the purpose of generating new knowledge.

The intimate and potentially therapeutic nature of the person's disclosures does raise unique ethical issues for qualitative research that at least do not appear on the surface to be as relevant for quantitative studies. These issues primarily involve what constitutes an adequate level of information for consent to be truly informed; what potential effects might be brought about through the participant's involvement, both for the participant and also for others; and what responsibility, if any, the investigator carries in relation to these effects and their longer-term repercussions. For further discussion of these important ethical issues, the reader is referred to the growing literature on this topic (e.g., Baez, 2002; Boman and Jevne, 2000; Cieurzo and Keitel, 1999; Hadjistavropoulos and Smythe, 2001; Orb, Eisenhauer, and Wynaden, 2001; Piercy and Fontes, 2002; Price, 1996; Punch, 1994; Raudonis, 1992; Stewart, 2000).

Despite these important differences, qualitative interviews and psychotherapy share an interest in eliciting and exploring rich, narrative accounts of the person's experiences. As such, they share several principles related to the structure and function of narratives in people's lives. We have found the following principles, derived from one or both of these traditions, useful in training and supervising psychologists in the conduct of qualitative interviews. First the don'ts:

1. Avoid asking closed-ended questions that can be answered by yes, no, or other one- or two-word answers;
2. Avoid asking questions that begin with "Why," as they tend to put people on the defensive, feeling that they are being asked to explain rather than describe;
3. Avoid asking vague, general, or abstract questions, and avoid using technical language or jargon;
4. Avoid asking complex or compound questions that require the person to answer more than one thing at a time;
5. Avoid asking people *about* their thoughts, feelings, or other "internal" states and avoid saying "Can you tell me . . ." as all of these tend to introduce distance between the participant and his or her own experience (as well as between the participant and the interviewer); and
6. Avoid interrupting the person or showing any other signs of impatience with their efforts to respond to your questions.

And now the do's (if they are not already self-evident):

1. Ask open-ended questions for which you do not know the answer ahead of time;
2. Ask questions beginning with "How" or "In what ways";
3. Ask specific, detailed questions and couch them as much as possible in the participant's own language;
4. Only ask one question at a time;
5. Ask questions that imply a temporal framework of before, during, and after rather than a static state;
6. Communicate respect by following the person's lead and not pursuing any areas in which a participant clearly communicates discomfort;
7. Communicate interest nonverbally by squaring one's posture, making an effort to look in the person's eyes, nodding at appropriate times, etc.; and
8. Demonstrate comfort with the content of the person's story by having a relaxed disposition and posture and refrain from extreme reactions to any particular details.

As we are aware that such a list is far from adequate in clarifying the nature of good qualitative questions, and as we remain convinced of the importance of this topic in designing qualitative studies, we offer an illustrative example from our own research. This example illustrates the process of moving from a vague interest in a general topic to a more focused and narrative approach to interviewing people about their relevant experiences. Following this illustration, we return to the issue of how to frame qualitative questions before moving on to the question of what then to do with the participants' answers.

On the Way to an Illustrative Example: The Importance of Context

We mentioned in the introductory chapter that in the past, once diagnosed and hospitalized, people with schizophrenia often lost the opportunity to make substantive decisions and to speak and act on their own behalf. Having their everyday lives in the hospital regimented and supervised by others, they became almost entirely recipients of the ameliorative and custodial efforts (or neglect) of others. These others included hospital staff, clinicians, family members, clinical investigators, and public policymakers. Such a situation is necessary, we acknowledged, when an illness takes over the entirety of the person as it eventually does, for example, in Alzheimer's disease. Such a situation may be considered problematic, however, when the person wishes—despite the disorder—to act, speak, or make decisions on his or her own behalf, as would likely be the case in schizophrenia should recovery, in fact, be possible.

A number of years ago, we had an opportunity to begin to explore this issue in some detail in an area that had important policy implications and decided to do so using qualitative methods. The opportunity was presented by a hospital downsizing initiative, mandated by our state mental health authority. This initiative constituted the last wave of deinstitutionalization in Connecticut, completing a 40-year process of moving long-stay patients out of state hospitals back into the communities from which they had come many years before. This last wave was in preparation for closure of two of the three remaining state hospitals and involved relocating to the community long-stay patients who had been deemed too disabled to be discharged in previous waves. In other words, these individuals not only had experienced extended stays at the state hospital but also were considered by the staff to be particularly "refractory" (i.e., nonresponsive) to previous treatment and rehabilitation. The community mental health center at which we worked was asked by the state mental health authority to facilitate the return of 16 of these people back to the New Haven community.

What does any of this have to do with the phenomenology of schizophrenia? What difference does it make where these people live in relation to the nature of their disorder? Aren't we interested primarily in the person's role in influencing the course and outcome of schizophrenia? What does the over 40-year history of the policy of deinstitutionalization and a more recent hospital downsizing initiative stemming from it have to do with our qualitative interest in the person's role?

The answers to these questions actually bring us to the heart of another common misunderstanding of qualitative inquiry. The questions seem to imply that it would be not only possible but also preferable for us to explore subjective experiences of schizophrenia divorced from any particular geographical, historical, or social context. They seem to imply, that is, that we can have unobstructed, uncontaminated access to psychosis and to the person's role in influencing its course and outcome, without having to take into account such seemingly irrelevant details as where the person happens to be living at the time. Can there be, however, a phenomenology of schizophrenia as experienced, as it were, in a vacuum? Can there be experiences of schizophrenia or of recovery, for that matter, that are not grounded concretely in particular geographic and social contexts and that do not occur concretely at particular times in history to particular people? We suggest not.

Early phenomenological studies, like early approaches to the social sciences, in general, made the unfortunate mistake of viewing their findings as independent of context. Like the Platonic forms, these findings were taken to represent timeless, universal truths about human nature or the essential structures of (any) human consciousness. It is true that Husserl viewed philosophical phenomenology in this way, arguing initially that it provided access to universal and timeless essences. Husserl, however, was a mathematician by training and was interested primarily in establishing the a priori foundations for logic and science. At the philosophical level, such a quest for essential truths may be appropriate even as it remains difficult to accomplish. For his part, late in his career even Husserl had begun to let go of his philosophical insistence on timelessness in order to explore more fully the nature of the person's immediate social environment as constituted through historical and cultural institutions (1970a). Regardless of one's philosophical convictions in this regard, however, at the level of the social sciences it is an entirely different matter. At this level there is no escaping the conclusion: Context counts.

It is true that the WHO's International Pilot Study of Schizophrenia described in the Introduction, as well as other studies conducted since, consistently have documented that prevalence rates for schizophrenia are constant across countries. It also is true, however, that these studies discovered, and then later confirmed, significant differences in course and outcome across cultures, indicating that the person's experience of psychosis and his or her ability to manage in the face of it differ considerably depending on context. One need only compare Pat Deegan's (1993) or Carol North's (1987) experiences of psychosis and its treatment in the mental health system of the late 1950s and 1960s either with the lives of people being wharehoused in the state hospitals of the 1930s and 1940s or with the experiences of people early in the course of illness at the beginning of the twenty-first century to see how different experiences of serious mental illness and its treatment can be over time and across different contexts.

Even without these contrasting experiences as examples, it is obvious upon reflection that there cannot be an experience of schizophrenia without that experience occurring at a specific time, in a specific place, to a specific person, etc. There can be no experience without an experiencing agent, and that agent is always an embodied human being with a certain past, present, and future living during a certain historical period and in a certain social and cultural environment. We were wrong to think, however, that these particularities obstruct or contaminate our access to the nature of schizophrenia. Far from these personal particularities posing problems for our qualitative method, it is these very parameters of particularity that bring us right to where we want to be in eliciting stories about living with schizophrenia. If you are able to remember back to several pages ago, you will recall that we diverted your attention to this particular example in order to illustrate how to frame questions so that they elicit narratives full of rich, descriptive detail. With our discovery of the context-dependent nature of experience, we have now found our way to the answer. We elicit narratives full of specific details by asking specific people to describe specific experiences they have had at specific times in specific places. To this type of specific query, they typically respond with specific answers.

An Illustrative Example: Hospital or Community Living?

With this in mind, we return now to the example of our recent hospital downsizing initiative. What makes this particular initiative relevant to our present interest is that in the case of schizophrenia, major policy decisions such as this, that is, whether or not to close two large state mental hospitals, historically have been made without input from the people affected most directly by them: the patients themselves (Herman and Smith, 1989; Lord, Schnarr, and Hutchison, 1987; Thornicroft and Bebbington, 1989). Even more surprising, perhaps, is that evaluations of such policy decisions, and of the initiatives resulting from them, also have not included the patients' own perspective on the services, programs, or interventions intended to serve them. Nowhere has this been more the case than in the debates over deinstitutionalization and the related questions of where people with mental illness should live while they are being treated.

Our experience of the downsizing initiative reflected this same lack of attention to, or interest in, the patients' own preferences, in that the decisions to downsize the hospital and to transition these particular 16 individuals back to the New Haven community had been made with no consultation with the 16 individuals themselves. Shortly after the decision was made by the state mental health authority to move some people back to the community, these 16 individuals were identified by the hospital staff as ready for discharge and then engaged in a process of gradually transitioning out of the hospital. During the next several months, they routinely visited New Haven (a 30-minute drive from the hospital) to find an apartment or other residential setting, to get to know their new mental health providers, and to refamiliarize themselves with the local community. Upon discharge from the state hospital, they then were offered extensive community-based clinical, residential, social, and vocational rehabilitation services in order to support them in their efforts to adapt to community living. At no point in this several month process were these individuals asked about their own preferences for staying in the hospital versus moving back to New Haven, or about what it was like, or would be like, for them to live in either place. In accord with the conventional presumptions about schizophrenia described in the Introduction—in which people with the disorder are viewed as empty shells of their former selves, no longer able to care for, speak for, or decide for themselves—these people were assumed to be too sick to participate in this way in determining their own fate. They were assumed not to have preferences or opinions on the matter or they were assumed to be too out of touch with reality for those preferences or opinions to count.

After working with these individuals in New Haven for about six months following their discharge from the hospital, we decided that we had been handed an excellent opportunity to test some of these presumptions and to attempt to add the patient's voice to the on-going policy debates by conducting a qualitative study of life with schizophrenia before, during, and after the transition from hospital to community living. In terms of our interests in narrative, we had before us 16 specific people who had been living in the same specific place and who had just gone through a process of transitioning over a specific period of time to another specific place. As clinical managers and researchers, we were interested in specific questions about specific dimensions and details of their experiences related to their day-to-day lives in both of those specific places. In addition to shedding light on several aspects of living with schizophrenia (including the aspect of having certain of one's major life decisions made by others), a qualitative study of these experiences would provide important evaluative feedback about the wisdom of this policy decision and about the quality and effectiveness of our efforts in implementing it.

How, then, to get people to tell us stories about their experiences in the hospital, during their transition to the community, and once resettled in the community? Keeping in mind the principles enumerated above, including our primary wish to avoid vague and abstract questions, how do we begin to ask questions that will elicit such narratives? One possibility would be to ask: "What has it been like for you to go from living in the hospital to returning to New Haven?" This is not a closed-end question, does not ask "why," is more specific than "What is it like to have schizophrenia?" and avoids the distancing language of "Can you please tell me. . . ." Unless we have already asked the person what life was like for him or her in the hospital, or assume that we already know without having to ask, however, this question violates principle no. 4 from the "don'ts" column: we are asking the person a compound question that requires more than one answer. In fact, this one question involves three separate questions concerning what life was like in the hospital, what the transition out of the hospital was like, and what life is like now that they are back in the community. It will be necessary to break these components apart and to ask about each one separately. As a result, we end up with the following three questions:

What was life like for you in the hospital, before you were discharged to New Haven?

How did the transition of leaving the hospital and coming to New Haven go for you?

How has it been for you to be living in New Haven since you were discharged from [the state hospital]?

These three overarching, open-ended questions were used to frame our inquiry. The only major issue remaining was the order in which the questions should be asked. Investigators who have extensive experience conducting similar interviews may be able to determine the most useful order for such questions by themselves, perhaps thinking that chronological order is a natural sequence to follow. We were not so confident that we could determine this in advance and instead explored this issue, along with several others, in a pilot phase of the study as we recommended above.

Informal, pilot interviews suggested that chronological order was, in fact, *not* best, as participants had difficulty shifting their orientation abruptly from the present to their past hospitalization. Following the clinical principle of meeting the person where she or he is at, we learned that—at least in this case—it was best to start with the present and ask the person to describe what life is like at the time before asking him or her to reflect back on previous experiences. Once engaged in the process of telling stories about their lives at present, it then became easier for people to shift in their orientation back to the past, as all of these stories had a past intrinsic to them.

We did not settle simply on a reverse linear chronology, however, as questions related to the discharge and transition process seemed to make most sense coming *after* descriptions of life in the hospital rather than

Figure 1

Order of Interview Protocol Relative to Linear Chronology

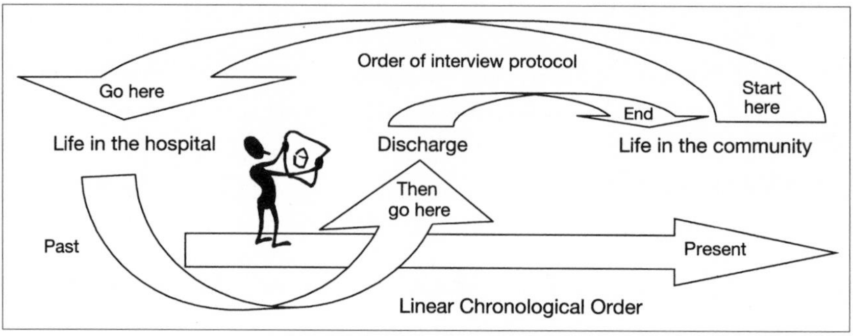

before. Once people had become reoriented to recalling how life had been in the hospital, the narratives flowed naturally into the discharge and transition process that brought participants back to where they now were. As a result, we eventually settled on an interview guide that, in terms of its temporal flow, did not direct the person step-by-step through a linear narrative (either forward or backward), as we might initially have expected. Instead, the progression of the interview may be depicted as in figure 1.

We are taking the time to review in some detail the process of composing a qualitative interview because, as we said above, this is an area most qualitative investigators do not elaborate to a sufficient degree to give new investigators a sense of the amount of work and attention involved. We did not simply sit down with these 16 people and ask them to tell us a story about their life experiences prior to, during, and following their discharge from the state hospital anymore than a quantitative investigator asks research subjects simply to rate how anxious, depressed, or psychotic they are. In both cases, "life is in the details," and it requires careful attention to the phenomenon under study to identify what those details might be and how to gain access to them (Strauss, 1996).

In the case of this qualitative study of the experiences of long-stay inpatients returning to the community (Davidson, Hoge, et al., 1995), the nonlinear nature of the narrative flow was one such detail we did not anticipate beforehand. Many other such details emerged from our review of the literature, our collective clinical experience, and our pilot interviews. These details suggested specific areas of inquiry that we could use to prompt people to flesh out parts of their narratives they might otherwise not have mentioned. Some of these details were consistent across time periods, while others were specific to one component or another.

For example, we found that experiences of food—where, with whom, and what the person ate—were important indicators of the person's involvement in, or lack of, relationships regardless of setting. In the state hospital, informal social gatherings typically occurred in the hospital canteen, where patients would go to buy cigarettes, soda, or coffee, and where they could spend unstructured time with their peers. For example, one woman described her daily routine in the hospital as follows:

> [I'm] at the canteen every day. My mother sent me money [so I'd] buy cigarettes, buy candy, buy coffee, buy gum, buy soda, buy tea, buy soup, saltines and cheese and ham and bagels; you know, buy food and listen to the music.

In the community, on the other hand, stories of having to eat meals alone in one's own apartment were prime indicators of social isolation, while pizza parties with residential staff or trips to fast food restaurants with peers offered temporary relief from loneliness. Described one participant when asked about his life in the community:

> I just sit at my table and drink soda or water and smoke and listen to the radio and get a few memories by listening to the music. Or occasionally, I'll turn on the TV and watch a pretty good movie. And we get together and sometimes we go out [to] McDonald's and have a little bite to eat.

Similarly, the issue of what people did to express their faith or spirituality or to get in touch with their relationship to the divine or sacred was equally important across settings, even though it was lived out differently in each place. During their stay at the state hospital, several participants reported frequenting the hospital chapel. Once discharged, however, they ended up relying on private prayer or religious programming on radio and television to feel part of a faith community. Details related to issues of stigma, sense of safety in the community, and resumption of experiences they had enjoyed prior to their hospitalization were specific to participants' experiences in New Haven, while details related to visits by friends and family, how they were treated by staff, and how they kept in touch with the rest of the world were specific to the time participants spent in the hospital. One of the more unexpected findings of this study, for example, was that participants felt more safe on the streets of inner city New Haven than they had on a state hospital campus, situated on a picturesque hilltop among the Connecticut mountains. As one participant explained, in the hospital "I was afraid that if I made one wrong move someone would knock me down. . . . You never knew who was going to hit you or if you'd wind up in restraints."

In order to give you a sense of how this looks in practice, we reprint below one section of the final interview protocol we eventually used for this study. Prior to this section, there were questions pertaining to the participant's demographic and diagnostic characteristics, current living arrangements, family involvement, and history of service utilization. These data were obtained through a combination of self-report, medical record review, and consultation with the person's current mental health providers. Following this section, there were similar sections for life in the hospital and for the transition from hospital to community living. Questions pertaining to life in the community and probes to use as follow-ups in each area were as follows:

Instructions to interviewer: Begin with first, open-ended question in each category and encourage the participant to elaborate on content spontaneously, then refer to specific prompts in each area that the participant did not address.

A. In the community: First I'd like to find out what it has been like for you to be living in New Haven. How has it been for you since you were discharged from [the state hospital]?

   1. How do you spend your time in New Haven?
      What kinds of things do you do during the day?
      How do you spend your evenings?
      How do you spend your weekends (particularly Friday and Saturday nights)?
      Do you go to any parties, dances, or other social events?
      Do you engage in any religious activities, by yourself or with others (e.g., go to church, synagogue, or mosque, pray or talk with God alone)?
      Do you celebrate any holidays? If so, how (where, with whom, etc.)?

2. What are your relationships with other people like?

> Do you have any friends?
>
> Do you see anybody from your family?
>
> Do you have any romantic relationships?
>
> How do people treat you in the community?
>
> How do you get your sexual needs met?
>
> Do you feel like a member of any group?

3. What is the community like?

> Are there any places in New Haven where you feel like you belong?
>
> Do you feel safe in the community?
>
> Are you able to buy the things you want or need?
>
> Are you able to get around as you would like?
>
> Do you get to use or do anything the community has to offer (movies, places to eat, etc.)?
>
> How do you take care of your daily needs (eating, doing laundry, etc.)?
>
> How do you feel about where you live?
>
> Do you get to do any of the things you used to enjoy, or that were important to you, before you went to the hospital (e.g., eat your favorite foods, get a good haircut, attend family events, etc.)?

4. Has anything been particularly difficult for you since you were discharged from [the state hospital]?

> Symptoms or psychiatric problems?
>
> Have you felt more lonely or hopeless?
>
> Have you had any problems with your health?
>
> Has it been harder to get along day to day (e.g., eating or filling your time)?
>
> Has it been harder for you to see or talk with your doctor or other healthcare providers?

5. What kinds of successes or good experiences have you had since being discharged?

> What kinds of things do you like about the community?
>
> Do you get to do more or different things that you enjoy now that you are in the community?
>
> How do you feel about your ability to take care of yourself to the extent that you can?

6. What have you found most helpful in your adjustment to living in the community?

7. Are there any things you miss about [the state hospital]?

    Particular people?

    Particular places?

    Particular activities or opportunities for work, school, or recreation?

    Feelings of being safe and taken care of?

8. As you look toward the future, what are your hopes?

9. As you look toward the future, what are your fears?

First, the attentive reader will note that several of these questions violate our own principles of qualitative interviewing. For example, questions beginning with "Do you . . ." or "Have you . . ." conceivably could elicit yes or no answers, even though in practice they seldom do. Questions beginning with "Are you able . . ." may put people on the defensive as much as "why" questions, especially if they are sensitive to being seen as incapable; a sensitivity that many people with schizophrenia have. Finally, questions like "Have you felt more lonely or hopeless?" not only ask *about* feelings but also could lead the participant into areas the investigator wants him or her to go, injecting the interviewer's biases into the participant's story. So what conclusions are we to draw from this exercise?

These interview questions were developed as part of one of our first qualitative studies. We would like to believe that we have learned a number of things about conducting qualitative interviews over the intervening years and would, for the most part, no longer use questions framed in these ways for the above reasons. Then why did we use these questions as examples? As this exercise was intended to illustrate the process of framing qualitative interview questions, this early interview was chosen on purpose to demonstrate a few additional points.

The first point, as is evident in the last paragraph, is that it is not so easy to develop optimal qualitative questions. The questions outlined above were developed following our review of the literature, reflection on our relevant clinical experiences, and a series of pilot interviews. Now, in retrospect and with considerably more experience under our collective belts, we would throw out two-thirds of these questions, especially the specific prompts. We included the prompts in order to focus the participants on the details of their experiences, however. If we are to throw out two-thirds of the prompts, how else might we ensure the specificity of the narratives and their inclusion of these important areas?

This brings us to a second point, which is that qualitative interview protocols are to be used flexibly as guides or cues for the interviewer; they are not to be administered verbatim in a standardized format, as if they were structured quantitative instruments. The single most important thing that a qualitative interviewer can do in eliciting a rich descriptive narrative from a participant is to listen actively to what he or she is saying. It is not possible to listen attentively in this way if one also is preoccupied with making sure that one asks all the questions provided in exactly the order and form they are provided. In fact, it would be highly unusual in a qualitative interview for the interviewer to use all the specific prompts or questions provided. To the degree that one sticks strictly to the questions and prompts outlined, one is at risk of conducting a structured or semistructured interview at best. Open-ended, narrative interviews, on the other hand, take on a life of their own and depart considerably from the written protocol. It was for this reason that the problematic prompts included in the above protocol did not do too much damage in the conduct of the actual interviews; many of them simply were not used.

This leads to the third, and final, point to be derived from this example, which is that it is possible to learn how to improve the quality of qualitative interviews over time. If we did not rely on the prompts we developed, how, then, was the participant encouraged to describe his or her experiences in detail? The key was mentioned in the first sentence of the instructions provided with the above protocol, but in such a way that it easily could have been overlooked as obvious. This sentence read: "Begin with first, open-ended question in each category and encourage the participant to elaborate on content spontaneously." In the intervening years since we developed that first protocol, we have learned that encouraging participants to elaborate on their own answers is more important than framing specific prompts as follow-ups to open-ended questions. In fact, the more experienced we have become in conducting qualitative interviews, the fewer predetermined questions we find ourselves asking. Rather, we have found framing follow-up questions in the participant's own words to be a more effective route to fleshing out unknown or implicit details in his or her narrative than our attempting to anticipate specific areas of focus as we did above with our prompts. The work of anticipating specific areas of focus continues to be important, however, as such prompts, even when they are not asked explicitly, remain in the back of the experienced interviewer's head, informing his or her framing of questions. As the task of framing effective follow-up questions poses yet another significant, if unacknowledged, challenge to qualitative researchers, it deserves a section of its own.

Encouraging Elaboration

We mentioned in the beginning of chapter 1 that we had the good fortune of working with a medical student a number of years ago who, in his naiveté, had an intuitive talent for conducting excellent qualitative interviews. Does this fact contradict what we said above regarding the role of experience in learning how to frame qualitative questions? In other words, if a relatively naïve medical student who knows little about schizophrenia can conduct excellent qualitative interviews with limited training, how can it be necessary to have a solid grasp of the literature on schizophrenia and have extensive experience doing interviews in order to do them well? We should note, however, that our medical student did not develop the interview protocol himself, but rather was trained in its use. More important, what is especially striking about his interviews is the way in which he asked many of his follow-up questions. It is to these that we turn now in order to explore ways to encourage participants to elaborate spontaneously on their own answers in fleshing out the details of their story. It is in this process that either a genuine naiveté or a well-trained and disciplined sense of curiosity is of value in keeping the investigator from making assumptions about what the participant is saying, thereby missing opportunities to ask for clarification.

The study for which these interviews were conducted was embedded within a larger, randomized community trial of one form of what we have come to call "supported socialization" (Davidson, Haglund, et al., 2001). In this larger study, 260 people with serious mental illness who also were socially isolated and withdrawn were given a stipend of $28 per month and encouraged to take part in social and recreational activities in the community. On a random basis, two-thirds of these participants also were offered the opportunity to be matched with a volunteer partner to join them in these social and recreational activities. This project, and the smaller qualitative study embedded within it, have both been described in detail elsewhere (Davidson, Haglund, et al., 2001; Stayner, Davidson, and Tebes,

1996) and will not be described at length here. For our present purposes, it is enough to know that the interviewer was asking people who had participated in this project to describe their experiences of being matched with and becoming friends with their partners and of their lives before and since being matched with a partner.

It was in her response to these questions that a woman we have called Jane gave the following description of her life prior to the project:

> I would open a can and eat right out of the can, because I knew I had to put some food in me, but I had no enthusiasm of wanting to make it because I was going to eat it by myself. The only person I had to talk to was the television. So I would open a can of beans, wouldn't even heat it, because I just knew that I had to put food in me. . . . I [wouldn't] go out to a restaurant because I don't like the emptiness. I mean you just sit there and you buy your meal. It doesn't taste the same as when you're eating it with somebody.
> (Quoted in Davidson, Stayner, Nickou, et al., 2001, p. 380)

There are a number of remarkable things about Jane's response, not the least of which is her ability to capture her sense of isolation through her description of sitting in front of the television eating cold beans out of the can because she knew "I had to put food in me." This description provides an excellent example of the kind of rich, descriptive detail a phenomenologically oriented investigator is hoping to elicit from qualitative interviews. Despite being seriously disabled by schizophrenia and exhibiting a bit of what psychopathologists might label "concreteness" in her use of language, Jane also provides an excellent example of how people with schizophrenia for the most part make sense when they talk. The only part of Jane's response that departed from the path of common sense, the one example of what some might describe as her inappropriate concreteness, was in her conclusion that food doesn't taste the same when she is alone as when she is eating with someone else.

Being attentive to the unfolding of Jane's story, and noticing when her narrative (somewhat abruptly) stopped making sense to him, the interviewer chose this moment to ask Jane to elaborate further on her story. His choice for how to frame this question exemplifies one particularly effective approach to encouraging elaboration and one we recommend be used whenever possible. This is the approach of reiterating the participant's own words but within the context of a question. In this case, the interviewer asked: "It doesn't taste the same?" To which Jane responded:

> No, because when, like when you go to Burger King, like on the first [of the month] I can go to Burger King [because] I've got money. I've got a reason to go in there because I've got money, but I'm alone. I sit down at the table. I eat a hamburger. I'm just eating a hamburger. But when I go in with somebody else, and I'm sitting there at the table and eating it, she'll say "Oh, is your hamburger good?" Then it becomes, the hamburger becomes noticeable, and then your mind starts to think about the taste. But when you're sitting there by yourself, you're just eating it and then you go out the door. . . . I don't want to eat really, because it doesn't taste good when I'm alone. [But] when you go out [and] you're not alone, you're able to eat talking to somebody, so that can of beans could have been in a gold bowl instead of just a plain, cold tin can. (Quoted in Davidson, Stayner, Nickou, et al., 2001, pp. 380–381)

As is the case in assessing the accuracy and timeliness of interpretations in psychotherapy (Casement, 1991; Edelson, 1993), the effectiveness of qualitative interview questions can be judged by the quality of the responses they elicit. Well-framed questions, like well-framed interpretations, generate rich narrative data like that seen in Jane's response above. Had the interviewer not asked Jane to elaborate on how the hamburger tasted different in the two situations, Jane most likely would not have offered the two stories of eating in Burger King with and without a friend. It is just this kind of story, however, that provides the most useful grist for the phenomenological mill of structural analysis to be described in the next chapter.

In the first example, it is likely that the interviewer genuinely did not know how the hamburger could taste differently in the two situations until the matter was clarified for him by the participant. Not to ask in such a circumstance is not so much a matter of overlooking the obvious as it is of being unaware of one's own ignorance. For this reason, it is important in conducting qualitative interviews to be intimately familiar with, and accepting of, one's own ignorance. Relevant to this circumstance is the additional principle of "When you don't understand something the person is saying, ask."

In the second example that follows, on the other hand, it is quite possible that the interviewer may have thought that he already understood what the participant was telling him but asked for clarification nonetheless in order to confirm, reject, or simply make explicit his implicit understanding. This is an equally legitimate, and more common, reason for asking people to elaborate on their narratives, as interviewers should not be content with an implicit or unconfirmed understanding. To do so is a sure way for the interviewer's own biases to creep into the participant's narrative undetected. As we all necessarily take for granted an indefinite number of implicit meanings in our interpersonal interactions in order to function on a daily basis, it unfortunately is harder to learn to recognize when one is making unwarranted assumptions concerning implicit meanings in an interview and needs instead to be asking clarifying questions. The following example illustrates the value of asking such questions in cases in which the responses may be expected to confirm one's implicit understandings, for it is not uncommon in such situations for there to be surprises that turn out to shed additional light on the phenomena of interest.

In this example, our highly talented medical student was interviewing a gentleman with a 20-year history of co-occurring serious mental illness and substance use who had been randomized into the control condition of the study described above. In this condition, participants received the $28 monthly stipend but were not matched with a volunteer partner to join them in the social and recreational activities they were encouraged to pursue. The point of having such a comparison condition was to see if the intervention of providing the monthly stipend and encouraging participants to go out and use the money to enjoy themselves and have fun was sufficient by itself to increase their involvement in social activities. Similarly, qualitative interviews with participants in the control condition focused on describing their lives before the project, how they used their monthly stipends, and what their lives have been like since joining the project and receiving the stipend. In this part of the interview, the participant we have called Tom was describing for the interviewer what his life was like before joining the project. In response to a specific question about how he spent the holidays, Tom said:

> For years I've hated Christmas because . . . [that's] the time that everybody
> gets together and everybody talks, and everybody sits at the table and they

start listing their accomplishments. And I don't have very many I can list. I'm in school. I'm in college, you know. Big deal. I'm only taking one course a semester. My brothers and sisters took double courses during the semester. I've got a brother who's a lawyer. I've got a brother who's going to be a priest. I've got a brother who's an insurance actuary. These are all high paying, real respectable type jobs. And then you look at me and what have I got and what am I doing? And it's very hard to try to compare yourself to these people. And everybody's getting together on a holiday and . . . they're usually comparing themselves like "I've done this," "Well, I've done that" and I don't have much to say about what I've done. And what I do say, I don't like saying, because, you know, just because of how things are. (Quoted in Davidson, Stayner, Nickou, et al., 2001, pp. 381–382)

At this juncture in the interview, the interviewer has at least three options of different directions to pursue, based on three different approaches to what Tom is describing.

One option is to assume that by "just because of how things are" Tom is referring back to the examples he provided earlier in the interview. In this case, the interviewer would be assuming that Tom didn't like to talk about what he was doing because he was only taking one course a semester and otherwise hadn't done much worth mentioning, especially in comparison to his high-achieving siblings. In this case, the interviewer might not ask a question at all, allowing Tom to continue uninterrupted or, if need be (i.e., if Tom stops and does not continue), asking the next question in the protocol, assuming that this comment is fully understood in this way. Note that in this case not only is the interviewer making an unwarranted assumption but also that there is nothing in Tom's story that is directly related to his having a serious mental illness, as this story is equally poignant for any of us who consider ourselves to be the "underachievers" in our families. We certainly do not want to assume that everything people tell us will be directly related to their mental illness, as this would be to perpetuate the very presumptions about schizophrenia that we are trying to challenge. As we will see, however, in this case not to have asked would have been to miss an important dimension of Tom's experience that otherwise would have remained undisclosed.

As a second option, the interviewer might ask what is intended to be a clarifying question but ask it in such a way as to imply that he already understands Tom in the way described above (i.e., in terms of his under-achieving in relation to his siblings), with this understanding simply to be confirmed by Tom in order for them to be able to move on with the re-mainder of the interview. Such a question might be framed: "By 'how things are,' Tom, you mean taking only one course a semester and not hav-ing accomplished much else?" These are precisely the kinds of questions, however, that are criticized for leading the witness, so to speak. By asking the question in this way, the interviewer may well have interpreted *for* Tom the meaning of his comment before Tom had a chance to become aware of its meaning himself. As many participants are loath to correct the inter-viewer, this is one way of sneaking in one's biases without knowing it. In order to avoid inserting such biases, a useful rule of thumb is: "If you un-derstand what the person is saying, don't ask for clarification, but if you don't know what the person is saying, ask for clarification in such a way that keeps all of the participant's options open." In other words, ask the follow-up question in an equally open-ended fashion.

With this rule of thumb we have arrived at the third option and the one chosen by our interviewer. Even though he also may have presumed that he understood Tom's story as a typical story of an underachiever, the in-terviewer was humble enough in accepting his ignorance to choose a more open-ended version of a clarifying question. In another illustration of the value of reiterating the person's own words within the context of a ques-tion, he asked: "Just because of how things are?" To which Tom then re-sponded: "Yeah, like 'I didn't go to the nuthouse this month, I guess I'm doing pretty good.' You know, what do you got to say" (quoted in David-son, Stayner, Nickou, et al., 2001, p. 382).

With this response we are given indications of the ways in which Tom's story *is* directly related to his history of serious mental illness, substance use, and repeated hospitalizations. By referring to the "nuthouse" in a self-deprecating manner, Tom appears to be connecting his inferior perfor-mance in comparison to his siblings, his lack of accomplishment, and, eventually, his hatred of Christmas and other family holidays to his history of psychiatric disability and institutionalization. With a hint of sarcasm directed unfortunately at himself, Tom lets the interviewer in on one of the ways in which his sense of identity has been affected by his struggles with his illnesses and their sequelae and, in turn, one of the ways in which his resulting negative self-image has impacted his family relationships.

Without blaming Tom for his negative self-perceptions, it is worth noting that many other individuals with a history of serious mental illness would find taking any college courses, regardless of how many per semester, to be a significant source of pride. This apparently is not the case with Tom, and we now have the beginning of an understanding of why that might be so. As we can see, even in those cases in which questions may be asked initially to confirm the interviewer's understanding, the person's responses typically not only confirm or disconfirm this understanding but also elaborate on it in potentially quite useful ways.

A Final Illustration

We bring this chapter to a close with a final example of the utility of well-framed follow-up questions, this time turning back to the earlier study described above of long-stay state hospital patients returning to the New Haven community. In this example, we do not find the interviewer reiterating directly the person's own words, even though doing so might have been an effective response. In this case, the interviewer chose instead an alternative approach that also is worth both describing and recommending. This approach may appear similar to certain cognitive-behavioral techniques, but within the phenomenological tradition it is derived from Husserl's notion of the "eidetic reduction" (1983).

The eidetic reduction is not to be confused with the phenomenological reduction discussed in the Introduction. The phenomenological reduction, you may remember, placed between brackets the existence of a world out there independent from our experiences of it. Even though it shares the mathematical term "reduction," the eidetic reduction is an entirely different matter. It is described more accurately, perhaps, and also with less of a chance of confusion, as involving the technique of "imaginary variation" (Husserl, 1983). As its name suggests, imaginary variation is a technique of varying the details of an object in one's imagination in order to determine which aspects of the object are essential to its being what it is. For ease of clarification, let us take a red metal chair as our object. What is it about the chair as we experience it, asks Husserl, which makes it precisely a chair and not something else, like a table or a couch? Is it essential, for example, for the chair to be red for it to be a chair? Similarly, is it essential for the chair to be made of metal for it to be a chair?

We can vary these particular details in our imagination in order to assess the status of these various aspects. We can imagine the chair to be green, brown, or yellow instead of red and in each case it would, for all intents and purposes, remain a chair. We can imagine the chair to be made of wood or plastic instead of metal and still in each case it would remain a chair. Obviously, it is easier to determine the nature of a chair (e.g., an object on which a person can sit) than to determine the nature of a work of art, an object of nature, or a person. In all these cases, however, the technique remains essentially the same.

Let us now see how this technique of imaginary variation might be useful in helping a qualitative interviewer to frame follow-up questions. We take our example from an interview with a female participant who had spent a total of almost one-third of her 36 years in the state hospital, suffering from a combination of schizophrenia and cocaine abuse. When asked by the interviewer if she engaged in any religious activities in the community, this young woman responded: "I don't own a dress." Taken out of context, this response might well be viewed as an example of the symptom of formal thought disorder found in schizophrenia, given that it appears to be a non sequitur. The interviewer, however, as a skilled clinician and an experienced qualitative researcher, understood that there might be a link between this woman's participation in religious activities and her wardrobe.

Given the context of urban poverty in which this young woman lived in the community, the interviewer took this response to suggest that perhaps she did not have appropriate clothes for attending church services. In this case, seeking clarification through simply reiterating the participant's words in the form of the question "You don't own a dress?" would have run the risk of offending her, no matter how unintentionally. We can imagine that to such a question she conceivably might respond with the statement "No, I don't own a dress" but said in such a way that you could tell she wanted to add "What's the matter with you, can't you hear" or, worse, "Of course I don't own a dress, don't you know what it's like to be on disability?" Either way, this question might have damaged, rather than promoted, the rapport between interviewer and participant, all the while failing to generate any additional information. A different approach was required to encourage her to elaborate on this rather intriguing response to an inquiry about her religious activities.

It is in such a case that imaginary variation can be useful for both interviewer and participant. Its use in this instance would involve varying the details of the participant's narrative in one's imagination to determine whether or not she perceived owning a dress to be the only necessary condition for her involvement in religious or spiritual activities. Accordingly, the interviewer responded by asking her: "If you had a dress, would you go?" This elicited the following response from the participant:

> No. Churches are crowded these days, and I wouldn't want to just go and try to mingle around them, you know. All I have to do is listen to the radio to the word of God if I wanted to hear it.

This response goes well beyond the sole issue of whether or not the participant owns an appropriate dress to wear to church. Her comments about anticipating difficulties in attempting to mingle with parishioners in crowded churches speaks to a broader sense of discomfort in public gatherings and begins to give us insight into some of the factors that might contribute to her social isolation. Had the interviewer simply assumed that this young woman's comment about not owning a dress was the end, rather than the beginning, of a story about her hesitation in joining religious activities, we would not have learned this additional, and important, information about her broader social concerns and discomfort. By posing the hypothetical question of whether or not this would be different if one of the details of the story were varied (i.e., she did own a dress), the interviewer was able to elicit a fuller account of the participant's life.

The reader may, based on this example, have two lingering concerns about our treatise on principles of framing qualitative questions. A first concern is that by asking this participant to imaginatively vary the details of her account are we not putting her back into the role of fellow psychologist that we rejected at the beginning of this chapter? Are we not asking her to explain her behavior in precisely the ways we said we wanted to avoid by asking her whether or not having a dress was essential to her reluctance to participate in religious activities? Note, however, that this is not what the interviewer asked her. He did not frame his question as a tentative interpretation for her confirmation or disconfirmation by asking, for example, "So are you saying that you would be too embarrassed to go to church?" or "Oh, do you think people would not welcome you because of how you dress?" Similarly, he did not invite her to interpret her own behavior by asking "Are you afraid that you might not fit in?" His question refrained from placing the participant in the role of psychologist by sticking to the level of descriptive, behavioral detail. The question was one of would she or would she not go to church if she owned a dress. It did not address the reasons for, or significance of, either choice, nor did it ask the participant to explain her choice in any way. It simply invited her to entertain in her imagination the possibility of an alternative twist in the plot of her narrative and asked whether or not this variation fit within her narrative as well.

A secondary concern would be that this follow-up question violates our first principle by being closed-ended, by posing a yes or no choice. The participant might have stopped after saying "No" and left her response at that. Isn't this what we are trying to avoid? There are two answers to this question. One is yes, this is what we are trying to avoid in principle. We can see, however, that in this case the question elicited more than a yes or no answer. Does this mean that our principle is wrong, and that yes or no questions are fine to ask? No, it does not, and the reason it does not is because this particular question was framed in the words and details of the person's unfolding narrative. We have found that once you begin to frame questions in the person's own terms you have more latitude in how you frame questions, at times not even needing to frame them as questions at all. This appears to be a result of the fact that when one is following closely another person's narrative, most questions asked in this context come to be taken as requests for further elaboration on the story being told (which is precisely what they are). Once the narrative flow is established, it may be sufficient to make a brief comment, utter an expression such as "wow," "really," or "oh," or even raise one's eyebrows without saying anything; all of which primarily have the aim of letting the person know that you are listening and following along, thereby encouraging him or her to please continue.

Caricatures of "hmmm"-ing psychoanalysts aside, this brings us to the second answer to the above question regarding our wish to avoid closed-ended questions. The principles for framing good qualitative questions enumerated earlier were meant to guide the interviewer into an actively listening and attentive posture. Following all these principles to the letter will not improve the quality of an interview, however, as long as this posture of actively and attentively listening is not present. We also have found the reverse of this to be true to some degree, in the sense that if the interviewer is, in fact, listening in an active and attentive way, following the person's narrative closely, then this opens up the kind of latitude in framing questions, making comments, or giving nonverbal cues as described above, conveying to the person that you wish him or her to continue to tell his or her story.

The principles we offer are intended to assist interviewers in achieving the kind of posture in which those same principles no longer matter. As in the Zen story of the disciple mistaking the finger pointing to the moon for the moon itself, it is the active and attentive listening promoted by these principles that is most important, not the principles themselves. There are many paths available by which people can learn how to listen. We offer our principles only as one such path. What is important is that the interviewer be able to listen, and that the participant feels that he or she is being listened to. Once this stage is set, the narratives, invariably, will flow.

3

■　　■　　■　　■　　■　　■　　■　　■　　■

Understanding Narratives

In the sphere of the human sciences . . . to say that [psychologists] "explain" human-scientific facts means that they want to clarify motivations, to make intelligible how the people in question "came to do it," came to behave in such and such a way, which influences they underwent and which ones they themselves exercised, what it was that determined them in and toward the community of action.

—Edmund Husserl, *Ideas II*

WE MAY NOW BE FEELING relatively good about ourselves. With a bit of patience and some practice we have learned how to elicit rich, detailed narratives even from an isolated population of people who are perhaps not accustomed to being asked about their lives. This leaves us, though, in possession of hundreds of pages of verbatim transcripts from (typically) between 12–36 interviews, each lasting (again, typically) between 45–90 minutes. It is at this phase of the research that doctoral students who choose to conduct empirical qualitative studies for their dissertations begin, at times unexpectedly, to have nightmares. Why didn't anyone warn me that it would be like this, they ask? What am I to do with this pile of unruly data? How can I fit hundreds of pages of only loosely structured interviews (at best) into a manageable and coherent "results" section? How am I to reduce this amount of data into something I can communicate to my thesis committee in a 20-minute presentation or publish in a 15-page journal article?

Despite the dismay we may experience when confronted with hundreds of pages of interview text, this challenge is not, in principle, unique to qualitative research. The occasional self-righteousness of new qualitative investigators who believe that they alone are burdened with an overwhelming amount of data is misguided. Doctoral students conducting quantitative studies are similarly confronted with the challenge of what to do with the hundreds of variables collected on dozens, if not hundreds, of people. How are they to reduce their piles of data—which will be literally piles of instruments or interview booklets—into a few tables? The strategies for reducing the data will differ depending on approach, but the challenge to both approaches is fundamentally the same: make some (manageable) sense out of the participants' (unmanageable) responses. Within the context of a narrative perspective, we can expect the sense that we make to be narrative in nature. Our challenge can be thus reframed as: How to bring the many stories we have been told by many people into one or a few coherent stories that convey their most salient, consistent, and, perhaps, integral common elements?

The following chapter addresses these questions, completing our outline of an empirical, qualitative research methodology for psychology by describing how narrative data can be reduced and made sense of within a phenomenological perspective. There are several components to this process, which we describe below. We may recall, however, that we already began this description in the Introduction, when explaining how qualitative methods differ from quantitative ones in their basic theoretical orientation. We did this through our use of the example of a tree bursting with fall foliage, arguing that experiences *of* the tree cannot be understood in the same way as the tree itself. It will be important in understanding what follows in this chapter to recall this example and its theoretical significance.

A Brief Return to Our Favorite Tree

In the case of our favorite red tree, we understood its identity as a physical object to represent a "union point of causalities" within the context of nature (Husserl, 1981, p. 179). We were able to experience the tree as the same despite changes in its appearance over time because the changes that occurred were ordered, predictable changes that abided by certain laws. The tree remains the same tree over time because its interactions with its environment consistently abide by the laws of possible changes that we identified as belonging to trees. It was the nature of the laws by which these changes occurred that we conceptualized as natural causality.

It also was because these same laws of causality were not sufficient to ground all psychological investigation and theory, however, that qualitative methods, we argued, are both possible and needed. In situating qualitative psychology outside of the scope of the laws of causality, we suggest that experiences—whether of trees or of anything else—cannot themselves be understood adequately through causal explanation. My experiences of the tree cannot be understood as if they were themselves objects *of* experience. As the realm of experience is that in which physical things are experienced through their multiple appearances, appearances themselves must be experienced in a way that differs from the way in which objects appear through them.

To translate these rather abstract notions into their implications for psychology, we turn now to a different example, that of eating. In relation to eating as a human behavior, we can say, on the one hand, that a naturalistic science of psychology will *explain* eating behaviors based on a causal model of the human body's metabolic processing of nutrients and their conversion into energy. A qualitative science of psychology, on the other hand, will understand eating behaviors based on a motivational model of experiences of being hungry. To paraphrase Robinson (1985), while the *cause* of my eating may be a lack of satiety, the *reason* that I am eating is that I am hungry.

On the basis of this distinction, we argued that approaches to qualitative psychology needed to develop methods suited to studying the subjects of experience rather than its objects. In this way, qualitative methods are experience-based, taking as their aim description and understanding of subjective experience as it unfolds immanently over time. Without rejecting the value of naturalistic approaches to psychology, we recognize that we experience ourselves as making decisions, as acting and behaving in accord with plans we have made (or not) based on *reasons*; based, that is, on motivations that involve our being directed toward goals.

Within this context we discover that there is a unity to this flow of experiences that does not need to be explained on the basis of factors external to the experiences themselves. The experiences carry within them an intrinsic continuity, a continuity that unfolds through meaningful relationships of motivation rather than through physical relationships of causality. That is, we discover the laws of motivation operating in this temporal flow by studying the meaning of the experiences themselves in their relationships to each other. We need not look anywhere other than to the realm of experience itself to generate knowledge about the structures and laws of experience.

As we will see in what follows, however, this is not as straightforward as it may at first appear. Like the Sirens beckoning Ulysses, we find ourselves tempted at every turn to abandon our slow-going but steady labor in the realm of experience for the lure of more accessible results through a short cut into causal explanation. As we find in most get-rich-quick schemes, however, such escapes into naturalistic causality lead inevitably to the bankruptcy of qualitative approaches. More so perhaps than other theoretical perspectives grounding qualitative methods, phenomenology is very clear on this score, and it is partly for this reason that we have chosen it. To understand experience *on* its own terms we must understand it *in* its own terms, and for this purpose we place in phenomenological "brackets" our usual notions of causality.

In the following sections we explore some of the challenges we encounter in our attempts to keep natural causality contained within these brackets, as we go about trying to make sense of the experiences of people living with schizophrenia in their own terms and from their own perspectives. We see how overcoming these challenges entails avoiding—in all instances and at all costs—a lapse into objectification, of making psychosis or people with psychosis into natural objects in order to preserve our interest in subjectivity and human beings as experiencing agents. We stand convinced, however, that only by successfully avoiding lapses into natural-causal explanation are we able to justify, and demonstrate, the distinct value of a qualitative approach. Let us be inoculated by this theoretical reminder, then, as we resist the call of the Sirens in figuring out what to do with all the stories we have now been told.

The Return to the Life-World

Following the guidelines we just established, the first step of our method is that of the "epoche of objective science," involving the so-called bracketing of our theoretical-scientific assumptions about the objective nature of our subject matter (Husserl, 1970a, p. 135). In the case of qualitative psychology, this means turning from the reigning attitude of natural science, in which the psychic is viewed as an object of nature toward the "life-world" that is the world of everyday experience. With this shift we simply describe what we find to belong to psychological subjectivity as it appears, or is experienced, in everyday life. We find our experiences of the psychic to include not only the material-physical aspects that have been isolated and studied by natural science but also the evaluative, ethical, emotive, and aesthetic aspects that previously had been excluded from our narrow natural-scientific focus on causality.

As a result of this shift, we find subjectivity to be embedded in a network of motivational relationships, carrying out activities that both presume and involve meaning. We find *persons* engaged in goal-directed activities, interacting with their environments in "meaning-bestowing" ways (Husserl, 1983). The environment with which these persons interact thus no longer appears solely as nature, as the one all-encompassing material nexus of causality, but as a sociocultural and historical world which engages their interests, arouses their aesthetic appreciation, appeals to their social conscience, and the like. It is this relation between person and world that constitutes our focus as psychologists.

Any psychology that is not grounded in naturalism—whether or not it is grounded in phenomenology—might begin with this purified descriptive sphere of subjectivity in its intentional relation to the world of everyday life (see Scanlon, 1982). The particular contributions of phenomenology begin to be introduced when we turn to the question of how these relations are to be studied and understood, and thus how we are to analyze and interpret the meaning of our narrative data. In order to delineate each of the steps toward our answer, including the unique contributions of phenomenology, we take an example from our research on the experiences of people with schizophrenia and follow this example through each of the steps of our method.

Having bracketed our naturalistic preconceptions and other theoretical constructs regarding the nature of schizophrenia, we begin with first-person, subjective accounts of the relevant experiences of people who may be characterized as having this disorder. We ask a young woman who has been diagnosed by *DSM-IV* criteria as having schizophrenia, for example, to describe with whom and how she spends her time on a day-to-day basis. She responds by telling us stories of her different experiences both in her apartment and at Burger King, in some cases eating alone and in others being joined by a friend; stories we quoted at some length in the previous chapter. Now that we have elicited an account of one aspect of this woman's experience, how are we to go about studying all of this?

Let us acknowledge that this may at first seem to pose an insurmountable challenge. After all, it is not only doctoral students or neophyte qualitative investigators who find the moving target of a flowing narrative hard to grasp. Husserl already recognized that "at first, to be sure, the possibility of [phenomenology] seems highly questionable, since the realm of phenomena of consciousness is so truly the realm of a Heraclitean flux" (1977, p. 49). Whether following Heraclitus, Husserl, or Holden Caufield, it is by no means obvious how one is to go about making sense of an ever-changing series of experiences that will never be the same twice. How are we to bring order to the seemingly chaotic flow of sensations, perceptions, memories, associations, desires, and emotions comprising subjective life?

We noted in the Introduction that physical objects of nature acquire their identity by persisting as the same through various appearances, even though we later came to realize that this "sameness" is actually a by-product of certain ordered and determinable changes based on the laws of causality. My favorite red tree will never be exactly the same tree twice either, after all, but will change in predictable ways over time, losing its leaves each autumn, etc. We also suggested in the Introduction that the Heraclitean flux of ever-changing experiences has its own parallel unity; a unity that does not have to be explained based on factors external to the experiences themselves (such as, e.g., the laws of causality). We suggested, that is, that these experiences carry within them their own intrinsic order; an order and coherence that is to be found consistent throughout the relationships of meaning that connect one experience to another. Where are we to look in order to locate this intrinsic order? How are we to determine its nature and the principles by which it structures the flow of experiences so that they are not as chaotic or arbitrary as they first might appear?

We have now arrived at our first fork in the road of qualitative data analysis. A decision must be made at this point as to where we shall look in order to locate the principles by which we can order and understand the stories we have been told. How are we to account for the descriptions elicited by our inquiry? Are we to look, for example, "outside" of this woman's experiences: to her diagnosis, her social class, her genetic predisposition, or her family of origin? Or are we to look more deeply "into" her experiences: to the meanings and intrinsic connections that inhabit her experiences as they unfold over time in the unified and coherent whole that is her psychic life? The path pursued at this initial fork in the road will determine the nature of our psychological understanding and practice.

It is possible, if not appealing, to turn at this juncture to factors external to our participant's experiences themselves in order to account for them. It would not be unusual, for example, to consider her description of eating cold beans out of a can in front of the television to represent the impairments in social functioning and daily living skills often associated with schizophrenia. We already had mentioned in our last chapter how her comment about her hamburger not tasting the same when eaten alone (as when eaten with a friend) reflected the kind of misplaced concreteness in thought and language also considered characteristic of schizophrenia. In these ways, our first step of obtaining descriptions of first-person experiences serve primarily to provide examples that we then account for on the basis of other, underlying, factors. Narrative and qualitative inquiry, in this case, are considered to play preparatory roles in the conduct of psychology, furnishing psychologists with experiential grist for their naturalistic-causal explanatory mill (Kockelmans, 1967, 1972, 1973; MacLeod, 1947, 1964).

In pursuing this path, however, we quickly have lost sight of the psychological subject as an intentional agent, and we also have drifted away from our focus on experience in the life-world with which we began. Such an approach constitutes a return to naturalism and its pre-"life-world" reduction naiveté: treating experiences as if they were natural objects brought about by physical-material causes. It certainly may be true that the woman we have named Jane finds herself eating cold beans out of a can in front of the television set *because*, in some sense, she suffers from schizophrenia along with the social impairments associated with it. This, however, is analogous to providing an account of *Romeo and Juliet* by explaining that it is a tragedy as opposed to a comedy or historical play. This explanation tells us very little about Jane, about her experiences of schizophrenia, or about the nature of psychosis and processes of recovery. It also does not take into account the fact that many of us who have not experienced schizophrenia nonetheless know what it is like to eat alone in front of the television or to notice how our hamburger didn't have any taste as we leave Burger King after a hurried lunch alone.

If we are to pursue qualitative research as anything more than simply preparatory to naturalistic-causal explanation, we must resist this call from the Sirens of objectification and eschew such external explanations of Jane's experiences. This is not to say that these explanations are wrong, or that there is no credibility to naturalistic-causal explanatory approaches to schizophrenia, of which Jane's unique experiences might, in fact, serve as excellent illustrations. Rather, it is to put such explanations into our phenomenological brackets and consider them, for the time being, irrelevant to our quest to understand our participants' experiences on and in their own terms.

The Phenomenological-Psychological Reduction

The other, less trodden, path to be pursued at this juncture is to limit our scope to what is immanent to our participant's experiences, looking more deeply into the experiences rather than outside of them. This path takes us to the second step of our method, that of the "phenomenological-psychological reduction" (Husserl, 1970a, p. 235). We place in brackets all realities ordinarily presumed to exist outside of this person's experience, including the causal context of nature, and focus exclusively on her experiences themselves as *the* realities in which we are interested. Rather than explaining her experience on the basis of underlying causes, we attempt to understand its meaning and structure from the perspective of the subject as it was *lived* (i.e., experienced) by her.

With performance of the phenomenological-psychological reduction, we make a fundamental shift in the determination of what is to be considered "real." Looking into our experiences in this way is intended to turn our usual way of looking at things on its head, abandoning our common-sense understanding of the real as consisting of things and their causal underpinnings in order to adopt an appreciation of reality as consisting of *the acts* of experiencing themselves. As a result, we take an entirely different sphere from that traditionally taken by science to constitute our subject matter. We shift our focus from a concern with objects experienced to concern ourselves with the experiencing *of* these objects in consciousness. By doing so, we leave the "natural attitude" of everyday experience and its one objective world behind and adopt the "personal attitude" of human science, described by Husserl as follows:

> In the personal attitude, interest is directed toward the persons and their comportment toward the world, toward the ways in which the thematic persons have consciousness of whatever they are conscious of as existing for them, and also toward the particular objective sense the latter has in their consciousness of it. In this sense what is in question is not the world as it actually is, but the particular world which is valid for the persons, the world appearing to them with the particular properties that it has in appearing to them; the question is how they, as persons, comport themselves in action and passion—how they are motivated to their specifically personal acts of perception, of remembering, of thinking, of valuing, of making plans, of being frightened and automatically starting, of defending themselves, of attacking, etc. (1970a, p. 317)

Restricting our focus to what is immanent to our young woman's experience, however, would seem to lead us to mistake something purely subjective for reality (Kohák, 1978). No longer rooted in the objective reality of the natural world, we have limited ourselves to studying Jane's particular and unique subjective perceptions of reality: a "personal world" that could easily be seen as arbitrary. Yet our pursuit of a qualitative psychology is built on the premise that the realm of subjectivity is *not* arbitrary in precisely this way but is ordered according to its own principles—which it is our job to discern. Regardless of its objective validity, we have before us in Jane's experiences an entire drama, the temporal unfolding of a distinctly human scenario contained in the simple experience of eating alone in front of the television (Politzer, 1974). How, then, are we to account for this drama? Now that we have resolved not to explain these experiences away in terms of objective factors external to them, what *subjective* principles might we use in order to bring some order into this flux?

Rather than looking outside of the stream of experience, we look to the inherent organizing principles for the flux of phenomena itself: the meaningful structures into which these diverse experiences cohere (Giorgi, 1985). For example, we may compare our subject's act of eating cold beans in front of the television to a scene in a play, to one act in the unfolding of a plot; we compare it, say, to Othello's gesture of giving a handkerchief to Desdemona in the unfolding of his jealousy. If we can comprehend the motivational structure of being jealous, then we have no need of appealing to factors external to experiences of being jealous. Jealousy as a distinctly human phenomenon need not be explained away in terms of other, not-so-human causes. It carries its own reason within it. As Kohák argues: "The principle of jealousy is not susceptible of any proof other than that based on it own intrinsic necessity" (1978, pp. 20–21).

What, then, is the nature of the necessity to be found in our subject's experiences? What was the motivational structure of Jane's acts? What was she trying to achieve in her life (the "plot") and how do these particular experiences (the "scenes") fit in, or not fit in, with her present plans and her imagined future? What principles are to be found inherent to these experiencing acts, binding them together into a coherent flow? And how are we to find them?

Exploring Jane's Motivational Horizon

If we are not to look outside of the realm of experience to locate these principles, then it would appear that we must restrict ourselves to this realm and locate these structures within it. Although this principle certainly seems reasonable on the surface, it is far from obvious how we are to implement it. We have Jane's description of her experiences and have quoted it verbatim. Are there any obvious intrinsic connections between elements of her experience that we overlooked? Is it possible to answer the questions listed above based solely on these specific vignettes? For example, are there any indications in Jane's description of what it is that she is trying to accomplish in her life and what roles beans, hamburgers, or friends play in this process? Within our narrative perspective, understanding Jane's experiences of eating beans and hamburgers entails placing these vignettes, what we might call her "microstories," in the context of the "macrostories" of her overall life-course; building on what we have called in previous work a "life context" model (Davidson and Strauss, 1995). But where are we to find this life context?

Can we ask Jane to provide it? We know from the Introduction that we are not to ask Jane to interpret her own experiences for us, to tell us what they mean to her, as this would place her in the role of fellow psychologist. It is our job as researchers to understand and interpret her experiences. But does that mean that we cannot ask Jane any additional questions about her life or encourage her to elaborate further on any details of her story that may not be obvious to us in their significance? Of course not, as we spent several pages in the last chapter suggesting how such questions might be framed to avoid bias and elicit rich narratives. But this begs the question with which we are presently concerned, which is that of how we analyze the data Jane provides. This assumes that at some point all of the relevant meanings inherent to Jane's experiences will be made obvious to us. But what does it mean for such meanings to become "obvious"—obvious, for example, to whom and on what basis?

We have now stumbled upon another key theoretical and methodological issue in qualitative research that is rarely addressed explicitly. At some point, we must stop asking Jane clarifying questions and move on to the phase of analysis. How do we know when we have enough information from Jane about her life experiences that we can *stop* asking such questions? We can assume that these particular vignettes are only small segments of a longer narrative provided by Jane in several hours of open-ended interviews. It certainly would be important to understand these particular experiences in the context of this additional material. But as Camus pointed out at a time when interest in phenomenology in France was at its peak: "To be really realistic a description would have to be endless" (1956, p. 270).

Jane's narrative conceivably could begin with her earliest memories of her childhood and proceed on from there, becoming, in essence, an autobiography. Even so, such an autobiography would then have to be placed in other contexts of meaning, such as those of Jane's immediate and extended family and of her social environment. The importance of these contexts in shaping experience is amply demonstrated both in clinical practice (e.g., the use of genograms and psychosocial histories) and in the art and science of writing biographies. Biographers know well the intensive and prolonged labor involved in coming to understand another person's life.

Years of research and study, including searches for archival material and information about the sociocultural and familial context into which the person was born, are required to produce a single biography. Is this the path we have chosen for qualitative research in psychology?

To put it simply: It is not. We are not suggesting that in order to do qualitative research one must become an expert in conducting psychoanalytic or sociocultural biographies of each participant in a study. Not only would this not be feasible based on the practicalities involved in such an undertaking, but it also would be unnecessary, inappropriate, and still not resolve the issue of "obviousness." Even biographers have to decide when to end their investigations. More important, however, is the nature and scope of our interest. We are not interested in Jane's biography per se. We did not embark on these interviews in order to develop biographical accounts of the lives of Jane and the other 179 people who were matched with volunteer friends in this particular study. Nor did we conduct interviews with 12 people who had returned to New Haven following extended stays at the state hospital in order to develop 12 separate biographies. We had hoped to use Jane's experience as one window onto the phenomena of social isolation and the processes of developing friendships for people with serious mental illnesses. Similarly, in the earlier study, we had hoped to gain some understanding of the differences between hospital and community living among people with serious mental illnesses. In doing so, we were not so much interested in each individual's uniqueness but in what these people *as a group* might have shared in common *across* their experiences of the same or similar phenomena. This is not to suggest, of course, that biographies or intensive case studies are not worthwhile endeavors in their own right—just that they do not address our present interest.

How, then, are we to examine commonalities across different people's experiences? From a phenomenological perspective, we first need to appreciate the nature of the experiences we are trying to examine. Experience, within this perspective, is taken to be temporal, directed, and "meaning-bestowing" in nature. As temporal, experience unfolds as emerging out of a past, through a present, and into a future. As meaning-bestowing, or what phenomenologists have come to label "intentional," experience in addition is always directed toward some object (e.g., an idea, a thing). In these ways, experience is directed both forward and outward. In the process, meaning is constituted as that *toward* which experience is directed; in other words, it is the meaning of meaning to be that of which we are aware in our experience. Given that this moving outward also entails moving forward, the act of intentional constitution can be described as generating new meaning based, in part, on the residue of meanings generated by previous experiences. In addition, the meanings so generated will then provide the basis for the generation of yet newer meanings by future acts of experience. Both ends of this temporal continuum intrinsic to experience come together in what is referred to as a "motivational horizon." The motivational horizon of an experience is comprised of the proximal past out of which the experience arose and the proximal (imagined) future toward which it is directed.

What is the point, you may be wondering, of all this talk of meaning and temporality? How does it relate to our task of understanding Jane's experiences of eating alone and with a friend? You may recall that the question we are trying to answer is: What was Jane trying to achieve in her life (the "plot") and how do these particular experiences of eating cold beans in front of the television and hamburgers at Burger King (the "scenes") fit in, or not fit in, with her present plans and her imagined future? Although we decided that we should not have to construct a biographical account of Jane's entire life to date in order to answer this question, we also know that the answer to this question is not given on the surface of these vignettes alone. With our new understanding of the intentional and temporal nature of experience, we can now take a first step toward an answer, having found the "motivational horizon" to provide a middle ground between a timeless present occurring in a vacuum and an exhaustive biographical account of the past.

We now know that intrinsic to the flow of experience there is a motivational horizon that contains both the meaning of the proximal past as it impacts on the constitution of new meaning in the present and the imagined future toward which the present experience is directed. Weren't these precisely the dimensions of Jane's experiences that we were trying to identify? If we are interested in exploring what Jane was trying to achieve in her life and how these particular experiences fit or don't fit in with her plans, we will find precisely what we are looking for in the motivational horizon intrinsic to these very experiences. Such a horizon may not be obvious at first, especially if we do not know what we are looking for, but its presence also means that we do not need to construct a biography of Jane's life. What is left for us to do is to identify those aspects of Jane's motivational horizon that had the most direct relevance to understanding the processes of intentional constitution involved in these specific experiences. While we do not yet know what these aspects are, we now have a map for exploring the dimension of Jane's experiences where they are most likely to be found.

To illustrate this point, let us return to Jane's narrative and see what indications we can find of the presence of such a motivational horizon at play in shaping her experiences. Jane reports that she would eat cold beans "right out of the can" rather than warm them up on the stove when she was alone. She describes having "no enthusiasm" for cooking the beans when she was going to be eating them by herself, with only the television for company. In this case, she appears to have viewed the beans solely in terms of their function as nourishment, as a source of the dietary intake required for her to survive; as she describes: "because I just knew that I had to put food in me." Similarly, Jane reports that she would not go out to a restaurant by herself due to the "emptiness" she would feel sitting alone in a public place and due to the fact that when she ate alone, whether in her apartment or in a restaurant, she couldn't enjoy her food. As she describes: "I don't want to eat really, because it doesn't taste good when I'm alone."

What we can learn from these descriptions is that Jane has spent a significant amount of time alone in her recent past; that when she has been alone she has been vulnerable to feeling isolated, lonely, and empty; and that when she has felt empty, isolated, and lonely she has not been motivated to take care of herself. All of these meanings are confirmed and expanded on in Jane's descriptions of eating with a friend. In these descriptions what also becomes apparent are Jane's desires for companionship. She sums up these wishes eloquently when she says: "[But] when you go out [and] you're not alone, you're able to eat talking to somebody, so that can of beans could have been in a gold bowl instead of just a plain, cold tin can." What we are left to surmise is that Jane is heading into an imagined future, in which she would like to have more friends, people she can spend time and share meals with, in order to be able to enjoy her life more.

We fully expect at this point that the savvy reader will be thinking: "Of course, that was obvious from the start. I could have told you those things when I first read the interview transcript." If, in fact, the savvy reader is thinking those very thoughts, then we have succeeded in proving our point both directly and relatively painlessly.

The Importance of the Obvious

We do not anticipate much disagreement about the content of the motivational horizon we have identified in Jane's descriptions. In retrospect it does, indeed, appear obvious. But this is as it should be. We understand that in most approaches to scientific investigation, discovering the obvious is considered tantamount to failure. Within the context of phenomenological inquiry, however, saying that certain meanings have become "obvious" does not suggest dismissing those aspects as irrelevant or as adding nothing new to our understanding. Quite to the contrary, it is precisely our task in this case to discover, or more accurately, to explicate the meanings intrinsic to the experiences in question in order to reveal them in their very obviousness. In other words, we strive to make the meanings that are implicit in an experience explicit so that they can be viewed with the same degree of obviousness as that which was originally explicit in the experience. Here, as in most aspects of phenomenology, it is a matter of a direct, intuitive grasping of meaning that is involved; the only real challenge is in uncovering the implicit meanings so that they can be grasped in this way.

In empirical qualitative inquiry, however, it is not enough simply to uncover these implicit meanings in their obviousness. An additional, and pressing, challenge for this kind of inquiry, whether or not it is phenomenological in orientation, is to find ways of presenting one's findings so that they appear to one's audience to be imbued with the same sense of obviousness with which they were initially discovered. No one can be convinced of the validity of qualitative inquiry solely by persuasion, by debate, or by the reporting of interrater reliability scores. When one has not been able to render the meanings involved in the experiences in question obvious to one's audience, *then* one has failed in one's efforts either to identify or to explicate those meanings. This is one of the several ways in which phenomenology stands conventional science on its head.

But what is the point, then, asks the savvy and unsatisfied reader, of uncovering the obvious? How does this advance our understanding of Jane's experience, in particular, or of psychosis, in general? Despite their obviousness, these findings hold several not so obvious implications for our understanding of the experiences, and behavior, of people like Jane. These findings are not so obvious in the sense that they contradict—or at the very least, challenge—aspects of the clinical view of psychosis currently holding sway in the field.

We suggested, for example, that Jane was lonely and desired companionship. This goes against the current view of asociality and withdrawal as characteristic negative symptoms of psychosis, in that these concepts imply that the person does not desire, or at best is indifferent to, social contact. Jane, despite her apparent isolation, would appear *not* to be indifferent to social contact. In addition, much has been made of the apathy, anergia (lack of energy), anhedonia (lack of pleasure), and avolition (lack of will) considered to be other core negative symptoms of psychosis in arguing against involving people in strenuous rehabilitative efforts or placing social or vocational demands on them. The most common complaint heard by supervisors of case managers or rehabilitation practitioners working with people who have psychosis is that they "lack motivation." Jane does not contradict this perception of lacking interest, energy, motivation, or pleasure—she tells us, after all, that she can't enjoy her food when eating alone—but she does offer a different perspective on these elements of her clinical presentation.

For Jane, the lack of motivation, pleasure, interest, and energy is experienced not so much as a core element of her psychosis but as an unfortunate side-effect of living an empty and lonely life alone. She has no enthusiasm for cooking, she says, because she knows she'll just be eating by herself. Perhaps a not uncommon sentiment among bachelors and widows as well, this perspective is reminiscent of the response offered by a person with psychosis with whom we worked when asked by her vocational rehabilitation practitioner (i.e., "job coach") why she refused to wash her hair and change her clothes before reporting to her job site, which was in the back room of a Salvation Army thrift store. She replied: "You want me to get all dressed up, but you're never willing to take me any place." Consistent with her response, we have since found that if we offer to take people places they would like to go, such as a nice restaurant or a baseball game, they will, in fact, "get all dressed up."

The Transcendental Reduction and Its Implications
for Psychology

Having unearthed the motivational horizon implicit in each act of experiencing, we can now return to our discussion of method and pursue the next step in our phenomenological data analysis. As suggested by the heading above, this step will consist of the so-called transcendental reduction (Husserl, 1970a).

But why bother to perform yet another "reduction"? Why distract our attention from Jane and her experiences of living with psychosis just as we (finally) are about to get to the really interesting part, only to muddle our heads with such concepts as the "transcendental"? Is it necessary to tackle the so-called transcendental question—the focus of considerable debate and controversy in philosophy—in order to conduct empirical phenomenological studies in psychology? Even Husserl agreed that psychology was not a transcendental science, dealing as it does with the worldly reality of psychological, as opposed to transcendental, subjectivity. Most phenomenologists have concluded, as a result, that psychologists need *not* be concerned with the transcendental, leaving that thorny set of issues happily to the philosophers (e.g., Drüe, 1963; Giorgi, 1970; Kockelmans, 1967; Merleau-Ponty, 1962; Ricoeur, 1966; Sartre, 1956). We have addressed (and, to our own satisfaction at least, refuted) this position at length elsewhere (Davidson, 1988, 1994; Davidson and Cosgrove, 1991, in press) and do not intend to go into it in any detail here. The concept of the transcendental remains important for our own concrete, psychological purposes here, however, for two related reasons. We will confine our discussion to these two issues.

The first issue pertains to the nature of the relationship between the multitude of meanings that we now understand to be inherent to experience on the one hand, and the one world we all share on the other. By "one world" we are referring to the world as objective, as existing independently of, and as the common ground for, psychological subjects. The second issue pertains to how we are to gain access to the meanings inherent to someone else's experiences. These issues are related in the sense that the answer to the first question necessarily dictates the answer to the second. For the sake of clarity, let us take the example of one possible theoretical position and see how this is so.

A common theoretical position implicit in many approaches to qualitative inquiry in psychology is to view the meanings constituted by experience to inhere, or exist, within those same experiences themselves. As a consequence of viewing meaning as existing inside of experience, each individual is viewed as having his or her own personal world of meaning constituted by him or herself. Given the highly individualistic existence attributed to meaning and the personal worlds it creates, it then becomes impossible in this view for one person to gain access to another person's experience or world. Fundamental questions of the nature of the person who creates such a world, of the existence of one shared objective world independent of all these subjects, and of how people can relate to each other despite their separateness, become unanswerable, if also irrelevant, because the world is restricted to whatever is within each individual's personal world. The world as a whole, as the common ground for billions of subjects and their various personal worlds, becomes lost.

We understand that questions of the existential status of meaning, of the subject who constitutes it, and of the world constituted by these meanings typically are not tackled, if not to say actively avoided, in psychology. In fact, psychology divorced itself from such "armchair" philosophizing over a century ago in order to become an empirical science. Yet, we would suggest, qualitative psychologies bypass these issues at their own peril. Neurocognitive approaches to psychology address these issues implicitly by assuming that meaning resides in our neurons. The world and its psychological subjects are physical entities, reducible in principle to their most basic elements of matter. All such approaches to science are grounded in physics and thus, fundamentally, in mathematics. If qualitative psychology is to stake out its own territory as an alternative, it must establish a non-mathematical ground for its science. How do qualitative psychologies typically go about this?

Quite simply, they don't. Grounded theorists, who are some of the more theoretically inclined of the empirical qualitative researchers, may, for example, refer to symbolic interactionism as their philosophical basis. Investigators utilizing narrative approaches similarly may point to social constructivism as providing their conceptual framework. Many investigators make no reference at all to an alternative theoretical framework to ground their investigations, being comfortable, apparently, with positivism. Without delving into detail regarding differences between social constructivism, symbolic interactionism, and existential-hermeneutic approaches to phenomenology, what is most relevant to our present purposes is that *all* of these approaches remain transcendentally naïve. Having yet to be transformed through the transcendental reduction, they remain on the worldly side of the transcendental (Davidson, 1988). But what does this mean, and, just as importantly, what difference does it make?

What is fundamentally at issue here is the nature of the act of intentional constitution. What status do we accord the process of meaning making, the meaning maker, and the meanings that are made? Based on our performance of the phenomenological-psychological reduction to the personal attitude, it would appear that the meaning maker is the psychological subject, the process of meaning making is itself a psychological process, and the meanings that are made by this subject constitute his or her personal world. But each psychological subject is understood to be an individual, embodied being that exists on the ground of this same world. At the same time that the psychological subject is viewed as creating a personal world through the process of intentional constitution, she or he is viewed as a worldly being who exists within the one objective world we all share. The problem is: How can psychological subjects who are a part of the world also be responsible for creating their own personal worlds? This is a problem not only of duplicative worlds, one personal and one objective, but, more important, a problem of the relationship between these worlds. Once the psychological subject is viewed as creating his or her own personal world, it turns out that there is no way to get back to the objective, shared world with which we started.

This is a problem that occupied a good deal of Husserl's mature works, being referred to variously as the "parallelism" or "paradoxical coincidence" of transcendental and psychological subjectivity, the problem of "flowing in," and the dilemma of psychologism (Husserl, 1970a). Without dragging the reader into the gory, if intriguing, bowels of Husserl's refutations of psychologism—a journey, as we said above, that we have taken elsewhere (Davidson, 1988, 1994; Davidson and Cosgrove, 1991, in press)—suffice it to say here that the only way out of this dilemma is to perform the final phenomenological reduction to transcendental intersubjectivity.

The problem with viewing the psychological subject as creating his or her own world, in brief, is that intentional constitution or meaning making cannot be understood to be a psychological function. The world cannot be created by one of its own worldly creatures, therefore, the function of world making must be located elsewhere. This elsewhere is what has come to be referred to within the phenomenological tradition as the "transcendental." Our only difficulty, and the only reason why we have to take this additional step of the transcendental reduction, is that we ordinarily view ourselves and our capacity for meaning making as psychological, and therefore as worldly, in nature. We do not appreciate, to the contrary, that we collectively are actually responsible for the world we create. It is as if the puppeteers were to forget that they, in fact, created the marionettes and continue to manipulate their strings, viewing themselves instead as sitting passively in the audience of a live performance.

It is important that the reader appreciate that we are not viewing the puppeteers in this analogy as psychological subjects who, in this case, are instead the marionettes. It is precisely our point that psychological subjects cannot be meaning or world making. According to this view, psychological theories, or the conceptual frameworks that inform them, that view meaning making as a worldly, psychic function are based on a fundamental misunderstanding of the nature of experience. Experience, as meaning making, is a transcendental function. To view experience as psychological in nature is to be transcendentally naïve; it is to remain in the audience with the puppeteers, viewing the marionettes as if they were themselves live actors on a stage. We should not be misled by this analogy, however, to think that we are each a (transcendental) puppeteer pulling the strings of a (psychological) marionette. As tempting as that image may be, it represents one last attempt on the part of the Sirens to lure us back into an objectification of experience, a final relapse into naturalism. It is in conceptualizing the transcendental differently, without resorting to objectifying language, that the real challenges lie.

Fortunately for us, these are largely philosophical challenges. As psychologists, we need not get caught up in the thickets of philosophical disputes related to the possibility and nature of the transcendental as different from the worldly sphere of the psychic. It will be enough for us in answering our original two questions to characterize the psychic in its relation to the transcendental in the following two ways.

We recall that the first issue pertained to the nature of the relationship between the multitude of meanings constituted by experience and the one world we all share. We now know these two dimensions to be one and the same. The meanings constituted by experience are what comprise the one world we all share. There are not a multitude of personal worlds separate from this one world and separate from each other, but one world of which there can be unlimited, diverse experiences. We recall that the meanings constituting this world are not only constituted in the present but also involve the residue of meanings constituted in the past and the horizon of the imagined future toward which these acts are directed. If psychological subjects are not to be viewed within this context as the agents of such experiences, however, then what becomes of psychology and the psychic?

Psychology, as a worldly discipline, pertains to the study of one constituted realm of sense (i.e., the psychic) as opposed to the acts of constituting. As a result, psychology becomes the study of the ways in which individual subjects may be motivated to act. A significant portion of its subject matter consists of the meaningful ways in which prior acts of a subject motivate his or her future activity. But while we can consider the residual meaning of any constitutive act to be an aspect of the psychic make-up of a person, we cannot consider that act itself to have been psychic in nature. The acts themselves, the active generation of what later becomes a part of the subject's motivational horizon as pregiven meanings, cannot be captured within psychology. These acts are transcendental. Psychology can only study these acts retrospectively, as having played a role in the constitution of the subject's motivational horizon. As transcendental, the acts themselves transcend the boundaries of psychology, just as they transcend the boundaries of the psyche. They do not lie within the scope of the psychologist.

This is one of several implications of the transcendental reduction for psychology. With the transcendental turn, we now know the motivational horizon to be studied by psychology, as both the product of previous acts of constitution and the precondition for future such acts, to be only a small segment of an infinite transcendental landscape (Scanlon, 1982). It is in this sense that the notion of motivational horizon most differs from that of personal world. "World" carries with it the connotation of being self-contained; an enclosed orb surrounding, if not entrapping, the person. "Horizon," on the other hand, preserves a sense of incompleteness, of opening onto infinite depth and distance. As with a perceptual horizon, the horizon of experience is defined partly by one's position in relation to it; partly, however, it also transcends any one person's particular perspective in that it serves as a horizon for others as well. A horizon is a shared vista; equally accessible to all who stand nearby.

In restricting psychology to the study of the motivational horizon for individual activity, we have limited significantly its competence as well as its scope. It is obvious, for example, that a transcendentally grounded psychology cannot consider itself to be predictive in nature. It cannot presume to explain in a deterministic manner each new action of a subject as simply being an effect of the operation of previous experiences acting as causes. Although it may be able to delineate the horizon for a given action, including its preexisting possibilities, it is not able to guarantee that this action will actualize any of the already given possibilities as opposed to creating a new one. Nor is it able to explain how the creation of a new possibility came about, nor why it came about in this instance as opposed to that one, etc. Able, perhaps, to delineate "typical" patterns of experiencing (Giorgi, 1970), it is not able to know *in advance* how a given subject will act in a given situation. But this, also, is as it should be. With a primary aim of qualitative research in psychology being to attempt to preserve that which is distinctly human, we should view this eschewing of prediction to be a virtue, rather than a limitation, of our science.

We recall that the second issue pertained to how we are to gain access to the meaning of someone else's experiences. It is in response to this question that the transcendental reduction generates perhaps its most important implications for empirical psychology, as well as for all the other human sciences. Thus far, we have defined the transcendental primarily in terms of what it is not; that is, it is not the psychic, the worldly, or the mundane. Fundamental to these definitions *via negativa* is the view that the transcendental is not constitut*ed by* experience but is instead the very act of constitut*ing,* which, as a result, cannot be taken as an object of its own experiencing. With our differentiation of motivational horizon from the personal world, we can now add that the transcendental is intersubjective rather than individual in nature.

Were the transcendental simply to be a mirror image of the psychological subject at another level, the problem of solipsism would reemerge. It would be a question of how one transcendental subject can relate to another when each has its own sphere of meaning. It was to avoid such a position that we insisted that the puppeteer could not be just another marionette whose strings were being manipulated by yet another puppeteer, etc. To do so lands us in an infinite regress. The only way to escape the infinite regress is to view the transcendental no longer as the function of an individual, as *a* transcendental subject, but as intersubjective in nature.

The intersubjective nature of the transcendental is of crucial importance to us for two reasons. First, it reinforces the point that the real is not any one thing, any constituted realm of meaning, large or small, black or white, but the real is the *act* of experiencing itself. This is true regardless of what it is an experience of or whose experience it might appear to be. The very fact that it is an act of experiencing is what is key, what makes it transcendental.

Second, the intersubjective nature of the transcendental resolves our second question of access to another's experience by making experiencing itself intersubjective in nature. In other words, we do not start out separate from each other to begin with, having to find a way to cross the chasm between two distinct worlds. We start out already sharing a common world, participating together in the transcendental constitution of the one objective world we both experience. I do not experience the world as being my personal world, but rather as a world that is co-inhabited by other subjects. It is our world. This is what phenomenologists often refer to as the "being-with" aspect of experience, the fact the world is always given to us as shared with others who experience it alongside us. I have a direct and immediate sense that you are another subject experiencing the same world that I do and that you experience me as a subject experiencing the same world as you.

We had not intended to produce a tongue, or brain, twister. Establishing the intersubjective nature of experience is essential to our method, however, because without it we would have no access to the meanings other people experience. For phenomenology to be used as an empirical psychological method, we must have direct access to the experiences of those people we are interested in understanding. Such access is only possible due to the fact that subjective experience is not the personal possession of any one individual. It is not confined within the boundaries of the individual subject. Rather, individuals are constituted as domains of experience within the intersubjective sphere of the transcendental. It is intersubjectivity that is primary, with experience as a function of the individual subject a derivative domain of meaning constituted within it. We are always already connected to others by virtue of sharing in an experiential reality larger than ourselves. Access is thus not a problem to be solved but rather is a fundamental given of our experience. This approach to access and inter-subjectivity then provides a most useful context for reconsideration of the role of obviousness in our science, as we will see below.

Exploring the Culture of Psychosis

With the transcendental reduction we have achieved a radically different view of subjectivity than that which we typically assume in the natural attitude of our everyday lives. As Kohák has described, this shift "is subtle but significant. As lived, reality is the *experiencing of* an object. As common sense interprets it, the reality is *the object,* the experience is incidental to it" (1978, p. 32; italics in the original). We ordinarily view subjectivity as an epiphenomenon of nature, as tacked onto the species *Homo sapiens* as if it were an accidental by-product of evolution or an afterthought in the mind of God. In scientific circles, a common phrase used to dismiss someone else's views is to declare that they are "merely" subjective. In contrast to this view of the subjective as incidental, as the fluff of life so to speak, the transcendental reduction establishes intersubjectivity as *the real,* providing a transcendental basis for all of objective (i.e., constituted) reality. Transcendental intersubjectivity is neither incidental, accidental, peripheral, nor fragmented into billions of separate personally relative spheres like shards of broken glass, nor is it arbitrary or dependent on the whim of the person. It is universally structured as goal-directed, or teleological, in nature (Husserl, 1970a). The laws of motivation pertain to all experiences, connecting one to another in lawful ways. Despite their diversity of appearances and the fact that they don't always, if not often, appear so on the surface, acts of experiencing uniformly manifest this teleological structure.

This is important for our purposes, and worth the several page digression, because it is this teleological structure that replaces naturalistic causality as the explanatory vehicle in our qualitative science. We come to know our favorite red tree as an identical entity because it abides by determinable changes over time; these changes being determined by the laws of natural causality. Similarly, we come to know ourselves, and others, as identical agents because our experiences abide by determinable changes over time; these changes, however, being determined by the laws of motivation.

As causality is the fundamental law of nature, so motivation is taken to be the fundamental law of psychic life (Husserl, 1989, p. 220). There are two implications of this view that provide the final components of the conceptual foundation upon which analysis of our narrative data becomes possible, thereby completing our methodological discussion.

The first implication of this view is that if, in fact, all experience abides by the laws of motivation, then all experience in principle becomes understandable. It simply is a matter of uncovering the motivational relationships at play in shaping the experiences in question or rendering explicit the motivational horizon that is the implicit context in which these experiences take place. Although an important implication relevant to all of psychology, this principle becomes especially important when applied to investigations of serious mental illnesses such as schizophrenia.

Perhaps more so than any other group of people, individuals with psychotic disorders tend to be viewed by their communities as irrational and nonsensical and as exhibiting behaviors that are, almost by definition, impossible for others to understand. Some clinical investigators, such as Jaspers (1964) and Rümke (1990), have gone so far as to suggest that it is precisely by virtue of a person appearing to us as having experiences and behaviors that are impossible for us to understand that we have come to identify and recognize schizophrenia. Our emerging view of all experience as abiding by the laws of motivation poses a fundamental challenge to this view. In principle, the laws of motivation would be no less applicable to the experiences of people with psychosis than to the experiences of anyone else.

This is not to say that there may not be varying degrees of difficulty involved in uncovering those laws as they operate in different experiences or in the lives of different people. It is possible, for example, that some experiences of schizophrenia pose a particular challenge to our understanding in that the laws of motivation that shaped them may be difficult to identify or explicate. Other experiences, however, may be readily understandable and pose no challenges at all as, for example, were Tom's unpleasant experiences of family holiday gatherings quoted in the last chapter. The view we are proposing suggests that between experiences of frank psychosis and more readily understandable experiences of people with psychosis—or of any of us, for that matter—lay only a difference of degree on a continuum (Strauss, 1969). That is, differences between what appear to be nonsensical or irrational behaviors and behaviors whose meaning is readily understood are quantitative rather than qualitative in nature. The only difference lies in the amount of work involved in coming to an understanding of the experiences or behavior in question. No experience or behavior lies outside of the scope of such understanding.

What kind of "work," the skeptical reader may be wondering, is involved in coming to an understanding of another person's experiences? Especially when confronted with the challenge of understanding psychotic experience, what is the psychologist to do in order to uncover and explicate the laws of motivation at play in these experiences?

We suggest that it is useful at this point to borrow an analogy from our sister discipline, anthropology. Using one of the phenomenologist's most important tools, our imagination, let us imagine for a moment that a person with psychosis comes from a different culture than our own. There will be limitations to this analogy, for sure, but to the extent that someone who has psychotic experiences appears to be having experiences foreign to our own, we may find the analogy of a foreign culture useful in our explorations. We find this analogy to be particularly useful because we now have come to a point, as a society, that we value (or at least tolerate) people from different cultural and ethnic backgrounds. Although racism and bigotry continue to exist, they no longer have the explicit backing of the law to sustain them. In addition to providing a useful analogy to guide phenomenological explorations of the culture of psychosis, we offer this analogy in the hope that the current umbrella of tolerance might be extended to weary travelers from this foreign land as well. Let us take an example.

In concrete terms, were we to be standing behind someone in line at the grocery store who was having difficulty counting out change, we might have a number of different responses, in part, depending on our interpretation of his or her difficulty. If this person were to speak in a foreign language or in very broken English, we would assume that she or he was from another country and was not familiar with American currency. For most people, this would be an occasion either to offer to be helpful or at least to be amused at the person's confusion, perhaps imagining ourselves to be in the same shoes were we to visit this person's country. If the person was elderly and possibly beginning to suffer from dementia, we also might offer to be helpful or we might become irritated at his or her fumbling (depending most likely on our relationships with our own elderly relatives). Similar reactions are likely to be elicited by someone who has a developmental disability, our assumption being that it was not this person's fault that he or she finds counting change difficult. In some cases, in fact, we might even admire the courage we imagine it to have taken for this person to attempt to go out shopping on his or her own.

But what if the person happened to be mumbling to him or herself while fumbling, appeared perhaps a bit disheveled, and appeared neither foreign, elderly, nor developmentally disabled? In such a case most of us would react with fear and trepidation, looking to put a safe distance, physical and emotional, between ourselves and this person. Even if, in an altruistic moment, we were to consider attempting to be helpful in the face of an uninterested cashier, we might restrain ourselves out of concern that we don't know how the person will react to our benevolent offer. We typically view such people as alien and unpredictable, and, especially when any anger is involved, as potentially assaultive, as a powder keg that could explode at any minute. Even our offer of "Could I help you with that?" might be enough to set off an avalanche of uncontrollable affect and behavior.

Regardless of the source of this stereotype (e.g., the media, stigma, or misperceptions of risk factors for violence), we would like to suggest that the cross-cultural model is the more appropriate, and more useful, in such circumstances. That is, in the case of serious mental illness, we appear to have two basic options to consider. Option one is to be afraid of this person based on an assumption that he or she is irrational and unpredictable, concluding that we cannot understand his or her behavior because it does not abide by our cultural, linguistic, and other predetermined rules. Option two is to at least tolerate this person based on an assumption that his or her behavior does make sense within the context of his or her own culture, but that for the moment she or he is a "fish out of water." We are clearly preferring and suggesting for the reader's consideration option number two. Not only is it the more respectful and humane of the two approaches to our fumbling change counter, but it also turns out to be more accurate and useful, as we will see below.

What does it mean to suggest that we adopt a cross-cultural attitude toward experiences of psychosis? It means to assume, as we did above, that all experience is in principle understandable and determinable by the laws of motivation, and that it is just a matter of doing the "work" to uncover and explicate the laws at play in any given situation. What the cultural analogy adds are time-tested tools and approaches we can use in the process. Cross-cultural anthropologists have amassed a repertoire of knowledge, skills, and techniques that can be used to orient explorers to foreign cultures. On a more introductory level, tourists may buy a *Fodor's* and read up on a country's customs, currency, celebrations, and cuisine to start familiarizing themselves with a foreign culture. Learning the language and rituals ahead of time, when possible, also facilitates the acculturation process. Beyond these basics, different cultures will require different amounts of preparatory "work" depending on a number of considerations: for example, how different the language and customs are from the person's country of origin or how potentially hostile the environment is. Without belaboring the obvious (which is not a good thing, even in phenomenology), there are many things one can do to prepare for an exploration of a foreign culture. We are suggesting that this is precisely the kind of work that is involved in uncovering and explicating the laws of motivation at play in experiences of psychosis.

Our international travel analogy can be used in this case because the nature of the work involved in identifying a person's motivational horizon requires that the investigator take up the perspective of that person, that is, "go native" into his or her culture. A person's horizon can be seen accurately only from where he or she is standing. This point may have been obvious to the attentive reader, but it bears repeating. If there is one fatal flaw that accounts for the poor quality of much qualitative research, it is in the failure of investigators to appreciate the importance of occupying the role of the person whose experience is being investigated.

For qualitative research to remain qualitative in nature—as opposed, that is, to generating grist for the mill of causal explanation—it is crucial that the work of exploration be carried out explicitly from the perspective of the subject. In situating an experience within its motivational horizon, we have had to take over the perspective of the experiencing subject or agent whose previous experiences and imagined future inform this horizon. We cannot stand "outside" of the experience at a safe distance in order to interpret, speculate about, or otherwise judge its meaning. We have access to this meaning only from the inside, only from the perspective of the person who is emerging out of a particular past and heading into a particular (imagined) future within the context of a particular culture, etc. In addition to our travel analogy, we take this perspective to be similar to the Native American tenet that you should not judge another person until you have walked a mile in his or her shoes.

Building Empathic Bridges

What we are suggesting, in less theoretical language, is that the only route to accessing and understanding another person's experiences or behavior is through *empathy*. We take empathy in this sense not to be a so-called touchy-feely, sentimental identification with another person void of meaningful content, but to be a highly disciplined and demanding posture involving an active and artful use of all of one's faculties of memory, imagination, sensitivity, and awareness in coming to understand another person's experience from his or her own perspective. This kind of empathy may be similar to that employed by certain psychotherapists but, as we noted above, it takes place within a different context and with a different aim. Not only do we not feel responsible for changing, or being helpful to, the person, but in analyzing our qualitative data we also are no longer in the person's presence. Relieved of the burden of being helpful, we are left up to our own devices to make sense of the data.

Husserl describes the process of empathically uncovering and explicating the motivations at play in another's experience as follows:

> I secure [the person's] motivations by placing myself in his situation, [with] his level of education, his development as a youth, etc., and to do so *I must needs share in that situation*; I not only empathize with his thinking, his feeling, and his action, but I must also *follow* him in them, his motives becoming my quasi-motives, ones which, however, *motivate with insight* in the mode of intuitively fulfilling empathy. (Husserl, 1989, p. 287; italics in the original)

By "motivate with insight in the mode of intuitively fulfilling empathy," Husserl means to suggest that we share in the person's motivations *in our awareness* without thereby being motivated *by* them in our own experience. We employ empathy to identify his or her motivations as they unfold and influence his or her actions over time, imaginatively putting ourselves into his or her role and position in order to understand the actions that emerge out of these motivations without, of course, actually acting on the motivations ourselves. It is only in this way that the meanings of the other's experiences can be "secured" by us, imbued with the requisite air of obviousness. In fact, this is how we now have come to understand the nature of obviousness: to perceive a meaning to be obvious is to perceive it as if it were being constituted in one's own experience, as if it were part of one's own motivational horizon, without thereby being motivated by it.

It is in this way that cultivating empathy and achieving a degree of obviousness in understanding another's experiences requires preparation. We have to take incremental steps toward imaginatively occupying the person's motivational horizon by incorporating into our own awareness those dimensions of his or her culture and experiences (e.g., education, social class, family life, etc.) most relevant to the experiences in question. A good example of the cultivation of this kind of empathy within a phenomenological framework is provided by Frank and Elliot (2000) in her description of her two-decades' worth of efforts to gain a first-hand understanding of the life of a woman with physical disabilities. It was in preparation for this work that we acquired the tools of cultural anthropologists. We also can imagine that it is such a process of gradually coming to inhabit the other's shoes that unfolds over the course of the mile walk.

In addition to gradually coming to internalize aspects of the other person's motivational life, there is another kind of work we have to do in clearing the way, or setting the stage, for these motivations to emerge in our awareness. This work also is entailed in performance of the transcendental reduction, in the sense of coming to recognize the subjective origin of our own motivational horizon. In other words, in order to come to occupy the perspective of the other, we have to be willing to place our own perspective in abeyance, to place it squarely and securely within phenomenological brackets. If we cannot suspend our own cultural, historical, and personal signposts, we will be unable to explore this foreign territory in its own terms. We will insist on using our shiny new Euros at the grocery store, only to get exasperated with the cashier for his refusal to accept our currency. To perhaps stretch the metaphor beyond its customary limits, we cannot walk a mile in the other's shoes unless we first are willing (and able) to take our own shoes off (i.e., place them in brackets) on at least a temporary basis.

To concretize these theoretical meanderings for use in our empirical psychological method, let us pursue a bit further our current example. It is possible, for instance, that not everyone on first hearing Jane's interview would understand immediately what she meant by her hamburger not tasting as good when eaten alone. Especially those of us who have been blessed to raise young children may find it hard to imagine why eating a quiet lunch alone would not be a most welcome opportunity to savor one's meal undisturbed. We can recall vividly times in our lives when eating an entire meal while it was still hot without the frequent interruptions of getting up to get additional items, cut up someone else's food, clean up a spill, or reassure a crying child, would have stood out as a landmark event. This obviously represents a different motivational horizon than the one Jane appears to have, however. How are we to understand *her* experience of eating alone?

In cultivating empathy for another person's experiences, we have found it useful to build imaginative bridges between his or her experiences and our own. We do this—especially in cases in which the meaning of the experience is far from obvious—as one might do in certain acting classes, by recalling experiences in our own lives that have similarities to the experiences in question. These similarities may take many different forms, from similarities in affective tone or state to similarities in content, as well as involving experiences of works of art, music, and literature. In this case, for example, one of us remembered an experience of dining out at an elegant restaurant in Washington, D.C., during a professional meeting. Despite being alone, this person, who fancies himself to be a bit of a gourmand, had decided to go out to a nice restaurant for a treat. Unfortunately, he could not enjoy his meal, didn't remember tasting the wonderful food at all, and completed the meal and returned to his hotel as quickly as possible, with only a serious case of indigestion as a souvenir. This experience seemed to parallel Jane's experience in Burger King in a number of ways and, once recalled, could be explored productively from the inside, so to speak, to identify additional clues as to the meanings of Jane's narrative.

The experience of the Washington, D.C., restaurant began, for example, with the maitre d' approaching the person with a quizzical look and the question "Just one for dinner?" This was followed by being seated at a small, out of the way, table but one that appeared to be intended for romantic dinners for two. Despite being sequestered off to the side, our diner very quickly became aware of being the object of scrutiny from other tables; an experience that he imagined at the time would most likely be intensified for women who dared to dine alone. Trying to ignore the scrutiny, the almost embarrassed wait staff who appeared not to be comfortable being the focal object of a diner's attention when they approached his table, and the self-conscious need to appear to be enjoying a fine meal, left little room in our restaurant patron's awareness for even tasting, much less savoring, his meal. Eating as quickly as possible in order to escape from this uncomfortable situation, it is unsurprising that he returned shortly to his hotel room with indigestion.

What do we learn about Jane's story through this exercise in constructing an empathic bridge to her experience? We learn that Jane's dislike of hamburgers eaten alone at Burger King may have several additional dimensions that were not obvious to us at first glance. Like our disappointed diner, Jane appears to be self-conscious about being in a public place alone ("I've got a reason to go in there because I've got money, but I'm alone"), as well as feeling a sense of urgency to get out of the situation as quickly as possible ("When you're sitting there by yourself, you're just eating it and then you go out the door"). Jane's discomfort with, and aversion to, eating by herself in public suggests that she too may be uneasy about transgressing societal norms. She most likely has experienced even less enthusiastic welcomes from proprietors than the curt "Just one for dinner?"; suggesting in her interview that she has been asked to leave or to "move along" by people who perceived her to be loitering in similar circumstances. Eating with a friend appears in this context to serve a number of functions, from putting Jane at ease in a public place and allowing her to concentrate on and enjoy her meal to turning a biological necessity (the need to "put some food in me") into a fulfilling and uplifting social occasion ("that can of beans could have been in a gold bowl").

Are all these explanations of Jane's experiences just so many more elaborations on the obvious? We sincerely hope so. If these elaborations come across as obvious to the reader, we take that to be a sign of our success in conveying the power of the phenomenological method in explicating implicit meanings. But has this exercise advanced our understanding of Jane's life, in particular, or of psychosis more broadly?

We are left with the picture of a lonely woman who self-consciously wishes to avoid breaking social norms and becoming the focus of negative attention, but who simultaneously hungers for companionship and a sense of fitting into the larger social sphere. Is this an obvious, or even typical, portrayal of a person with schizophrenia? Are these the kinds of experiences and concerns we would expect from someone who, according to the clinical literature, lacks insight and self-awareness, has a diminished capacity to attend to and interpret social cues, shows a disregard for societal norms, and is at best indifferent to, if not aversive toward, social contact?

The only clinical perspective consistent with the portrayal of Jane above that we could discover was that contained in Harry Stack Sullivan's adage that people with schizophrenia "are much more simply human than otherwise." Sullivan, somewhat of a proto-phenomenologist himself, based his clinical theories on intimate and in-depth knowledge of the experiences and lives of people with psychosis including, as it turns out, his own (Swick Perry, 1953). We will see in the two chapters that follow some of the ways in which Sullivan's discovery can serve as a useful guide in phenomenological explorations of the lives of people living both inside, and outside, of schizophrenia.

4

■　　■　　■　　■　　■　　■　　■　　■　　■

Living Inside Schizophrenia

> Even in conditions so far removed from the reality of the external world
> as hallucinatory confusional states, one learns from patients after their
> recovery that at the time, in some corner of their minds, as they express
> it, there was a normal person hidden, who watched the hubbub of the
> illness go past, like a disinterested spectator.
>   —Sigmund Freud, *An Outline of Psychoanalysis*

WE HAVE COLLECTED OUR MAPS, filled our backpacks with supplies
and our canteens with water, and are ready to set off on a more systematic
exploration of lived experiences of schizophrenia. Conventional clinical
wisdom cautions that this may be a journey from which there can be no return. "Once a schizophrenic," this clinical voice murmurs, "*always* a schizophrenic," believing schizophrenia to be an invariably life-long condition.
"Once a schizophrenic," this voice murmurs, "*only* a schizophrenic," believing also that schizophrenia subsumes the entirety of the person affected
by it (Davidson, Chinman, et al., 1999; Harding, Zubin, and Strauss,
1987). This chapter gives us an opportunity to explore the subjective experiences that all too often lie buried and hidden underneath such beliefs
(Davidson, 1997).

Our review in chapter 1 already offered counterevidence to these clinical claims, with first-person accounts of recovery and longitudinal studies demonstrating heterogeneity both in course and outcome for schizophrenia. These studies documented significant variability over time, between people, and across domains of functioning within an individual. Apparently, some people will lose the entirety of their lives to schizophrenia and will remain profoundly disabled by it until they die. It is apparently equally true, however, that many people will not lose their lives to schizophrenia and will only be affected by the illness for a brief to moderate period of time. For some it is a short journey from which they return relatively unscathed, for others a black hole from which they never fully escape. Knowing that both of these extremes are possible, and that the vast majority of cases lie in the gray areas in between, makes our present task particularly daunting.

We mentioned at the end of the previous chapter that we have found Harry Stack Sullivan's impression that people with schizophrenia "are much more simply human than otherwise" (Swick Perry, 1953) to serve as a useful guide in our explorations. We invoke that principle here as one way to begin tackling our challenging task. We interpret Sullivan's principle to mean that people with schizophrenia should be accorded at least the same rights as people standing trial for a crime; they should, that is, be presumed to be innocent (i.e., healthy) until proven guilty (i.e., suffering from an aspect of the illness).

This use of Sullivan's adage is particularly appropriate in this case, as people with schizophrenia frequently complain in interviews about instances in which other people assumed that an aspect of their behavior (e.g., becoming angry or anxious) was due to their illness when they, in fact, considered it to be a normal response to a given situation (e.g., being criticized or trying something new). Given that we readily acknowledge that we do not yet know what this thing called schizophrenia is, or the multitude of ways in which it may affect people, we proceed in what follows with precisely the opposite attitude. That is, we will not assume that any aspect of our participants' experiences is due necessarily to their illness, unless we have clear and compelling reasons to think so. Like Sullivan, we assume that it is so-called normal people who become afflicted with schizophrenia and that most, if not all, of their ways of dealing with this illness are likewise normal responses to being affected by a disabling condition.

Other than having a psychotic disorder, they were and remain "much more simply human than otherwise."

Far from being an obvious matter, this point of departure stands in stark contrast to that of most investigations of schizophrenia, which we suggest are contaminated somewhat by unacknowledged assumptions based in stigma. Most psychiatric research begins with the premise that people with schizophrenia are different from the rest of us, the result being that any possible markers of difference that are identified (e.g., the size of their ventricles, their use of language) are then attributed to their illness. Beginning with this premise is what gets investigators into trouble, however, as we saw in chapter 1. At that time, we appeared to have landed in a "catch-22" situation, in which research on schizophrenia could not be considered relevant to people who have recovered because they were no longer ill, while at the same time research on recovery could not be considered relevant to people who are ill because they are not yet well. We have only encountered this problem, we suggest, because we start with the assumption that people who have schizophrenia are no longer simply people like the rest of us. Once relegated to a species apart, it becomes impossible for such people ever to return to normalcy without once again crossing this categorical divide.

It is precisely this divide that is ultimately responsible for our dilemma. Insights about A cannot be used to understand B, and insights about B cannot be used to understand A, as long as A and B are conceptualized as separate and distinguishable entities. As in the nursery rhyme about Humpty Dumpty, once separated it becomes impossible to put the pieces back together again. It is only our acceptance of Sullivan's adage that allows us to overcome this dilemma, cross the categorical divide, by insisting that people with schizophrenia ("B" in our analogy) remain fundamentally the same as everyone else ("A"), except, of course, that they have an illness. In this case, we do not introduce a chasm to begin with and therefore do not have to face the challenge of finding a way to bridge it. Rather, and in order to overcome the problem of viewing illness and health as mutually exclusive categories, we follow Estroff's reasoning in asking: "Who and what existed *before* the illness, and who and what endure *during and after*?" (1989, p. 191, italics in the original) (also Davidson and Strauss, 1995).

As a result of our following this principle, we have been criticized in the past for "normalizing" psychosis, for making light of, or minimizing, the differences between people with schizophrenia and the rest of us, thereby failing to appreciate fully the degree of suffering involved in this potentially catastrophic illness. It is striking to us, however, that this criticism has never been leveled against our work (to our knowledge) by someone who has actually experienced the disorder. To the contrary, the findings we will be presenting below are typically well received by so-called consumer audiences; those who presumably would know best. Even if this were not the case, we would continue to feel comfortable with this principle as an antidote to the last two hundred years of institutionalization, stigma, and neglect—not that the years before were any better, of course.

But how, the inquisitive reader may be wondering, does this principle simplify our daunting task? Are we not still faced with the difficulty of who we should interview and at what point in the course of the illness or recovery process? For example, how can we assume that aspects of the lives of people early in the course of illness are at all relevant to the lives of people who appear to be stuck in the later, more chronic stages of severe disability? How could we possibly aspire to a complete and comprehensive picture of such a multidimensional and complex disorder, based on a limited number of open-ended interviews?

Obviously, we cannot; issues of sampling alone make it clear that the number of interviews that can be accommodated within a qualitative approach by any one investigatory team will only be able to offer glimpses into this rich and variegated landscape. Taking into account all the factors thought to influence course and outcome, such as premorbid functioning, age of onset, duration of untreated psychosis, gender, culture and ethnicity, phase of illness, level of functioning within and across various domains, treatment responsiveness, family and social milieu, opportunities for rehabilitation, vicissitudes of the labor market, would result in an almost infinite number of combinations and permutations to consider. Even large-scale quantitative studies cannot take many of these factors into account in any one study or in any series of studies.

It may be obvious by now to the reflective reader, however, that these considerations are beside the point in pursuing an empirical phenomenological investigation. It has never been our ambition to discover an all-encompassing structure, one grand theory, which can account for the phenomenon of psychosis in its entirety. We will leave such aspirations to our colleagues who use grounded theory. Our transcendentally grounded empirical psychology eschews claims to comprehensiveness or exhaustiveness as much as it does to prediction. Experience is too complicated to lend itself easily to such simplistic solutions. Rather, we again follow the lead of our good friend and colleague, Sue Estroff, who has encouraged us to "keep it complicated"(1994).

Then what is it that we will be presenting in what follows? We will be describing a number of themes—some related, some not—that we have distilled from interviews with over 100 people who have lived with schizophrenia and from our review of first-person accounts. These individuals have had disorders of varying severity and duration, are at different phases of the illness/recovery process, differ from each other on many of the factors listed above, and, in general, have had different experiences of the disorder. Despite all these differences, the themes we will be describing represent concerns shared, issues that are common, across their diverse narratives. To continue the travel analogy from the last chapter, rather than offering one all-encompassing theory of schizophrenia we will be presenting our own version, as it were, of a *Fodor's* introduction to the culture of psychosis. We will describe some of the central aspects of living with schizophrenia and will highlight those elements of experience that our participants reported as most important to them. In the process, this chapter will lay the foundations for describing, in the chapter that follows, key processes that appear to be involved in recovery.

What we are striving for, in our aspirations of offering a *Fodor's* style introduction, is a travel guide to the once-foreign territory inhabited by people living with schizophrenia. As a guide, we will not attempt, in these two chapters, to *explain* our findings. We will leave what few explanations we tentatively offer to our discussion in the concluding chapter. Also as a travel guide, we should not expect every person living with schizophrenia to experience every one of the themes to be described below. A travel guide to France is right to include escargot in its description of classic French cuisine, but we do not on this basis expect every French person we meet to consume a plate of snails on a regular basis.

Finally, a travel guide should never be (mis)taken to be a substitute for an actual visit to the territory. We are not thereby encouraging the reader to develop schizophrenia or insisting that only people who have had firsthand experience can understand psychosis. As a psychology text, we are rather encouraging any reader who finds her or his intellectual appetite whetted by the findings below to go out and meet with, talk with, and get to know people who live with schizophrenia. We are self-consciously offering a travel guide because we do not believe that anything can replace direct and personal involvement with the phenomena in question. In other words, do not read the following two chapters and even imply to anyone that you now know schizophrenia. We would rather you use these chapters for getting oriented as you embark on your own journey through the territory or for reassuring landmarks when you begin to feel lost. In any case, know that the degree to which these narrative data come to life depends not only on our talent and skill in conveying them but also on the reader's imagination and fund of first-hand experience. Some experiences, like turning a street corner in Rome and unexpectedly facing the Coliseum or another imposing antiquity from over 2,000 years ago, simply cannot be captured adequately in a travel guide.

"I May Be Crazy, but I'm Not Stupid"

A popular refrain within the Mental Health Consumer Movement, this heading pertains to the theme with which we choose to begin our journey. It is the issue of insight or awareness of one's illness. Insight represents a key issue for us, as the remaining data for our study rely on the awareness, memories, and reflections of people with schizophrenia. If, as clinical wisdom suggests, people with schizophrenia are unaware of their illness and its sequelae, what will they be able to tell us? How can we rely for our data on a population of people described as lacking insight, showing an unawareness of their condition, or, more actively, denying their deficits and dysfunction?

The quote we used above to describe our first theme, as well as the quote from Freud with which we opened the chapter, suggest otherwise, however. Fortunately for us, our interviews consistently have suggested otherwise as well. In fact, we have found one of the more distressing aspects of the disease to be precisely in the person's all too acute awareness of the losses, difficulties, and disappointments he or she is suffering due to the disorder. Not only are most people aware of their condition, but—in stark contrast to Freud's impression of "a disinterested spectator"—they are also keenly distressed both by the destructive impact the illness has had on their lives and by the ways in which it has changed the way others interact with them. Particularly given this sensitivity to others' reactions to them, it should not be surprising that people with schizophrenia are not always forthcoming about their awareness of their own difficulties. In other words, awareness of illness does not always translate into disclosure about illness to others.

The following interchange, in which a participant appears willing to talk about her illness—up to a point—represents both forms of awareness we have found to characterize this aspect of life with the disorder; that is, awareness of the impact of the illness both on the person's own functioning and on the ways in which others perceive him or her as a result. It comes at the end of an interview with a woman who appeared to have difficulty focusing on some of the questions she was being asked, at times showing signs of thought disorder such as loose associations and, as she recognizes, tangentiality:

> *Participant:* I'm really sorry for running off on tangents today. . . . People think, you know, I'm mentally ill and I don't know my weaknesses and everything, but I do. You know, I'm not stupid.
> *Interviewer:* What weaknesses are those?
> *Participant:* Running off on tangents. Talking about things that other people aren't talking about at the time.
> *Interviewer:* Do you feel that other people think that you are just not aware of what you do?
> *Participant:* Exactly, or what I'm saying. I'm not even aware of what I'm saying sometimes. And like how can you hold a conversation with a person you can't understand, you know? And I'm not ignorant to this. I know myself and I know I'm not well right now, you know. And I don't know why this is happening to me, I really don't. It is really blowing my mind. And that's all I have to say.

This passage captures well several aspects of awareness of living with psychosis. We note, for example, that this woman is both aware of some of her difficulties in communicating ("I know I'm not well right now") and of the ways in which they impact on others ("How can you hold a conversation with a person you can't understand"), yet does not know why she is having such difficulties or what has brought them about ("I don't know why this is happening to me"). In other words, she can be observant of her own behavior and be sensitive to how it changes other people's perceptions of her ("People think I'm mentally ill and I don't know my weaknesses"), without understanding these changes or their origins as it were from the inside.

In this way, schizophrenia appears to be similar to other illnesses that manifest certain signs and symptoms behaviorally without, or prior to, more internal changes. Unlike a fever, in which the person feels hotter than usual, diabetes, for example, may at first be suggested through frequent urination but then is diagnosed through blood tests. Prior to experiencing what one comes to recognize as the effects of low blood sugar, there is no experience of diabetes per se. Even in cases in which the signs or symptoms of an illness may be experienced subjectively as well as observed behaviorally, such as the difficulties in breathing characteristic of asthma, the person is not aware of the nature of the illness until these signs have been explained through a healthcare provider's assessment and diagnosis. The same appears to be true of psychosis; there is no definitive experience of psychosis per se from which a person might then infer independently "I am suffering from a psychotic disorder."

Is this what is meant by the lack of awareness of illness in schizophrenia? It would be unreasonable to describe people with schizophrenia as lacking insight just because they were unable to determine the nature of their disorder on their own. The same can be said of most illnesses. We typically reserve such pejorative labels as "denial" for people who have a more than sufficient basis upon which to understand the diagnosis of their condition or identification of their deficits. People can only be said to lack insight after they have had their condition explained to them by a healthcare professional. For lack of awareness to be considered so common that it has been suggested as a diagnostic criterion of schizophrenia (Amador et al., 1991) must mean that from the outside, from a perspective external to the person's own experience, it appears that people do not understand, or refuse to accept, that they have psychosis, despite the efforts of others to educate them in this matter. Although this may appear to be true in many cases—particularly early in the course of illness—this observation alone tells us little about the internal experiences of the person with the disorder.

Once we accept the illness view of schizophrenia it becomes more productive to wonder what the first signs, symptoms, or indications of the illness are that people experience prior to being offered a diagnosis and being informed about what is happening to them, and therefore prior to deciding what to do with this information. How does psychosis become manifest, as it were, from the inside?

In retrospect, people have described their experiences of the first indications of psychosis in a number of ways. For some, it was the more classic, positive symptoms of auditory hallucinations, commonly referred to as "hearing voices." For many others, however, there were more subtle changes preceding the emergence of such full-blown symptoms. In most cases, in fact, the first things people noticed, or remember experiencing, were cognitive changes. As one young man described: "When I became mentally ill I lost a lot of my memory. I was a straight A student and everything went down the drain. . . . I'm a very confused individual at this point." In similar terms, another participant described her experience as: "Once I started getting ill my memory wasn't as good. I didn't feel as comfortable and things like that, so I guess that goes with the territory."

In addition to noticing difficulties with their memory, participants described difficulties in attending, concentrating, and focusing their cognitive energies on objects that interested them. In place of these former faculties, and appearing in part to be responsible for their distractibility, participants also reported a heightened sensitivity to certain phenomena. In our previous review of first-person accounts, we described this heightened sensitivity as "a kind of added brightness or extra dimension to everyday things," "as if someone had turned up the volume," "everything's brighter and louder and noisier," and "as if I am too wide awake—very, very alert" (Davidson, Stayner, and Haglund, 1998, p. 106). As suggested in these descriptions, this sensitivity and attraction to certain phenomena unfortunately is something over which people feel they have no control. As a result, one participant described this increase in sensitivity as the acquisition of a new kind of intelligence, different from the kind he felt he was losing, but a kind of intelligence that was not necessarily welcome. He described:

> I became very sensitive when I became mentally ill. . . . See, when I was mentally ill, I was losing some of my intelligence but yet I was gaining some. . . . I'm sensitive now and I really don't like it.

This combination of heightened sensitivity and the unwelcome burden it adds to the person's life was captured eloquently in the words of a consumer advocate, who described it as follows:

> We must learn to go through life experiencing our surroundings with a greater intensity than others do. Sounds are louder, lights brighter, colors more vibrant. These stimuli are distracting and confusing for us, and we are unable to filter their impact to lessen their effect. In addition, I believe we are more sensitive in an interpersonal sense as well. I have noticed that others like myself are easily able to pick up emotional nonverbal cues and feelings that may be "hidden." (Leete, 1993, p. 119)

Anyone who has known well, or worked closely with, a person with schizophrenia is most likely familiar with the kind of heightened sensitivity of which Leete speaks. In a clinical setting, for example, people with schizophrenia are notorious for being the ones who will address embarrassing or potentially problematic elements of a situation that everyone else would be content to keep "hidden" or unspoken. Often seeming unaware of the consequences or impact of their doing so, they will not hesitate in pointing out the so-called elephant sitting in the middle of the room. In social settings, it is not uncommon for a person experiencing psychosis to be attending to, and distracted by, details that others might find irrelevant or uninteresting. This idiosyncratic focus on details, along with the sense of repeatedly losing the person to his or her preoccupations, can be a source of considerable frustration for someone trying to relate to a person with schizophrenia.

More important for our present purposes, however, is the impact of these experiences on the person with schizophrenia. How does becoming aware of these cognitive changes affect the person? One participant described this impact as follows:

> It's like being sick. It's like being nauseated or having a really bad headache and you're trying to relate, but there's something bothering you. It's a distraction, you know. . . . Like if you have a headache or something, you can relate, but there's always that pain, so you're going to be thinking of that pain. . . . It was like I was trying to relate and yet . . . I was having to struggle to make conversation or to concentrate on something. My attention span

was low and my concentration was low. And I think that's a very common problem with people who are mentally ill. Their attention span and their concentration seem to wax and wane and . . . they're not always there. . . . People take for granted that you just do things. A person with mental illness, it's sometimes hard . . . it's like you're distracted, you can't get involved because you're not sort of all there.

As suggested by this gentleman, common consequences of having to deal with increasing cognitive confusion, distractibility, and heightened sensitivity are withdrawal from social interaction and the social isolation that results. As the woman with whom we opened this section had already told us, if you know that you're not well and that you can't hold up your end of a conversation, you will be unlikely to pursue interpersonal interactions. In the similar words of another consumer advocate:

Aggravating matters more is the painful knowledge that you can't talk to anybody about these things. Not only are these things hard to talk about, but if you admit to having any of these kinds of problems you are likely to get puzzled looks or face immediate and often final rejection. Most people will put you in the category of "crazy," or "looney tunes" or "nutcase" or something similar. So to avoid this kind of abuse you are forced to hide or conceal your thoughts and feelings from others, and then ultimately from yourself, which only serves to worsen your situation. This is why persons with mental disorders are often passive, withdrawn, and avoid human contact. [We] are engaged in an inner struggle [we] can't express and which consumes [us]. . . . The invisibility of [our] struggle . . . and the isolation that results is what makes [our] situation so tragic. (Weingarten, 1994, p. 374)

"I Feel like I Am Being Punished a Little Bit"

In the passage above, Weingarten suggests that the social stigma accruing to mental illness is one factor that may contribute to people not talking about, not seeking help for, or denying the cognitive changes and other indications of psychosis they may be beginning to experience. We return to the issues of stigma, withdrawal, and isolation below, when we take up more fully the social dimension of the disorder. Before leaving our initial focus on awareness, however, there is more we can learn about how people deal with the first indications of psychosis.

We have suggested that people often are aware of changes in cognition, of the ways they appear to others as a result of these changes, and perhaps of some of the positive symptoms of the disorder (e.g., hearing voices) as well. We know both from clinical experience and from research, however, that people do not then promptly make an appointment to see a mental health professional as a result of their awareness of these changes, nor do they consult their own volume of the *DSM-IV* in order to determine that what they are experiencing is a diagnosable psychiatric disorder. It is at this point in the process that awareness of psychosis begins to differ from awareness of other conditions, such as diabetes or asthma, and not only in relation to stigma. If they do not seek help, what are people likely to do about their emerging awareness of these changes and their resulting difficulties? Prior to being handed a diagnosis they can either accept or reject, how do people deal with the range of troubling and distressing experiences they are having?

In brief, participants describe attempts to make sense of these changes as best they can based on their own previous life experiences. Unfortunately, there rarely are elements of their previous life experiences that are terribly helpful in this process, unless they have had a family member or other person with whom they have been close who has gone through similar changes in the past. Such cases are considerably complicated by the nature of the other person's condition and his or her experiences in and out of the formal treatment system. The frequent familiarity that people in such circumstances have with the mental health system typically cuts both ways, in that these individuals may be more familiar with the signs and symptoms of psychosis and be more comfortable entering the treatment system on the one hand, but then also be more afraid or determined, on the other hand, not to become like their father, aunt, or close friend. Common remarks of people in this situation are "I didn't want to believe that I was going crazy too" or "I was going to be damned if I was going to end up like my dad."

In the majority of cases in which people have no personal reference point for experiences of psychosis other than media portrayals of "madmen" and "psycho killers," each person is left up to his or her own devices and to socially and culturally available strategies for sense making. These include religious accounts of such things as demonic possession or visitations by God; persecutory ideas about the activities of foreign powers, aliens, or various versions of the secret police (e.g., CIA or FBI agents); or more up-to-date beliefs about being under the influence of different forms of technology, such as computer chips implanted in the brain, infrared or ultraviolet surveillance, or electronic thought broadcasting.

In clinical practice, and upon the reader's first reading of such ideas, these ways of making sense of early psychotic experiences may be dismissed as "delusions"; that is, as another symptom of the person's developing psychosis. By now, however, we would recognize dismissing these accounts as mere delusions to be yet another form of objectification, to be the result of our having stepped outside of the person's experience to grasp after a convenient, if external, explanation. Having been inoculated against such eventualities in our last chapter, we will avoid giving in to the Siren's temptations and consider these accounts instead from the inside.

To do so, we will need to consider a few concrete examples. These examples provide us a first opportunity to practice our craft of building empathic bridges in our imagination to the lives of people with psychosis. We remember that we need to construct such bridges whenever the person describes something we cannot intuitively grasp as obvious. The temptation to dismiss these accounts as delusional should serve as a clue that we now have stumbled across an aspect of the experience of psychosis that we do not yet understand. And so we pause.

We can start with the passage we used for the heading of this section. In this interview, a young man was describing the difficulties he had been having, which had resulted in feeling, in his words, that "I don't have a mind left." He described:

> *Participant:* I would say I feel like I am being punished a little bit.
> *Interviewer:* How so?
> *Participant:* Like in my mind, you know. . . . The spirit, sometimes before I go to sleep, I feel like I hear satanic stuff in my head.
> *Interviewer:* And that feels like a punishment of some sort?
> *Participant:* Yes.
> *Interviewer:* What do you think you may be punished for?

Participant: For that I don't even really know. I don't know. . . . There was a murder that happened with me and my brother about thirteen years ago. I think it's from that.

Interviewer: Was this something you were involved in?

Participant: Yes.

Interviewer: And you think it is because of that that you have these problems, these experiences?

Participant: Yes.

Although seldom connected to a murder, we have found this notion of the signs and symptoms of mental illness being experienced as a punishment for previous acts not to be uncommon among people with psychosis. Whether considered as justifiable retribution for a heinous act (e.g., murder), as a sanction from God for one's sins, as a tragic consequence of earlier illicit drug use, or as undeserved suffering imposed by evil forces, the cognitive changes, disruptions, and intrusions that people experience are often viewed as being imposed on them against their will.

One could argue that any serious illness may be experienced in this way, with history providing examples of AIDS, cancer, epilepsy, and tuberculosis being viewed at various times as punishments from God or as consequences of living an unhealthy life. What our narratives suggest is that psychosis continues to occupy such a sociocultural niche into the present day for some people. What appears to be unique about psychosis is the alien, ambiguous, and intangible nature of the onslaught that people experience. Things I used to be able to do (e.g., remembering details), faculties I used to be able to control (e.g., directing my attention), and senses I used to be able to trust (e.g., not hearing voices when no one else is around) are experienced as being taken over and being under the influence of something, or someone, else. "When I was going through the psychosis or mental illness I knew that wasn't me," described one female participant: "It felt like I was outside my body and someone else was inside my body. That's the only way I can explain it."

Based on intricate phenomenological analyses that Husserl offered in the second volume of his *Ideen,* we have previously explored in detail the basis of this kind of displacement of agency in schizophrenia (Davidson, 2001). Without duplicating those analyses here, we can summarize the key points as follows.

Ordinarily we think of human agency as a sense of volition involved in making choices, in pursuing goals, and in preferring certain things over others. This may be seen as a secondary sense of agency, however, if we consider how a more basic sense of agency first emerges out of our sensory experiences. Husserl suggested that a basic sense of will emerges out of kinaesthetic experiences of being able to move our bodies; being able to act *in* the world is predicated on being able to act *on* one's own body. A corollary to this is that our sense of being affected is predicated on our sensory experiences of being acted on or being moved. Out of experiences of being touched emerges the sense that I can be impacted from the outside, that I am susceptible to stimulation from a world external to me. In the experience of most people, there ordinarily develops a complementarity between these two kinds of sensory experiences such that the person develops both a sense of moving and of being moved, of acting in and of being affected by the world. Husserl captures this complementarity in the image of the hand that can both touch and be touched, allowing the person to experience both the capacity to act and be acted on (1989, pp. 155–161).

The basic sensory experiences that allow for development of a sense of action and affection take place on the foundational level of self-awareness. That is, prior to the integration of my experiences of intending my arm to move and sensing it move there already exists the awareness that both the intention and sensation are indeed mine. There already is a sense that it is I who am directing my awareness to my arm and I who am receiving the kinaesthetic sensations of the arm in motion. It is here that we find the foundational sense of agency that is operative on the level of awareness, in that prior to the development of a sense of what I can do to my body or in the world, I already have developed a sense that I can direct my own attention, that I am the originating locus of my own awareness (Davidson, 2001).

It appears to be precisely in this sphere of the direction of their own attention that people with schizophrenia experience a kind of difficulty that is not common to other illnesses. As a person begins to struggle with the cognitive disruptions and intrusions that we have discovered to be the first prominent indications of this illness, it may become at times difficult, at other times impossible, for the person to continue to feel in control of his or her own awareness. For example, hallucinated voices typically are experienced as coming and going as they please, competing for airtime, so to speak, with the person's own thoughts. One participant described the effect of these experiences to be the feeling of someone else having invaded his mind, demanding use of his brain and body, and taking them over at will. In this way, a man who is besieged by satanic voices when trying to go to sleep, or a woman who is unable to filter out distractions in order to focus on something of interest, will have difficulty continuing to experience themselves as agents of their own experiences. The vacuum that results then renders the person vulnerable to having the role of agent become occupied by someone or something else. It simply becomes a matter of naming or labeling the alternative source of agency.

Being unable to retain a sense of oneself as the source of the direction of one's own awareness may thus deprive the person with schizophrenia of the most fundamental sense of ownership of his or her own experiences. Without this basic self-awareness, people may then lose their secondary sense of themselves as agents active in and affected by the world. The impact of voices and cognitive disruptions in this way reverberates throughout the person's experiences of self leading to the constitution of a sense of personal identity built more on feelings of being controlled by and vulnerable to external influences than of being the agent of one's own thoughts, perceptions, and feelings as well as actions.

It is important to note here that we are not talking about *actual* levels of passivity or agency in the behavior of people with schizophrenia, but only in their own sense of themselves as objects of external control. People with schizophrenia can be as active as anyone else. They can doggedly pursue certain projects with a persistence that is impressive, often to the point of being considered "irrational." But even in these cases they may not experience themselves as the origin of these projects nor may they experience themselves as striving toward these goals. The determinant both of the projects themselves and of the efforts involved may be situated outside the person and his/her own sense of agency. It may be the neighbors who control my actions, or God, or a hidden or invisible machine. In any case, these actions are not based on my own decisions or desires but are dictated by external forces. I do not experience myself as having any choice in the matter.

"I Had to Be Either a CIA Agent or a Mental Patient. Which Would You Choose?"

For those of us who have not experienced psychosis first hand, it may require some mental work to get a grasp on how the loss of a foundational sense of agency can reverberate throughout the person's life. Many of us will have encountered limitations on our own sense of agency routinely through such experiences as losing a football pool at the office, not getting a promotion we worked hard for, or doing battle with a chronic illness. In each of these cases, it is the results of our efforts that lie outside of our control, however, not the efforts themselves. So while these examples offer an initial step toward an empathic understanding of the loss of agency, they fall well short of the degree of loss experienced by people with schizophrenia. In what circumstances might it become the efforts themselves that we no longer experience as under our own control?

A more extreme example might be that provided by various forms of addiction, in which it is common for people to describe losing control of their lives to alcohol, cocaine, or gambling. In these cases, as perhaps in compulsions, it is no longer just the outcomes of the person's actions but certain of the actions themselves that no longer feel under his or her control. Even in these cases, however, people maintain the basic sense that their experiences are, in fact, their own. Likewise, in dissociative identity disorder, or multiple personality disorder, each self has its own discrete domain, in which there is an awareness of these experiences as belonging to their respective self and no other. In what more extreme cases might there be a sense of even the experiences themselves no longer belonging to the person?

We take another example, this time provided by a young male participant we will call Kyle. Kyle's interview occurred after he had already been sick for approximately 14 years, with onset of his psychosis traced back to his late teens. For the first seven or so years of his illness, Kyle fit the profile of a so-called treatment-resistant person, who lacked awareness or insight into his condition, refused to take his medication or participate in other treatment or rehabilitation, and cycled as a result through emergency rooms and psychiatric inpatient units with prominent auditory hallucinations and delusions of control (in addition to other symptoms). He had become alienated from his family and friends, was unable to maintain employment, and remained on the periphery of the mental health system, being discharged from group homes and day treatment programs due to his lack of interest and refusal to abide by program rules and expectations. Considered "permanently disabled" and on state and federal entitlements, Kyle wandered aimlessly from program to program. Or so it appeared.

This description and account of Kyle's life obviously comes from the perspective of the clinicians and others who knew him, not from his own subjective perspective. Kyle's account of these first seven years was quite different in some respects, although he did not disagree with the facts of his multiple hospitalizations, inability to maintain employment, etc. Kyle reported that during these seven years he was engrossed in the life of being a CIA operative with an extremely important role to play in thought broadcasting experiments the United States was conducting in its cold war efforts against the Soviet Union. The voices that spoke to Kyle even when he appeared to be alone identified themselves as coming from the CIA. As these voices and related thoughts were experienced as coming and going as *they* pleased and were not at all responsive to Kyle's own wishes to be left alone, Kyle at first believed the voices when they told him that he had been selected by the CIA to be enlisted into high level intelligence experiments. The credibility both of the CIA and of the thought broadcasting techniques they were testing on him was evident to Kyle in that he heard these voices and was invaded by related thoughts even when no one else was around. Where else could they have come from, how else could they have been delivered to him, and to what other purpose?

For his part, all Kyle had to do was listen to what the voices and thoughts told him to do, including following their instructions that he not tell anyone else about them or the experiments in which he was involved. Given the nature of the cold war and the covert intelligence operations in which he was involved, Kyle could never be certain when he might be crossing paths with counterintelligence agents or with operatives of the KGB. He could never be too careful.

The behaviors that Kyle exhibited during this period seemed odd to others and included sitting alone for hours at a time, talking out loud to himself, neglecting his personal hygiene, and refusing to leave his bedroom or any residential setting in which he might have lived at the time. He was uninterested in returning to school or getting a job, expressed little to no interest in dating or sex, and became increasingly disorganized and incoherent if pushed by others to get involved in social or vocational activities. Kyle was transported to the emergency room and/or hospitalized when his self-care deteriorated to the point of grave disability. Even when outside of the hospital, however, Kyle didn't seem to understand what was happening to him, as he struggled against the efforts of his family and the mental health system at every turn without proposing any of his own alternatives. Even if we do not describe Kyle's course as deteriorating during these first seven years, it certainly was the case that there was little progress in his condition.

Another seven years or so later, however, Kyle participated in a study of people who had shown significant improvement. At the time he was living independently in his own apartment and working part-time, spending his free time with friends. In his interview he described in retrospect a turning point in the course of his illness that had occurred around his seventh year of being sick, when "the thirty-sixth psychiatrist told me I had schizophrenia." Apparently, the first 35 psychiatrists Kyle had seen during his first seven years of psychosis had had only a limited, if additive, impact on him. It was only after the thirty-sixth psychiatrist independently told him the same thing that Kyle began to wonder if perhaps there was something to what they said. "I started to think that not all 36 of them could be wrong," he said. "It wasn't like they all knew each other or anything," he reasoned, so how else "could they all have come up with the same thing?"

This is not to suggest that Kyle became convinced about his condition at the time or that he adopted an altogether different attitude toward treatment as a result of these considerations. Rather, the possibility that all 36 psychiatrists might have independently come up with the same diagnosis—and thereby the possibility that he might not be a CIA agent after all—offered Kyle a glimpse into the possibility of a very different life. It then took Kyle an additional seven years of what he called his "experiments" before he came to any firm conclusions.

The intervening period of seven years following Kyle's period of severe disability and leading to his eventual recovery consisted largely of his efforts to figure out which of these scenarios was the true one. Under the rubric of these so-called experiments, Kyle alternated between seeing what happened when he believed his voices as compared to when he believed his psychiatrists. Over time he discovered a pattern that confirmed his initial impression that the thirty-sixth psychiatrist was indeed telling him the truth.

Kyle noticed that when he listened to his voices, he felt important and special in his role as a secret agent but found himself withdrawing from the day-to-day world and from any other activities that interested him. In addition, he stopped taking his medication, spent more and more time alone, was unable to maintain a job or an apartment, and was eventually hospitalized. On the other hand, he noticed that when he listened to his psychiatrist, Kyle took his medication and stayed grounded in the day-to-day activities of maintaining his apartment, holding a part-time job, and spending time with friends. He got along better with his family and had even begun to date. He felt, however, like "nothing but a mental patient." When asked by the interviewer how this might have influenced his eventual decision to believe his psychiatrists over his voices, Kyle explained that this was, in part, why his "experiments" took so long to conclude. Losing the sense of importance that came with being a CIA agent was the major barrier he faced in accepting that he had schizophrenia. As he explained: "I had to be either a CIA agent or a mental patient. Which would you choose?"

"I Thought Changing Geography Would Stop the Voices"

Kyle may have been particularly eloquent in describing some of the personal and emotional challenges involved in accepting that he had a mental illness and giving up his life as a CIA agent during the cold war. In less dramatic terms, perhaps, and with less eloquence, however, most people who experience psychosis (and who have no personal reference point for understanding it as such) find themselves grasping after explanations that help them to make sense of these experiences. For these explanations to make sense they have to be based, at least in part, on the person's own experiences. As we noted above, however, there often is little in a person's previous life experience that can provide a ready-made account for psychosis. As a result, people may appear to be stretching their imagination, with more or less degree of desperation, in order to come up with any account at all—regardless of how this account may strike others.

To appreciate the unusual nature of the efforts involved in coming up with such accounts, we need to consider the unusual nature of the experiences in question. One young man described as his primary concerns the difficulties with memory, attention, and concentration described above. He did not know why he would begin to have such difficulties in his late adolescence when he had never experienced anything like this in the past. He had been a good student, a hard worker, etc. The only explanation he could even consider as a possible source of these kinds of difficulties was brain damage, but he was born with no birth defects and he had not been involved in any serious accidents that would have caused a traumatic brain injury. While he had not had such difficulties from birth, they also did not come on in a sudden or abrupt fashion. They seem to have gradually built up over time over the last several years in a slow, incremental fashion. What would account for this?

Having ruled out birth defects and traumatic brain injury, the only other thing this young man could imagine causing slow but steady brain damage was something exerting a toxic effect on his brain. He hadn't been poisoned and he didn't have a brain tumor, so what else could account for the brain damage that must have been causing his increasing cognitive difficulty? Based on the fact that he walked to work each day a mile or so alongside an interstate highway, he guessed that it must have been the carbon monoxide he inhaled from car exhaust that had been slowly poisoning his brain. He blamed his parents for making him walk to and from work—ultimately, he blamed them for his brain damage as well—but located the source of toxicity in the exhaust fumes of the cars and trucks passing by only a few yards away from him. In this case, the young man eventually was relieved to know that his condition was not due to irreversible brain damage but to a psychiatric disorder for which he could take medication and receive other treatments that would be useful in improving his condition. As his cognitive functioning improved, he became less concerned with possible brain damage, less focused on his prior exposure to carbon monoxide, and less angry with his parents.

Another participant who experienced auditory hallucinations assumed that the voices he was hearing had to be coming from people he couldn't see, but who had to be nearby nonetheless. In this case, his attempt at a solution was to get away from the people who continued, for reasons unknown to him, to harass him. As he described: "I went to Florida when I started hearing voices. At first I thought changing geography would stop the voices from here, so I moved down to Florida." Once arriving in Florida, however, this gentleman realized that the voices unfortunately had followed him down south. Many years of battling the voices ensued, during which alternative explanations of their origins were considered. By the time of his interview, he had come to identify these voices as symptoms of a psychiatric disorder that was (at least partly) responsive to treatment and his condition was slowly improving.

What can we learn from these various examples? Apparently, many people experiencing the first indications of psychosis do not experience these signs or symptoms as indicative of mental illness at all. They grasp, with more or less desperation, at explanations grounded in their own life experience and fund of knowledge, with psychiatric disorder often being the explanation of last resort. This may be due to any number of factors—some of which are listed below—but it was not uncommon for our participants to have experienced an extended period of distress associated with unrecognized, and therefore untreated, psychosis, prior to seeking or being offered a psychiatric diagnosis or explanation to account for their difficulties. As one woman whom we call Maria described when asked when her difficulties began:

> Well, actually when I was thirteen and I became pregnant with [my son]. I can remember episodes from that far back, but people really didn't notice anything until I was twenty-six, or if they noticed it they ignored it.

In Maria's case, there thus was a 13-year period of episodic psychosis and the dysfunctions associated with it before anyone began to consider there might be something wrong that was medical or psychiatric in nature. Such prolonged delays in seeking help may be due partly to the fact that most people do not receive any education or information about early signs of mental illness or ways to understand psychiatric symptoms and to seek appropriate help. Many delays also are undoubtedly due to the stigma that rushes to fill in this void and to the images people grow up with of psychiatric disorder. For example, Deegan describes the images of mental illness she had in mind when she first started to experience indications of psychosis and first came into contact with the mental health system.

> To me, mental illness meant Dr. Jekyll and Mr. Hyde, psychopathic serial
> killers, loony bins, morons, schizos, fruitcakes, nuts, straight jackets, and rav-
> ing lunatics. They were all I knew about mental illness, and what terrified me
> was that professionals were saying I was one of them. (1993, p. 8)

Regardless of whether extended delays in identifying psychiatric disorder
are due to stigma, inattention, ignorance, denial, or a combination of all
the above, Maria had had 13 years to try to make sense of her distressing
experiences on her own. Like the handcuffs and restraints used to bring
people to the emergency room or psychiatric hospital against their will,
such efforts are likely to leave additional scars of their own.

Before moving on to explore those scars and their effects in the social
sphere, we should conclude the construction of this particular empathic
bridge in our imagination. We recall that the examples we have been con-
sidering were introduced to help us imagine what it might be like if even
our experiences themselves were no longer experienced as belonging to us.
If we put these several examples together, we begin to get the sense that
experiences are no longer experienced as mine because I am no longer experienced as their agent. One man described the most terrifying aspect of
his schizophrenia to be the times when he no longer was aware of himself
as a person. In these moments, what awareness he retained seemed to him
to be that of an object (should objects have awareness). Described another
person:

> Things just happen to me now and I have no control over them. I don't
> seem to have the same say in things anymore. At times, I can't even control
> what I want to think about. I am starting to feel pretty numb about every-
> thing because I am becoming an object and objects don't have feelings.
> (Quoted in McGhie and Chapman, 1961, p. 109)

In our own experience, the closest we have come to feeling so bom-
barded with unwelcome sights and sounds that directing our attention or
concentrating on anything in particular became very difficult, if not impossible—and our own status as an agent was called into question as a result—was when one of us took a train to Rome for the first time during his
honeymoon. It wasn't so much the train ride itself, even though our rider
did have to stand for three hours on a train that was so overcrowded it

would have broken all U.S. fire codes. It was emerging from the train station into the congested and noisy streets of Rome that was overwhelming. As we often do in our training program and through writing groups led by John Strauss, this person was encouraged to write a narrative about his experience.

I had spent the last half hour or so studying my map of Rome, thinking that this would help with my anxiety, hoping that when we left the station the well-traced route to our hotel would somehow spring to life and usher us the few straightforward blocks to a comfortable and waiting bed and bathroom. I had been in Italy long enough to know that I couldn't really trust these maps. I had already gotten us lost twice: once in Venice and once in Florence. Why did I think it would be different this time? But the woman we had met on the train had told me that it would be an easy ten-minute walk from the station to our hotel.

"Just head for the big fountain," she said, "and turn left. You can go straight from there, won't take more than ten minutes. You don't want to take a taxi. They'll drive you around all over town first and charge you a fortune. It's an easy walk."

Our travel agent had already warned us about cab drivers in Rome. After this train ride I didn't want to have to deal with them too. So we'd walk. Our bags weren't that heavy and on the map it looked easy.

It started the minute we got off the train. Lots and lots of people shouting and shoving, grabbing bags, grabbing each other, all moving quickly in one direction. We followed. We could barely hear each other above the din when I turned half way around to check with my wife and make sure she didn't mind the walk to the hotel. I had shouted and she had shaken her head. We followed the crowd. Not that we had any choice. I had already begun to feel that I had lost control of my legs, that they no longer looked to me for direction, when I was approached by several men shouting at me in English, asking if I needed a hotel or a taxi. Maybe I looked vulnerable, maybe I looked like a stupid American tourist, maybe they were just shouting and I took it to be directed at me, feeling like I had to respond. But I couldn't tolerate the barrage. Being pushed and pulled in the crowd, hearing several people at once addressing harsh and intrusive questions at me made my pace quicken. I darted for the opening that I saw ahead where the crowd spilled out onto the street just trying to get away. The closest I can come to this feeling was memories of dodge ball in junior high: I was one of the smaller but slower targets.

It didn't end, though, when we got to the street. There was no big fountain in sight, just a McDonald's sign. I'm not sure if I picked that direction, or if that direction picked me. I don't even like McDonald's. Maybe because I hadn't seen a McDonald's sign in Italy and it was at least familiar at a time when everything else seemed so foreign. Or I was attracted too, I think, to the anonymity that it offered.

You see, by this time I wanted not to be so obvious. I didn't want anyone else asking anything of me. I just wanted to be left alone. I was having a hard enough time carrying my bags and trying to find this elusive fountain. Couldn't all of those people shouting at me see that? Couldn't they see that I didn't know anything, that I was paralyzed by all of the sights and the sounds and the people and the unfamiliarity of it all?

We got to McDonald's and the crowds thinned to that of a normal city street. We would have thought that we were in Manhattan, except that no one was speaking English and the cars were going much faster. We had some breathing room. No one was asking me for anything, no one was shouting or gesturing toward me. So I took out the map. I couldn't find any of the streets we were on or near, any of the streets we had been on since leaving the station. The map just didn't match. There was no clue as to where we were, where we should be, or how to get there from here. My brief respite ended with this realization and the sounds and sights started to crowd back in. The people passing by us on the sidewalk, the cars whizzing by on the street, seemed to be moving *too* fast, their voices, honks, and screeching brakes seemed *too* loud. I couldn't shut it out, I couldn't do anything to change it, I hadn't asked for any of it, and my new wife stood there looking at me expecting me to have something intelligent or helpful to say. I was supposed to be able to find this on the map, I was supposed to be able to get us to the hotel. I just wanted to disappear. And then I started feeling obvious again.

As we were lugging our luggage up yet another hill on the way to yet another street that was not identified, an elderly British gentleman stopped and offered to show me his map. He even asked if he could help me find something on it. I waved him off perfunctorily with a "Oh, no thanks, I've got one right here." I was lost all right, and nothing matched my map, but I found myself feeling too vulnerable, too exposed already, to deal with a stranger who could see just how lost I was. Just let me disappear, I thought, just let me get out of this place to where its safe and quiet and clean, and where nobody can see me. Or see how helpless I am. Because somebody else could use this map, like that elderly British gentleman, or somebody else could have found the fountain from the station, like the woman on the train. It's just that I couldn't, like I couldn't deal with the noises or the cars, or the scalpers at the station. Other people were doing fine: they were hugging their loved ones as they got off the train, or eating their hamburgers at McDonald's, or browsing leisurely in the shops on the unnamed street. I was the one in trouble, and yet all I wanted to do was to be left alone, to disappear.

Perhaps this is a familiar scene for men who have traveled to urban areas in other foreign countries as well, perhaps not. We have been assured on several occasions by female colleagues, however, that only a man would turn down an offer of assistance in such circumstances. Men simply do not ask for directions. On the other hand, female travelers might have been more concerned with their personal safety in such situations, avoiding eye contact and other interactions out of a sense of fear and vulnerability. Gender stereotypes aside, this experience—while still far from actual experiences of psychosis—comes closer in suggesting the kind of sensory onslaught, vulnerability, and diminished sense of agency described by people with psychosis. It's just that in this case, our traveler eventually found his hotel (without asking directions), became assimilated to Rome and its own intrinsic chaos, and was able to enjoy the rest of his stay. For people with schizophrenia it typically is not so easy, with their involuntary onslaughts lasting days, weeks, months, or even years instead of hours. Still, many people, as we will see in the next chapter, are able to find their way to clean, well-lit places (Hemingway, 1964), figure out ways to manage their internal chaos, and find aspects of the rest of their journey enjoyable as well.

Readers who do not find this example useful in their own efforts to empathize with people experiencing early indications of psychosis are challenged to reflect on their own experiences in order to dredge up memories that can serve as more suitable examples. We offer this example as only one illustrative attempt to make such a bridge. Should these efforts fail, there also now exist audiocassettes that may be obtained from educational and advocacy organizations that simulate the experience of auditory hallucinations. Listening to a cacophony of voices through a set of headphones while trying to accomplish daily tasks can provide a similar revelatory experience for those whose imaginations may need a bit of additional encouragement and/or data.

"I Wouldn't Fit In Because I'm Bipolar"

In addition to the diminished sense of agency, the story of the Rome train station contains another element that is reflective of the experiences described by people with psychosis. Broadly speaking, this is the element of sociality, or how people with schizophrenia perceive others, are perceived by others, and relate to others on an interpersonal level. Our traveler's refusal of assistance when he was clearly in distress is reflective not only of a typical male reluctance to ask for directions, but also of the fact that many people early in the course of psychosis do not accept what help may be offered them. They may turn down offers of help from concerned others, refuse to seek medical or psychiatric care despite being encouraged to do so, and, once seen (voluntarily or otherwise), either refuse to accept the healthcare professional's assessment and diagnosis and/or choose not to follow through with the recommended regimen of treatment. These are some of the visible elements of behavior early in the course of illness that have earned persons with schizophrenia such labels as "lacking insight," "being unaware of illness," or "being in denial." As we have seen thus far, however, people appear to be keenly aware of the changes they have been experiencing and have actively been trying to make sense of them. Are there other reasons that they would be so reluctant to seek or receive help for these concerns?

Our traveler's story suggests two additional and related motivations for turning down offers of assistance. The first is captured in his wishes to disappear. What he is describing are experiences of such vulnerability that they led him to withdraw from all stimulation and to try to protect himself from any further intrusions from others. We have come to think of this aspect as the "raw nerve" phenomenon, borrowing from extremely unpleasant experiences we all have had at the dentist's office. When nerves are exposed and stimulated externally, the pain—and therefore the impulse to protect oneself—can be quite intense and involuntary. Like our traveler, we suggest that people early in the course of schizophrenia may feel equally exposed and vulnerable to external stimulation and experience an equally pressing need for self-protection through social withdrawal and the wish to disappear. Deegan described eloquently such efforts to withdraw and protect herself from further violations in the following passage:

> The professionals called it apathy and lack of motivation. They blamed it on our illness. But they don't understand that giving up is a highly motivated and highly goal-directed behavior. For us giving up was a way of surviving. Giving up, refusing to hope, not trying, not caring: all of these were ways of trying to protect the last fragile traces of our spirit and our selfhood from undergoing another crushing. (1994, p. 19)

Like Weingarten's description quoted above ("[We] are engaged in an inner struggle [we] can't express and which consumes [us]. . . . The invisibility of [our] struggle . . . and the isolation that results is what makes [our] situation so tragic"), this passage demonstrates how a person's behavior may be misinterpreted by others to represent a lack of something—whether motivation or insight—rather than the active struggle for survival in which the person often is engaged.

Such a misinterpretation of the self-protective function of withdrawal is only one example, however, of the many negative perceptions to which people with psychosis become exposed early in the course of their illness. Not only, then, may a person withdraw due to feeling exposed and vulnerable but also the person may find it even more difficult to return to the interpersonal sphere once she or he begins to get a sense of how others' perceive her or him as a result. In other words, being given negative labels for withdrawing only acts to compound the person's initial needs for self-protection, thereby increasing his or her need to withdraw. This leads to the second, related motivation for turning down assistance from others and rejecting psychiatric diagnosis and treatment: the fear, or actual prior experience, of being rejected, shunned, and stigmatized as a result of being mentally ill. We have touched on this briefly above but focus more explicitly on it here as an important dimension of the person's exposure and vulnerability and as a key factor in perpetuating what we will come to see as a spiral downward from withdrawal to extrusion to further withdrawal.

Unfortunately, there are many examples of this process in our interviews with people with schizophrenia. One man, for example, when asked how the person who knew him best would describe him replied: "Probably that I sound very ill, stupid, and pathetic . . . [but that he] tries his best. [He] feels bad for me . . . because I'm nuts." When asked by the interviewer if he participated in any social activities, another participant replied: "No. I wouldn't fit in because I'm bipolar." Finally, a third participant, when asked how she felt she was treated in the community, replied: "People treat me like not a person." When asked "How's that?" by an interviewer who was looking for clarification and details, she replied: "They ignore me . . . [they treat me] like crap. I felt like I belonged [in school], but now I don't feel like I belong anywhere."

The importance of feeling like you do not belong anywhere, if taken seriously, cannot be overestimated in its impact on people with schizophrenia. We say "if taken seriously" because, in our experience, this aspect of schizophrenia is as difficult to get a handle on as the loss of agency described above. That is, we have found this experience to occur at the same kind of foundational level as the person's loss of self; a basic sense of loss that most of us will not have experienced first-hand.

Upon first reading that people with schizophrenia feel like they do not belong anywhere, for example, the reader may recall experiences of not "fitting in" at certain social gatherings or may have associations with a more general sense of alienation that at times characterizes adolescence. As a basis for building more empathic bridges, these examples fall well short of capturing the degree of alienation and isolation described by people with schizophrenia. This sense of alienation and isolation is better approximated by the experience of a person becoming lost in a foreign country, where no one speaks his language and there is no one else around who does, or the experience of a person trying to get to sleep in a hotel room in a city in which she knows no one, afraid that if she dies in her sleep no one will know to come looking for her until her body starts to smell from decomposing.

It is very possible, in such circumstances, that people with schizophrenia may find the inevitable peer group of other people with serious mental illness as the most accepting social sphere to which they have access, and, with that, the "mental patient" identity that comes along with this affiliation. In many cases, it will be preferable to come to see oneself as a mental patient who can socialize with other mental patients than to see oneself as a nobody who belongs nowhere. As one elderly participant described

Figure 2
Some Elements of Life "Inside" Schizophrenia

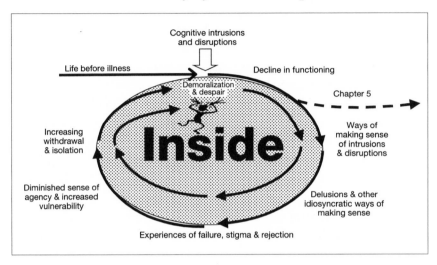

the limited kind of social interactions he had during a long-term inpatient stay that seemed to follow him out into the community following discharge: "I had nothing in common with the other patients except that I was another nut with them, you know." If you feel that you don't belong to the broader world because you are "bipolar" or a "nut," and that people will shun you because of it, then it is understandable how you would come to limit your social interactions to hanging out with other people who share this tragic fate.

"I'm Really in a Coma Somewhere and Waiting to Wake Up"

In Figure 2 we outline several of the elements of life with schizophrenia as described above. This figure is not meant to encompass the entirety of the person's life nor is it intended to provide a complete theory of the disorder. Rather, it is proposed as a way to understand several of the central aspects of the experience of the disorder in relation to each other. As a self-contained oval, the solid arrows are used to represent a downward spiral, in which a person may become entrapped at times during the course of her or his illness.

This spiral involves (1) cognitive intrusions and disruptions that (2) bring about a decline in the person's functioning which (3) the person then may make sense of in delusional or other idiosyncratic ways, making (4) the person's failure at normative life tasks and rejection from others more likely, leading to (5) a diminished sense of agency and increased vulnerability which can have the effect of (6) increasing the person's need to withdraw, resulting ultimately in (7) demoralization and despair.

There are, of course, possible escape routes that allow the person to leave the spiral of illness, as represented by the dotted line in Figure 2. These will be described in detail in chapter 5. For this chapter, we remained within the parameters of life "inside" the illness, so to speak, in order to explore the various components of the illness in relation to each other. In the next chapter, we focus instead on the various components of recovery or on life "outside" of schizophrenia. The reader should not be misled, therefore, to think that there is only an inside to life with schizophrenia. You should not be left with the impression that everyone with schizophrenia is doomed to forever perpetuate a downward spiral. Understanding the spiral and its various components, however, can shed useful light on some of the more stark characteristics of schizophrenia, such as denial of illness, rejection of treatment, and withdrawal into a passive and seemingly empty state.

These dramatic and troubling behaviors, we suggest, are better understood from the person's own perspective as self-protective in the best case and as signs of demoralization and despair in the worst case. The following report, reminiscent of the woman in chapter 3 who didn't want to get dressed up because she was never taken anywhere, expresses the growing sense of demoralization and despair that comes as the person descends the spiral. A participant describes:

> I have no good feelings and I've been hearing voices all the time. The only thing that really cares about me that I really care about is [my cat]. And my house isn't that clean and I got to do that. Some of these things just aren't as important to me as they used to [be]. I used to have some wonderful hygiene. That's not important to me anymore. What do I want to do it for?

In even more stark terms, the following description excerpted from an interview with a middle-aged male participant captures the subjective underside of the "giving up" Deegan described above as serving a basic survival function:

> Well, there's nothing really out here for me. . . . I'll say a prayer, say God help me or heal me or take [me], but it hasn't worked so far. . . . It's hard for me to concentrate, and sometimes when someone says something I may get a reminder of the past. I live in the past. Every day is the present, but it holds nothing for me. As far as the future, I have no future worth mentioning. . . . I know I'm going to die mentally ill. I don't know what else I'll die from physically, but as far as hopes, I don't see any hope. . . . I fear that I'll get sicker and linger on and suffer more than I'm suffering now.

Some readers may be skeptical at this point that so much in the way of suffering could be brought about by so little in the way of cognitive intrusions and disruptions. We offer, in no way to diminish the profound suffering of people with schizophrenia, the analogy of the *Princess and the Pea*. In this fairy tale, a king, queen, and their son, the prince, are able to determine that a young maiden who has sought shelter in their castle, and with whom the prince falls in love, is indeed a princess and thereby eligible to marry. They are able to establish her royal pedigree by virtue of the fact that she could feel a pea that the queen had placed on her bed through the numerous mattresses she had placed on top of it, complaining in the morning of having difficulty sleeping and being bruised by a lump in the mattress. Our analogy, though far from perfect, speaks to the heightened sensitivity that people with schizophrenia seem to share with the princess and to the fact that this sensitivity is still operative through many layers of protective covering.

What this analogy also suggests is that while some people with schizophrenia may appear at times to be quite different from the rest of us, their strange, preoccupied, withdrawn, or empty appearance is most likely due to many years of experiences of failure, rejection, vulnerability, and loss being layered on top of each other, all of which contribute to an encrusted self-protective shell formed around the original experiences of cognitive confusion. Earlier in the course of illness, people with schizophrenia are unlikely to appear as different from the norm or to be as inaccessible to others. These more extreme states are more likely to occur later due to the layers upon layers of self-protective cover they then accrue over time.

Now that most people with schizophrenia live the majority of their lives outside of institutional settings, it is much less common to see people in such extreme states of alienation or apparent emptiness—except perhaps among people traumatized by persistent homelessness. Much more common are complicated pictures of people who have areas of dysfunction co-existing with areas of intact health (Davidson and Strauss, 1995). In these cases, there remain more opportunities for escaping the downward spiral of chronicity and more avenues of possible improvement and recovery. It is to these that we now turn.

5

■　　■　　■　　■　　■　　■　　■　　■

Living Outside Schizophrenia

I'm nobody till somebody loves me. That's the way I look at it.
—Man with schizophrenia speaking with interviewer

IF WE HAVE PAINTED a vivid enough picture of the downward spiral that appears to unfold inexorably, and to lead thereby to the end-state of premature dementia first described by Kraepelin, then you should be left wondering how, or even if, recovery is possible in a condition like schizophrenia. If so, then we have done our job well in portraying the uphill, almost Sisyphean, battle people face in trying to overcome the effects of the disorder. We know from the outcome research reviewed in chapter 1, however, that partial to full recovery is, in fact, possible over time for many, if not the majority, of people afflicted with the disorder. How is this so? How is it possible for people to break away from the centrifugal force of the spiral in order to stake out, or reclaim, a life outside of the illness?

There are several answers to these questions that we will *not* explore in any detail in what follows. First and foremost among these is the issue of anti-psychotic medication. We are convinced, both from our own clinical experience and from the research literature, that anti-psychotic medications properly administered and properly taken can make significant differences in the lives of many people with psychotic disorders. This fact is also well reflected in our interviews, with participants saying things like: "Without the medicine I wouldn't be here right now. I would have committed suicide." Medications are increasingly effective in targeting the more dramatic positive symptoms of the disorder, such as hallucinations, but thus far have remained relatively ineffective in decreasing negative symptoms or disorganization or remediating cognitive deficits. As we have seen in the previous chapter, these are some of the more virulent and durable sources of the impairments associated with schizophrenia. We also know from the outcome research, as well as from autobiographical and biographical accounts of such people as Nobel laureate John Nash (Nasar, 1998), however, that people also recover without the assistance of medications.

From the perspective of qualitative research focused on the person's experiences of living with the disorder, both of these possibilities—namely, recovery may or may not be facilitated by anti-psychotic medications—are important to note. Equally important are how people may perceive the medications and their needs for taking them, and the reasons they so often choose not to take the medications (although they do so at no higher a rate than people with most other chronic medical conditions). There already exists a significant body of literature addressing these issues related to medication use, its effects and side-effects, reasons for nonadherence, and strategies to increase adherence, including our own phenomenological review (Davidson, Stayner, and Haglund, 1998). Given that our primary focus is on the person's role in recovery, however, the only dimension of this literature directly relevant to our interest relates to factors influencing the person's decisions of whether or not to take the medications and the meanings the medications hold for the person (e.g., if I take psychiatric medications that must mean I am a psychiatric patient).

To the degree that we remain primarily interested in the person's role in recovery, the same could be said of other forms of psychiatric treatment and rehabilitation. Our interest is not so much in the intervention itself, by whom or how it is delivered, but in the person's experiences of the various resources offered by the mental health system, whether helpful or not. In the following, we thus limit ourselves to the first-person perspective on processes of improvement and refrain from speculating about other ameliorative or therapeutic influences that lie outside of the person's awareness. On the one hand, this limits the scope of our investigation. On the other hand, by exploring the data accessible and appropriate to qualitative inquiry, we discover a little used window onto a rich landscape.

"When I Was Going through My Psychotic Changes She Was Always There for Me. She Never Turned Her Back on Me"

People who have experienced some degree of improvement in their condition almost invariably identify another person as having been of crucial importance to them in the process of recovery. It is not always the first thing people mention; they may talk initially about medication or about their own determination to get better, for example. It is most often, however, what people identify as having played a crucial role in bringing about a turning point in the course of illness. As described by Leete: "A supportive, accepting, and loving relationship with others . . . has been the key element in my recovery" (1993, p. 114). If we are interested in how people might initially escape from the downward spiral of illness and isolation, this then provides a good place to start.

A young woman whom we have called Betty, and whose eloquent narrative we have used to illustrate several components of the recovery of self in previous publications (Davidson, 1992; Davidson and Strauss, 1992), for example, has been equally articulate in her description of the importance played by one of her nurses during a period of extreme disability. At the time, Betty was experiencing persistent hallucinations and was highly fearful and paranoid, being unable to participate in any social activities on the inpatient unit where she was being treated. As a result of being overwhelmed by the stimulation of her voices and being crippled by her paranoia, Betty was placed in locked seclusion on the unit. This was primarily for her safety but also for the safety of others on the unit against whom she might have struck out in fear. Betty identified the attention offered by a particular nurse as providing a key turning point in this episode of her illness, which she described as follows:

> It may have been because [my nurse] really seemed to pay a lot of particular attention to me . . . and I started waking up and I started knowing that there were possibilities for life outside that room and things really started opening up for me. And she knew I had potential and talent and all this and that I

could get better, and I knew it too. And I just woke up. I wasn't hallucinating as much, and I was active and eager, and I was also more social. . . . She ended up being very helpful in that she let people know, "Well, Betty's ready to come out, Betty can attend unit meetings, Betty can take a half hour out twice a day," etc.

At its most basic level, Betty's nurse stood by her and believed in her and her potential for improvement, no matter how severely incapacitated she had become. The same sentiment was expressed by the female participant from whose interview we extracted the heading for this section when speaking about her grandmother. Her grandmother was there for her, never turned her back on her, but continued to stand by and believe in her, even while she was exhibiting signs of active psychosis. Other people identified a similar degree of support as providing a foundation for their recovery as described, for example, by the person who said that his clinician "believed in me when I no longer believed in myself" and by the woman who claimed that her friend is "always taking my side even when I am wrong."

Is there more to this element of recovery than the kind of support or encouragement that everyone can use at times? In other words, does this need for having someone believe in the person have anything to do with schizophrenia per se or is it simply one of the many ways in which people with the disorder remain like the rest of us? Certainly, we would not expect people who have recovered from schizophrenia to no longer need support or encouragement from others. On the other hand, we have come to understand some aspects of the disorder, like hallucinations, to differ from "normal" experience only as a matter of degree on a continuum. This element of recovery appears, similarly, to be a matter of degree. The challenge here, as it was in the previous chapter with respect to the loss of agency, is to build an empathic bridge that allows us to appreciate the extremity of the situation and the many challenges it poses for the person with the disorder.

We touched on this issue as well in the previous chapter, when we began to explore the importance of experiences people with schizophrenia described, in which they felt that they no longer belonged anywhere. In this case, the closest we came to approximating the degree of isolation and alienation involved in these experiences was that of the person trying to go to sleep in a city in which she knew no one, afraid that if she died in her sleep no one would know to come looking for her. What is at stake in such experiences is thus not simply feeling a need for encouragement after a bad day or to shore up one's fragile self-esteem. Rather, it is more of a fundamental question of one's place in the world.

People with schizophrenia may feel at times that there *is* no place for them, at least not among the community of human beings into which they were born. The one thing that appears to be the most effective antidote to such an extreme sense of isolation and estrangement is the care, acceptance, or love of another person. Having some place where the person feels that he or she belongs is predicated on there being at least one other person who views him or her, and accepts him or her, not as "a schizophrenic" or as a mental patient, but as a fellow human being, as a peer. As our opening quote for this chapter quite literally attests: "I'm nobody till somebody loves me."

This somebody does not always have to be a real, flesh and blood, person as was described in the examples above. For some people, for instance, this function of acceptance can be provided by God; one of the several ways in which spirituality can be of benefit to the person in recovery. As one participant explained when describing the ways in which she continued to feel accepted despite her illness: "In the Lord's eyes we're all about the same. It's in the book of Genesis." Losing such faith in God, in a higher power, or in the sanctity of life, on the other hand, can be devastating, as described by one woman who said that she had come to a point in her life in which she felt that "even God didn't love me anymore." For others acceptance may be provided initially by a beloved pet or animal, as in the following example offered by a participant in a horseback riding program that we also found to contribute to the lives, and thereby recovery, of individuals who had become socially isolated:

> I think [riding the horse] helped me with my depression. I went home, I went to sleep. It relaxed me. And, well, I guess it made me feel like the horse loved me. Spending time with the horse, it felt like unconditional love. And, I think this would be an excellent program for everyone because you connect with the animal and you connect with yourself and you're outdoors and it does something to you. It's hard to explain, but when you go home you think, "Wow, another lesson! Wow, I'm getting better!"

The lack of any direct evidence of, or faith in, acceptance by another, even a divine or animal other, appears to serve as an additional source for the kinds of beliefs labeled by clinical psychiatry as delusions. People will take desperate measures to obtain or maintain a sense of belonging in the face of radical rejection or estrangement, these measures at times taking on delusional form. In extreme cases, for example, paranoid and persecutory ideas can serve the function of allowing the person to continue to feel important to someone, even if that someone, or group of someones, have nothing but the most malevolent of intentions toward him or her. At least if one is being sought out to be punished or even to be killed, one then has yet to disappear from the human community all together. One must, in fact, be considered quite important in order to be the object of the efforts of so many other people. What this suggests is that when people feel accepted, when they have places where they feel they belong among their peers, they will have much less of a need for paranoid beliefs. As one participant confirmed:

> If I feel comfortable in an environment that would make me feel less paranoid. I think I'm more apt to be paranoid if I am in an environment where I don't feel like I'm that welcomed.

To elaborate on what we hope is becoming obvious, we are suggesting that the only way for a person with schizophrenia to feel less isolated and alone is to be with other people, real or imagined, who care for and accept the person despite his or her illness. What may be unique about this need that is specific to schizophrenia is that acceptance appears to be the only thing that allows the person to hold onto, or regain, the basic sense of being a human being that most of us carry around within us. In the case of schizophrenia, this sense may compete in the person's awareness with an equally convincing sense of being a machine (a common delusion following on the heels of the industrial revolution), for example, or, more recently, a computer or robot. The loss of agency described in chapter 3 leaves a vacuum where there previously was a sense of personal identity. This vacuum makes the person particularly vulnerable to being defined by others; others who may want nothing to do with the person, who may be afraid of the person, who may refuse to return the person's phone calls or to respond to his or her overtures, or who simply may pass the person

Figure 3

Trying to Climb Out of a Hole without Help

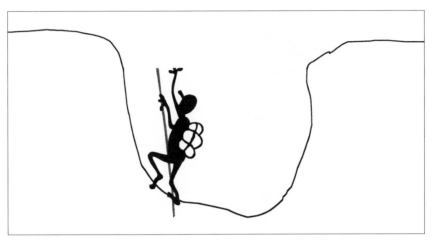

by in the hall of an apartment building or on the street, pretending that she or he does not exist or is not another person deserving of minimal recognition.

This is not only a matter of stigma, which, as we will see below, can manifest with various degrees of subtlety in the person's relationships with others. Stigma is important, but what appears to be even more important is the space the person is left to occupy as a result of the effects of stigma in combination with a variety of other factors, such as those described in the previous chapter. As described by Weingarten (1994), the person may lose all vestiges of his or her previous identity and be left with the desperate and despairing sense of being "a nobody nowhere." Climbing out of such a deep hole is extremely difficult, if not impossible, to do by oneself, as pictured in Figure 3.

Our interviews have suggested that a more common way of escaping from such a hole is, at least in part, by being offered a hand by another person, as pictured in Figure 4. As one person explained, at this point in the course of illness "you need someone to believe in you 'cause you don't believe in yourself" (quoted in Hatfield and Lefley, 1993, p. 138). This particular element of recovery is thus something over which the person with the disorder may have little to no control. In many cases, people are saved from falling into such a hole to begin with by family members or steadfast

Figure 4
Climbing Out of a Hole with Help

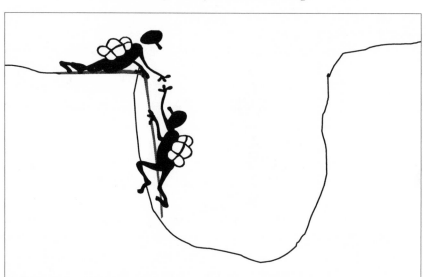

friends who stand by them, withstanding the effects of the illness, like the grandmother who was described above as never turning her back on her granddaughter. It also is possible for the outstretched hand to be offered by a healthcare professional, as it was in Betty's experience with the nurse who helped her to get out of locked seclusion. In other cases, in which neither family, friends, nor genuinely caring others are available, however, the person may be left to depend, in the words of *A Streetcar Named Desire*'s Blanch DuBois, "on the kindness of strangers" (Williams, 1947).

"People Talk about Chemical Imbalance. Well, [My Friend] and I, [Together We Made] a Chemical Balance"

Lest the skeptical reader be unimpressed by the importance we have attributed to acceptance by others or a sense of belonging in recovery, we will provide a couple of illustrative examples from our previous research. In both of the studies we describe, we found that the simple—if difficult to manufacture—gesture of genuine friendship made a significant difference in the lives of people with prolonged psychotic disorders. We may speculate why this is the case in the discussion that follows. Regardless of the reasons why, it will be useful in appreciating these examples to note beforehand the difference between artificial, institutional, or professional forms of caring, which are often directed toward the person as a patient on the one hand, and what we will label genuine caring, which invariably is directed toward the person as a fellow human being on the other.

Pointing out such a difference should not be taken to imply that mental health professionals are limited to providing only artificial forms of care; that the care service providers offer can never be genuine. Betty's description of this particular nurse's attention to her, for example, provides a case in point that professionals can transcend the limitations of conventional professional roles. What this does imply, however, is that such a gesture of genuine caring is not something that can be made or mandated as part of a person's job description. It requires the provider to give of him- or herself in a way that cannot stem solely from his or her responsibilities as a clinician but is based on his or her recognition of the common humanity of both people. Although you may find such a distinction more intangible or abstract than you would like, it represents a difference that is clearly both important and readily apparent to those people who are on the receiving end of the services. As one young man described:

> I see a mental health worker as just a person who functions as a mental health worker. . . . They're just doing their job, so therefore, it's not up to them to like me or be my friend or anything like that.

In contrast, a woman who derived more from her relationship with her clinician based on his validation of her as a person—in addition to being a patient—described the following:

> I often felt at odds with my therapist until I could see that he was a real person and he related to me and I to him, not only as patient and therapist, but as human beings. Eventually I began to feel that I too was a person, not just an outsider looking in on the world. For a patient and therapist to work together . . . they must establish a bond that is professional, certainly, but also based on the commonality of humanness that exists between two people. (Anonymous, 1986, pp. 69–70)

If the foundation to recovery that we are exploring here is the need for the person to feel that he or she is still a person too, alongside other people, then it is reasonable to suggest that sense be obtained through experiences of other people accepting and treating the person as such. It is very difficult, if not impossible, for me to continue to feel like a worthwhile individual if no one else in my life treats me as one. After a while it is much easier to assume that their perception of me is the right one, especially if I already have doubts about my own judgment and/or grounding in reality.

We first learned this lesson in a study of friendship among people with psychiatric disorders. Paralleling recent advances in psychiatric rehabilitation in the areas of housing (supported housing), education (supported education), and work (supported employment), we developed a strategy to increase the involvement of people with psychiatric disabilities in social relationships with their peers (what we now call "supported socialization"). What all of these approaches have in common, under the broader rubric of "supported community life" (Ferguson et al., 1990), is the provision of the in vivo supports needed to enable people with disabilities to take part in the naturally occurring and normative activities of their choice in the community, that is, beyond the boundaries of the mental health system. We did this in the social arena by transforming what started out as a companionship model of a volunteer visiting a disabled person (Skirboll and Pavelsky, 1984) into a reciprocal model of friendship between two willing and interested adults. Readers who wish to know more about the details of the design, quantitative evaluation, and qualitative component of this study are referred to our previous publications (Davidson, Haglund, et al., 2001; Stayner, Davidson, and Tebes, 1996).

For our present purposes, what we take from this study are the lessons it taught us about the role of belonging, care, and acceptance in recovery. Participants in this study were adults with serious mental illnesses, who were receiving psychiatric services as outpatients from community mental health centers, but who were assessed to have moderate to severe impairments in social and occupational functioning. A relatively stable but withdrawn cohort, these were people who had few, if any, friends and who rarely participated in activities other than attending treatment appointments at the mental health center or programs at a local consumer-oriented clubhouse. Living for the most part outside of hospital settings, participants tended to remain in their own apartments, suffering in relative silence and isolation. Given this profile, these participants presented an excellent opportunity to test the inherited clinical belief that people with schizophrenia become so asocial over time that they no longer desire human contact or companionship.

Contrary to the "empty shell" view of people with serious mental illness as choosing and protecting their isolated and marginal place on the periphery of the community (Davidson, 1997), the majority of people invited to participate in this study did so and with enthusiasm. Two out of three people offered the opportunity to be introduced to someone who had agreed to befriend them responded by becoming a friend; that is, they participated actively in the development of a reciprocal relationship with the volunteer with whom they were matched. The benefits they ascribed to these friendships were multiple (see Davidson, Haglund, et al., 2001; Davidson, Stayner, Nickou, et al., 2001), but for present purposes, we will limit our focus to the laying of a foundation for recovery. As described above, this foundation appeared to be secured when the person began "to feel that I too [am] a person, not just an outsider looking in on the world."

People involved in this study participated in a wide array of social and recreational activities in the community, many of which they reported not having been able to enjoy since the onset of their illness, if at all. These ranged from talking on the phone, sharing informal lunches together, or gardening and fishing together to drives among the autumn New Hampshire foliage, going to movies, and taking part in family and other group activities like holiday celebrations. What participants enjoyed and valued most about all of these activities, however, were the friendships themselves. As one woman described, life before the program "was a lot lonelier":

> But then [my partner] called me and stuff to see how I was doing because she genuinely cared about me and I cared about her, and that was a nice feeling.

Even though, by virtue of the experimental design, these friendships invariably began with feelings of artificiality, most people came over time to like their partners, enjoy their company, and care about them as friends. Participants sensed this and relished being the object of another person's positive attention and affection. These displays of affection need not be dramatic or unusual in any sense, but most often occurred at the concrete level of spending time together, regardless of how that time was spent. As one man described: "[My partner] just wanted to hang out with me, and I was kind of flattered by that." Said another participant when describing what had become routine early morning phone calls from his partner: "We might talk for two minutes or a minute, but it's so good to hear from him because I know that he cares." In a final example, after listing the many virtues of his partner and describing her affection for him as providing a welcome antidote to his persistent, disabling depression, an elderly male participant quipped: "People talk about chemical imbalance. Well, [my friend] and I, [together we made] a chemical balance."

In the same way, and to the same degree, that they valued being cared about by another as a person, instead of as a mental patient, participants also valued the opportunity to care *about* another person. This, too, was an experience they often reported not having had since becoming disabled. For many, in fact, this felt like the first chance they had had to form a "true" (i.e., reciprocal) friendship since their adolescence, both giving and receiving care based on who they were rather than on what the other person did for them. In describing this dimension of their new friendship, for example, participants referred back to their earlier, preillness, experiences with peers, typically in high school. Said one participant when asked what the most important aspect of the study was for him: "Having a male friend who I was friends with in much the same ways I was friends with the kids I knew when I was growing up." Other men described their growing relationships with their partners as similar to the "male bonding" they had experienced in the context of high school athletics. Women, on the other hand, were more likely to refer back to the hours they spent on the telephone engrossed in "girl talk." Throughout these and other, less stereotypic, examples, the most prominent aspect of participants' narratives was their delight, and at times surprise, in discovering through these experiences that they *could*, in fact, still care for someone else despite their continuing disability.

Those of us who have not struggled with a prolonged and disabling condition may not at first appreciate why people with schizophrenia would be surprised that they could still care for other people. What we learned in the previous chapter, however, is that the illness can take over the person's identity, replacing a sense of self as a human being with a sense of being an illness or a delusional sense of being something other like a machine or an object. People whose lives have been derailed by schizophrenia for an extended period of time may come to feel that, in addition to their selves, they have lost many of the other dimensions of their lives that were integral to being a person as well. We will see in what follows that this includes pleasure, faith, a sense of accomplishment, and a variety of other experiences that we humans value. Most fundamental among these appears to be the sense of being capable of caring about another person and being cared about in return.

The experience of participating in a caring relationship that is both mutual and between equals provides a contrast to the asymmetrical experiences of only receiving, which people with prolonged psychoses tend to experience with family and mental health providers, and serves to reaffirm several important aspects of the person that she or he may feel they have lost to the illness. The things that I find that I can contribute to a reciprocal relationship are things that I must be capable of and therefore things that reflect aspects of whom I am. These opportunities often are not present in the hierarchical kinds of relationships to which people with schizophrenia have become accustomed. As one participant in the supported socialization study described:

I didn't consider [my partner] to be like a doctor or a nurse or a social worker. He's just a friend, you know, he's in the same boat. The only difference is that he drives and I don't, and that he does certain things that I don't, but I do certain things that he doesn't. So we were pretty evenly [matched]. It wasn't like he was, you know, talking down to me or being condescending or like that, and that was a good thing. Whereas sometimes the mental health professionals tend to be condescending. . . . But [my partner] wasn't like that at all, so that was good.

Primary among the aspects of the person reinstated through such experiences is the sense of being a worthwhile human being who has something of value to offer to others. As an elderly woman who had spent over four decades in a state psychiatric hospital before becoming involved in this study explained: "I'm just so tired of taking, taking, taking all the time" without ever having the opportunity to "give back." As a result of being limited largely to such one-sided relationships, people came to view themselves more as "charity cases" than as worthwhile human beings. Having a friend offered them a chance to give something back, and by virtue of doing so, to learn what other parts of them had survived the illness. As one young man described in relation to his partner:

> It seems that I helped him, too. So I feel good about that. He just said that it helped him to have . . . me for a friend. He gets lonely and bored and I figure I added something to his life, and I'm really happy I could.

"One Thing I Really Enjoy the Most Is Helping Someone Out"

Being able to add something to someone else's life, to give something of value in return for the solicitude of others, reacquaints the person with prolonged psychosis with those parts of him or herself that have survived the illness but, due to its devastation, may have been forgotten or may have suffered in other ways from disuse. Thus, the remarkable appeal and powerful effect of what would seem otherwise to be a mundane experience. So significant is this dimension of recovery that we discovered it even in the lives of some of those participants in our study who were not matched with volunteer partners; those in the so-called control condition.

To control for potential confounds, we included three conditions in this study to which participants could be assigned on a random basis. In the first condition, participants were matched with community volunteers who had no personal history of psychiatric disability. In the second condition, they were matched with volunteers who had a personal history of psychiatric disability, but who considered themselves to be in recovery and who had a sufficient social network into which they could introduce their partner. In both of these conditions, both participants and volunteers each received a monthly stipend of $28 to spend on their joint activities. In the third, control condition, participants were not matched with either a community or consumer volunteer but were still given the $28 per month stipend and encouraged to treat themselves to enjoyable social and recreational activities in the community. This allowed the only difference between the two experimental conditions and the control condition to be that of having or not having a partner with whom to do things.

What we found in the case of many people who were assigned to the control condition was that they experienced the study as providing them with permission to "splurge" on themselves; to spend the additional money on themselves in ways they otherwise would not have done in order to follow the project staff's instructions of "go out and have a good time." This did not typically mean, however, that participants took themselves out for expensive dinners, bought themselves presents, or treated themselves to special events such as getting their nails done or going to movies, concerts, or sporting events. Instead, many participants used their monthly stipend to buy things for other people. The elderly woman quoted above, for example, was able to give back by using her stipend to buy Christmas presents for her grandnieces and grandnephews and, as a result of having gifts to bring, was able to attend her first family Christmas party in years. She had stopped going because she disliked showing up empty handed. A male participant described in very similar terms what he did with his monthly stipend:

> Well, I went to buy my father a Christmas present. I bought my mother a birthday present. I was able to buy cards for my brothers' and sisters' birthdays. It was just little things like that that mean so much. Because when you've got no income at all coming in, you know, that seven dollars [a week], you can stretch that out a long ways to enable you to have a pretty good time. I enjoy myself by making other people happy also. I'm tired of being the one that's "Oh, we'll get Tom a Christmas card or we'll get Tom something for Christmas," but Tom can't return the favor. Well, Tom is able to now. I was able to get little trinkets for my nieces and nephews for Christmas. It wasn't much, but I didn't feel like I was on poverty row anymore.

With his stipend Tom also was able to treat acquaintances from his AA meetings to french fries and coffee after meetings. As a result, he added: "I didn't feel like a user. I felt like I was able to . . . pull my own weight, and that made a difference."

The difference made by these experiences appears to be one that takes on a significant role in recovery. That is, we are not pointing out the importance of these experiences simply because, as the adage goes, "it is better to give than to receive." Giving under these circumstances is not only pleasurable and gratifying—though these may be important as well—but it also serves a very valuable function. It allows the person to discover or reclaim a part of him- or herself outside of the illness and, by doing so, opens up innumerable other possibilities for him or her to explore. By experiencing "I have something to offer," the person appears to realize that "I must be some*body* to have something to offer." The very important (and somewhat exciting) question then becomes "Who am I other than, or in addition to, my illness?" Only then does the remainder of the recovery process become possible by virtue of the person's efforts to answer this basic question.

What we are suggesting, based on these qualitative research interviews of participants in our supported socialization study, is that a primary way of discovering that there *is* an outside to schizophrenia is by viewing oneself through the eyes of others, but only when those others view the person as a worthwhile human being, who still has something to offer despite continuing to have a disability. If there are no real others available who love the person, or at least can perceive him or her in a positive light, then the person may have to rely either on faith (i.e., God loves me), on beloved pets, on delusional others, or on "boot strapping"—that is, pulling him- or herself up based purely on his or her own efforts. In our experience, the latter two possibilities are much more difficult and also less common among people who have shown significant improvement. More usual is the sentiment expressed by the following participant in describing how he likes to help others:

> It made me feel like I was being helpful and in situations like that I don't think so much about my illness. It kind of goes on the back burner because sometimes I just think about my illness and it seems like when I'm helping somebody or somebody says something nice to me . . . as soon as people say that, oh, you look good, things like that, it makes me feel better about myself.

Patricia Deegan (1993), the consumer advocate whom we quoted often in chapter 1, has suggested that there must be a person standing outside of the illness in order for there to be someone who can take up the work of recovery in an active and determined fashion. We are suggesting that in many cases the room needed for this person to reemerge from out of the illness is opened up through others' perceptions of the

Figure 5
Establishing an Outside to the Illness

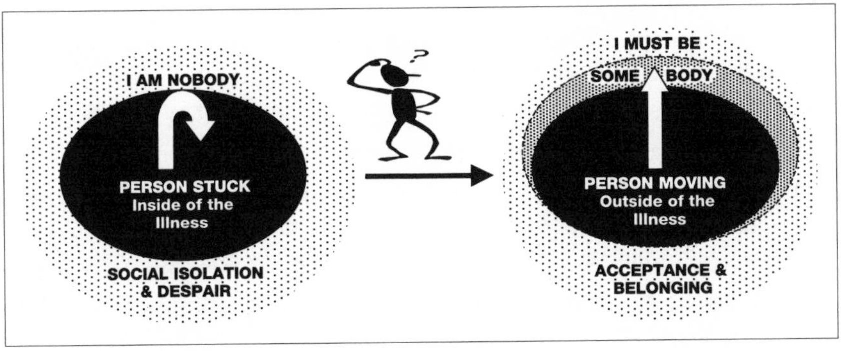

person as being more than his or her illness. As depicted in Figure 5, it is this "more" that then creates the room, gives the person the ground to stand on, to take up the work of redefining and expanding on this sense of self. Doing so appears to have the added benefit of reducing the amount of room left for the illness to occupy, thereby minimizing its disruptiveness in the person's life.

"When You Come In You're a One. To Go, the Goal Is to Leave as a Five"

Before moving on to explore the remainder of the recovery process, we turn to our second example to illustrate the ways in which social isolation and social inclusion provide bookends for the illness-recovery spectrum. Remembering our initial concerns about selecting participants who would represent the full range of severity and outcomes in schizophrenia, it is possible, after all, that some readers might be thinking that clinically stable but socially isolated outpatients do not represent the typical person with psychosis (if there is such a thing). Just in case this is a concern on the mind of our readers, we will describe briefly another study that involved a very different sample of people with psychosis. This sample was made up entirely of people who were experiencing significant difficulty establishing a basis for recovery in the community. Participants were identified by virtue of repeated hospitalizations and their failure to make effective use of outpatient care. As such, they represent a more disabled and less stable population; people who might be considered to be further away from embarking on the journey of recovery.

The opportunity to conduct this study of the experiences of people who were repetitively cycling in and out of the hospital was presented to us by the failure of a conventional, clinical approach to decreasing rehospitalization rates among a small, but costly, cohort of patients at our community mental health center (Davidson, Stayner, Lambert, et al., 1997). The initial attempt made by the clinical administration involved implementation of an early identification and intervention skills training approach based on the work of Max Birchwood and colleagues (e.g., Birchwood, 1995; Birchwood et al., 1989). These efforts consisted of a system for the close monitoring of early warning signs and detection of relapse and early intervention to prevent readmission. During their inpatient stay, people received education about their disorders and the need for continuing care, were assisted in identifying their unique relapse signature, and, together with their outpatient clinician, agreed to an action plan that stipulated what they should do in case of the reemergence of symptoms. In addition to inpatient psychoeducation groups, twice-weekly groups were begun in the outpatient clinic in order to provide for close monitoring of symptoms following discharge. The intent was to engage people in these groups while they were still in the hospital, in the hope that they would continue to attend following discharge.

For the first three months of this initiative, patients participated in both inpatient and outpatient groups while in the hospital. Not a single person out of the first 36 who were eligible returned to the outpatient groups following discharge, however. As a result, their rate of rehospitalization continued as before. When the limitations of this approach became evident, we were offered the opportunity to explore a different approach to preventing readmission among this population.

At this point, we adopted a participatory action research paradigm, inviting the people being targeted by this initiative, that is, those with histories of multiple inpatient admissions, to collaborate with us on finding solutions to the problem of recidivism. Our first step was to ask some of these patients about their experiences of hospitalization and their reasons for not using outpatient care once discharged. We conducted interviews following discharge with 12 people who had two or more hospitalizations within the last year. In the interviews we asked people to describe their experiences leading up to, during, and following their most recent hospitalization. Patients also were asked to describe their experiences of the relapse prevention program in which they participated during their hospitalization, the factors that led to their not participating after discharge, and any things they would find more useful in the future.

The findings of these interviews, described below, led us to question the widely held assumptions with which we had begun this initiative— namely, that hospitalizations were necessarily negative events and were caused primarily by relapses or exacerbations of patients' symptoms. What we learned instead was not only more complicated but also proved to be more useful. As a result of the success of this collaborative process, we redefined the problem entirely. We also became convinced of the necessity of involving the people in question as early in the research process as possible so that such unwarranted assumptions need not misdirect the investigation from the start. We return to this point in the following, concluding, chapter.

The most striking feature of these interviews was the fact that the overall agenda of preventing relapse and readmission being pursued by the clinical administration was not shared by the patients themselves. Rather than describing the hospital as a place to be avoided, participants described many attractions to the hospital that made it a place they appreciated being able to return to when needed. These attractions included safety, respite, food, privacy, and, most importantly, the personal attention they experienced there. In contrast to our initial assumption that recurrent admissions would be experienced by people as failures, for example, one person described how he had come to appreciate the hospital more each time he had been admitted, as the staff had come to know him better and his sense of being cared about had grown during each of three admissions:

> The first time I was scared, the second time I had been here before and I knew what to expect, the third time it was like coming home again. Everyone was like greeting me at the door. . . . The third time was the best I think.

The appeal of the hospital becomes understandable when contrasted to descriptions of what participants' lives were like outside of the hospital. Several people independently described hospitalization as a "vacation," for example, as it provided respite from lives they characterized as "homeless, broke, unemployed, the same harsh feeling everyday." Even one person who had been hospitalized involuntarily described his stay as a "forced vacation." Said another: "It's like a vacation, you take some time out, and you know, in a place where there is privacy and there is care and there are lots of people to listen to you." As suggested by this participant's description, what was most telling about participants' descriptions of life in the community was the striking *absence* of any mention of supportive friends or family. One person spoke of his lack of support in the community in contrast to the hospital when he said:

> At home you don't have to listen to nobody but yourself. When you come into a hospital it's different. You're around a whole bunch of people that care about you.

The sense of being cared about in the hospital that was repeatedly emphasized by participants provided a welcome relief from their feelings of being alone and abandoned on the outside, where they appeared to have no one who even knew or cared that they existed. As one participant noted in describing his valued access to clinical staff by phone:

> There's a number . . . and that's helpful that I can call and talk to someone when I have problems. That's a big thing; sometimes I just need somebody to talk to.

In addition to feeling alone and isolated, all of the people interviewed expressed a sense of demoralization, involving feelings of powerlessness, fatalism, and apathy in the face of their illness and other problems in living. Within this context of profound helplessness, active participation in outpatient treatment made little sense to people who felt like they could not even secure their own food or shelter. Far from feeling that they were in a position to manage their illness, participants drew a blank when asked what they could do to prevent future readmissions. Said one: "I can't answer that one. Nobody knows the future. I could be talking to you today and end up back in the hospital tomorrow." A few spoke of trying to ward off the effects of their symptoms through vague attempts to "keep stress free," to rest or "go slow," or to keep their minds "occupied," but their overall sense was one of having no control over their illness. This lack of control extended beyond their symptoms to their lives, in general, summed up by one participant whose mental illness was simply the last item in a long list of things in his life that he could not change; as he said:

> [It's] like living in poverty all your life, being oppressed, no income, unemployment, no good jobs, you know what I'm saying—guns, drugs, and all of that.

For a few people, the suffering associated with their illness and their lives had become so overwhelming and persistent that it was fading into an increasing sense of numbness. Numbness was not to be mistaken for lack of caring, however. Described one participant:

> My reaction to my suffering is less, less fierce, now I'm becoming cold about it . . . colder and colder. I don't mean I don't care no more, but you know I'm living in this situation for a long time and my reaction to it is like numbed.

Finally, participants gave as reasons for their lack of use of outpatient care their perceptions that treatment was of little use to them in dealing with situations they faced on discharge. Despite the psychoeducational efforts of inpatient staff, few expressed even a rudimentary understanding of their illness or of how medication and other treatments might be helpful. For example, one participant could think of only one thing she could do when she felt that she was getting worse: "I just know when I get too sick . . . it's time" to go to the hospital. Going to the hospital was understood in terms of respite as described above, however, rather than in terms of the treatment that would be received there. In fact, "treatment" was viewed more like classroom exercises for which people would be graded; having no more impact on their symptoms and lives than a history lesson. Described one participant when asked about the treatment he received in the hospital:

> Well, it was something like this where they ask you questions. It was like going to school [and] I passed. . . . I passed with flying colors. Everybody loved me after I left that place.

Like good students, some participants were quite willing to do what they were told while on the inpatient unit, following their doctors' orders, as long as they continued to be in the hospital. As one woman described:

> I loved it, because they knew what was wrong with me, and they were try-ing their best to help me; so I agreed with everything they said. . . . There were a lot of meetings, a lot of doctors, you know, doctors come around every morning to talk to you to see how you're doing. You get your levels, your levels are one to five. . . . When you come in you're a one. To go, the goal is to leave as a five.

Unfortunately, what participants took away from experiences like these was more of a sense of loss of the care and concern they felt in the hospi-tal rather than anything they might have learned in relation to managing their illness. As a result, compliance with hospital routines failed to trans-late into engagement in outpatient care for participants once discharged. Rather, outpatient care continued to be experienced by them as irrelevant and unresponsive to the needs and issues they faced in the community, while the hospital was remembered longingly as a place where they felt cared about, known, and even "popular."

"I Wasn't by Myself, I Wasn't Out There by Myself"

With the help of the participants, we thus redefined the problem to be ad-dressed from one of relapse leading to rehospitalization to one of social isolation, demoralization, and a lack of responsiveness in care as posing barriers to community tenure. Important implications for practice then followed from this reformulation. First, it was obvious that efforts to in-crease engagement in outpatient care following discharge would have to address participants' perceptions of the unresponsiveness of treatment to their basic needs and lives in the community. It also was evident that the hospital would continue to appeal to people until they were able to find several of its features—such as respite, privacy, safety, and, above all, social support—in the community. Finally, efforts to educate people about their disorders and strategies for self-care would be unsuccessful as long as they felt hopeless about potential for improvement and helpless to do anything on their own behalf.

To address these implications, we invited the participants as well as other members of the target population (i.e., people with multiple hospitalizations) to collaborate with us again, this time in developing interventions targeting the barriers of isolation, demoralization, and lack of responsiveness in care. We have brought this study into the present discussion because of the importance we came to attribute to social relationships, in particular, as providing the foundation for all of the various efforts made to address these multiple issues. In this study, as in our earlier supported socialization study, offering opportunities and encouragement for people to move from a stance of social isolation to a position of social inclusion appeared to provide a necessary foundation for developing other elements of recovery (i.e., remoralization and responsive care).

In this case, participants suggested that food would be an appealing incentive for their involvement in treatment-related activities following discharge, and that being able to meet with other people in their same situation (as well as staff), who also were focused on "making it" in the community, might replace the sense of comradery and concern they experienced in the hospital. As a result, we offered twice weekly peer-led group meetings to foster a sense of inclusion among interested members and weekly social and recreational activities to foster a sense of inclusion within the broader community. Groups focused on promoting mutual support between participants, instilling hope for recovery, and role modeling self-care. One group each week included lunch, and these groups, as well as peer outreach and community activities, focused on eliciting participants' interests. At the end of three months of participation in this program, members graduated to a less intensive mutual support group and were encouraged to continue to participate in social and recreational activities in the community.

The lessons we learned from this study were multiple, but all have in common the underlying issue of the important role of social inclusion versus social isolation as providing the basis for efforts toward recovery. For example, we learned that from the perspective of the person with the illness: (1) isolation is more often the precipitant of readmission than relapse; (2) the most important thing the hospital has to offer is the care of other people, not only of staff but also of other patients; (3) experiencing care in the hospital helps the person to feel more worthwhile; (4) feeling worthwhile encourages the person to take more of an active interest in his or her life; (5) taking an interest in life and in relating to others enables the person to begin to discover what he or she has to offer beyond, or in addition to, his or her illness; but that (6) any gains the person makes in the hospital in these areas rapidly diminish upon discharge, as long as the person returns to the same degree of isolation she or he experienced prior to admission. As a result of these lessons, and of the interventions crafted in collaboration with the participants on this basis, we also learned that if people feel they don't have to go it alone in the community but can continue to feel cared about and known as a worthwhile person following discharge, they will be much less likely to return to the hospital. Not feeling as much of a need for a "vacation"—forced or otherwise—they then are free to take up the remaining work of recovery (Davidson et al., 1997).

"When I Do a Good Job It Makes Me Feel Good"

What does the remaining work of recovery involve? There appear to be at least two remaining components integral to the process described by participants in our interviews. The first of these, which we have described previously (Davidson, 1997; Davidson and Strauss, 1992), involves the reconstruction of a functional and effective sense of self as a social agent. As we said above, a ground of possibilities for a life outside of the illness is opened up by the sense of acceptance and belonging that comes from experiences of being perceived (and treated) by others as more than one's illness. Within the context of creating such a life outside of the illness, the person is then required, and able, to re-create a sense of identity apart from the illness as well. As depicted in Figure 6 below, to be treated as somebody by others I must be somebody other than my illness. What that person is capable of, what he or she enjoys, and, in general, who that person is and will become remains to be determined by his or her future actions and experiences. Once this process is effectively underway and the person is successful in developing a significant, positive sense of self apart from the illness, the final component of employing this self in managing and compensating for the illness then becomes possible.

Prior to moving on to this final component, it will be useful to explore in some detail ways in which the process of defining the self apart from the illness can be facilitated and ways in which it can be impeded. We already have explored some of the ways in which this process may be facilitated

Figure 6

Expanding and Inhabiting an Outside to the Illness

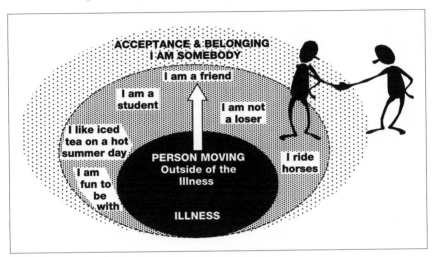

through the medium of social relationships. Feeling cared about, feeling capable of caring about others, and being involved in reciprocal relationships in which the person can give as well as receive are primary avenues of exploring what one has to offer and of discovering, thereby, who one is or may become. In addition to these experiences, people describe a sense of (1) faith and/or spirituality that opens them up to having (2) fun and pleasure, complemented by a sense of (3) being generative or productive as primary avenues for self-definition and the reconstruction of a life outside of the illness. We describe each briefly below.

There is a receptive element to experiences of improvement in schizophrenia that differs significantly from the sense of being a recipient of the care of others described above. Rather than diminishing their sense of agency, this form of receptivity is described by people as providing the basis for a sense of hopefulness and is often described in spiritual terms. Whether it be experienced through awe in face of the expansiveness of a natural landscape, through the beauty of a work of art or smile of a loved one, or through wonder at the unity of all creation as in religious traditions, the sense of sanctity common to all these experiences is given as bestowed upon the person, as a gift to be appreciated. Integral to this form of receptivity is the sense that the person cannot simply have such experiences at will, but that they require more than the person and his or her own efforts. These experiences represent a whole that is greater than the sum of its parts, the person him- or herself being only one part among many. Although the articulation of this receptive quality differs from one organized religion to another, and from one aesthetic or spiritual tradition to another, for our present purposes, it is best to frame it within the Western monotheistic, Judeo-Christian tradition.

Within Christianity, for example, this dimension of receptivity is best captured by the concept of "grace," which involves the unconditional receipt of the blessing of creation. According to contemporary theologian Frederick Buechner, grace "is something you can never get but can only be given. There's no way to earn it or deserve it or bring it about any more than you can deserve the taste of raspberries and cream" (1973, p. 38). Judaism has a similar concept of the gift quality of life, through which it affirms that life is given to all of creation by God in order to be sanctified and cherished. The sentiment shared by both of these religious traditions is captured well in the first book of the Old Testament, the book of *Genesis* (1:31), in which it is said in relation to creation "and God saw all that He had made, and behold, it was very good."

This sense of the "very goodness" of life often has been stripped from the experiences of people whose lives have been taken over or subsumed by their illness. Being trapped within their suffering and sense of disability, people can lose any sense that life is worth living. The experiences through which people describe regaining this sense of the goodness of life vary from person to person. Common to these experiences is the sense they offer that there is more to life than suffering and disability, and therefore there is hope that life will improve. This kind of experience was described succinctly by a young participant in our first supported socialization study. Although this young woman described being different from her partner in substantial ways—drawing contrasts, for example, between her partner's busy absorption in planning her wedding while she remained preoccupied with how she would manage to get through the grocery store without, in her words, "freaking out"—she also described her experiences with her partner as opening up a new window onto life.

> We always had a good time whenever we went out. We saw a movie, and it
> was fun, you know. Then I realized . . . hey, I can have more fun too. It just

opened my eyes that there are other things to think about besides mental illness. . . . It was just realizing that, you know, I could go places and have fun,
that life isn't one big horror.

This young woman's realization that "life isn't one big horror" may not
strike many readers as the kind of profound, affirmative stance required to
restore hope to those who are despairing. Following years of severe psychiatric disability, however, this is precisely how the first steps toward such
affirmation appear in the lives of those we have interviewed. To facilitate
your construction of an empathic bridge to this element of recovery, we
provide the following additional example.

Dave is a 64-year-old man with over a 40-year history of severe mental
illness in combination with a more recent history of serious medical problems that further impede his functioning. Upon enrollment into the same
supported socialization study, Dave was matched with a female partner
near his own age, a woman we shall call Florence. Dave's friendship with
Florence provides a good example of how the experience of affirmation
can at times appear in ways that are barely perceptible. For Dave, these experiences arose following an extended period of confinement, first in psychiatric hospitals and then in nursing homes. In this context, he had struggled with suicidal ideas and come to view death as a welcome relief from
his suffering. Initially, Dave accompanied Florence on excursions only as a
result of her indefatigable encouragement, but soon found these experiences to provide a stark contrast to his day-to-day immersion in misery. He
describes:

> She took me to places I had never been before. For instance, . . . we made
> several forays down to the Connecticut coast and took some nice long
> drives through the various towns, saw the beautiful old summer homes,
> stopped at a place where there was a really nice view of the ocean, and just
> sat there for a while and talked. And I remember one time in particular. I had
> never been to Masquawmacut, and so we went to Masquawmacut and Flo-
> rence came equipped. When I am at my best in terms of being mobile, I have
> a brace that I have to wear, and I have to use crutches. I get along fine, but
> those are things that are absolutely necessary for me to have in order to am-
> bulate. . . . [For] Masquawmacut, [Florence] had thought of everything. She
> had brought this huge beach umbrella and the tide was high so we only had

to walk a very short distance . . . fifteen feet maybe, and we were almost
where the water was lapping in, and I was having a great deal of difficulty in
the sand, and so Florence arranged for the kids that were lifeguards down
there to give me a hand, and they did. And she always had the beach chairs
which came out of the trunk and were unfolded . . . and it was just really
nice. And we sat there that day I have no idea how long . . . whenever Florence and I went someplace, it was always calm, peaceful. . . . I was getting
away from things, and it was just wonderful.

To this spontaneous description, the interviewer responded with the question: "Getting away from things was wonderful?" which then prompted
Dave to continue:

Getting away helped. That helped a lot. . . . I felt immeasurably better after
that outing. . . . [Wherever we went] I knew I was going to have a good
time. And I also knew that I was going to go to a restaurant that I'd be
very happy with. The best restaurant on the shore that we went to, and I
still, when I mention it, Florence laughs, was called the Fish Tail . . . and it
goes without saying that it's a seafood restaurant. And we went in there
and it was very sort of countrified, homespun, comfortable. And, as it
turned out, we got menus which were unusual. I don't remember how, but
they were unusual menus, in fact, I kept mine. And I didn't see fried clams
on the menu and I couldn't believe it. This is a seafood restaurant? No
fried clams? I don't think so. So I said to the waitress: "No fried clams?"
And she said: "We just got them in today. That's why they're not on the
menu." So I said: "Ah-ha! That's what I'd like." So that day we started off
with, I think they said, the menu said, a "mug" of clam chowder or maybe
seafood chowder. In any event, it really was a mug with a handle. And then
. . . when the clams came, I was overwhelmed. It was this huge mound of
clams and french fries and cole slaw. And the clams were so fresh and so
lovely, I think without a doubt they were the best fried clams I've ever had.
Ever, ever, ever. And I come from Boston, and there's a lot of seafood
restaurants in Boston, and I've been to them, but none of these have
equaled these fried clams. They also had a real nice perk at the restaurant
that I've never seen anyplace else, and this was a very hot day, and Florence
and I are both iced tea aficionados, so we both ordered iced tea. And we
didn't even have—it came in a huge thing and we were parched, so we dis-

patched those in record time and low and behold, the waitress came over and filled both of our glasses again. And we looked at each other, and sort of shrugged, and we drank that down pretty quick. And, this was all before we had a thing to eat, and when the glasses were empty, they were no more than empty, but the waitress came and filled them again. And so I said this time, I said to the waitress: "This is unheard of in my experience." And she said: "Well, everyone has bottomless coffee. We have bottomless iced tea." So I don't know how many glasses I had. I certainly outpaced Florence by a country mile, but I love iced tea . . . and oh! it was just wonderful. It was really a lovely day. Just a lovely day.

We have quoted this passage at such length in order to offer some sense of the subtle yet rich and sensuous character of the concrete details entailed in experiences that begin to provide people with a perspective beyond the limits of their illness. We often take such details for granted, just as we seldom stop to pause and reflect on our experience of tasting fresh raspberries and cream. Even though we may overlook the significance of such experiences in our daily lives, life for all of us consists precisely of such details; neither more nor less.

As suggested in both these examples, faith, hope, or affirmation lead naturally into an appreciation of enjoyment or pleasure as intrinsic to these experiences. We separate this component only because it is possible, if not, in fact, more common, for people to have experiences of enjoyment or pleasure without their being accompanied by a profound sense of affirmation, at least at the level of conscious awareness. In terms of their impact on recovery, however, experiences of joie de vivre do not appear to require a basis in a more fundamental sense of affirmation in order to facilitate recreation of a life and sense of self outside of the illness. As captured in the psychologist Csikszentmihalyi's (1991) concept of "flow," engaging in an activity that holds intrinsic meaning for the person is an enjoyable, pleasurable process that enriches his or her life. As described in very similar terms by Dave:

My life certainly was different [before]. I didn't think that I was going to live to be 120. I didn't think I was going to live very long; in fact, I wasn't sure that I wanted to. Now I feel totally different. I don't know how much or little [our] friendship has contributed . . . but certainly my life was enriched by my partner. And I think if one's life is enriched by whatever, then that is going to change your perspective on life *and* death.

In addition to joie de vivre, or perhaps as one variant of it, people find experiences of being generative or productive to be similarly enriching. This does not mean that the person has to take on, and succeed at, such ambitious and challenging tasks as completing college, working at a competitive job, or in other ways endorsing the conventional values of the "American dream." It does mean, however, that the person has to feel that his or her efforts are bearing valuable fruit. There are many ways to do so, of course, including by inhabiting the established social niches of employee, student, or friend. In addition to these conventional ways, there are ways people find to regain a sense of generativity that—similar to Dave's experiences of relishing fried clams and iced tea on a hot summer day—may well be taken for granted or overlooked by those of us who have not struggled with a severe psychiatric disability over a prolonged period of time. One example is provided by the young woman we described above, whom we have called Betty. She derived a sense of being generative in the midst of persistent symptoms by completing a few drawings while listening to music, as she describes:

> It is being active, and I take pride and I'm independent to a certain extent . . . like in my jazz music, like I'll turn on my jazz radio, and I'll love it . . . it's my interest. I turn the radio on myself, no one had it going to nourish *them*selves, to entertain *them*selves, like parents would at a house. *I* turn it on, *I'm* responsible, *I* enjoy the music, *I* make notes and draw while I'm hearing it. . . . Then I turn it off, then I have some evidence, I've got something done, I've been productive, I have the drawings to look at. . . . It was for me and by me. My own nurturing. So I'm proud of this effort.

As Betty makes clear through her emphasis on the words "*them*selves" and "*I*," what is particularly important about these experiences is that they reflect the person's own interests and abilities. Had someone else turned on the radio or chosen the channel that played jazz, or had someone else told Betty to draw pictures, these experiences most likely would not have had the same significance for her. Despite the fact that such activities may not appear on the surface to be significant undertakings, it is through such experiences that the person is able to come to discover and define what kind of person she or he is.

Prior to reflecting on this account, it is unlikely that many readers would have considered turning on a radio and drawing while listening to music to constitute an important achievement in the process of self-definition and recovery from schizophrenia. How are we to understand this? If we conclude that turning on her own radio is important for Betty simply because she has schizophrenia, for example, we have learned little about the illness itself or about processes of recovery. As we noted above in the case of delusions, inferring that such an event is important due to the fact that the person has a mental illness provides only an external explanation, a label for the particular experience that dismisses rather than encourages our exploration. How else are we to understand such experiences?

We now know that when encountering experiences whose meanings are not obvious to us we need, in order to understand them on their own terms, to build empathic bridges to our own experiences. What would our lives have to be like, we wonder, for us to find such simple and trivial actions to embody such significance, to offer such a sense of responsibility and independence? As an initial step in attempting to empathize with Betty's experience, we offer another experience one of us had which seemed to have similar significance. We encourage the reader, of course, to reflect on his or her own experiences in order to find one of comparable, or even increased, relevance.

At the time of this experience, I had just moved to a new town to pursue my clinical training and had moved into a basement apartment in an old house. I had begun the first inpatient rotation of my internship and was feeling very overwhelmed and inadequate at work, while knowing no one outside of the people I had just met at the hospital. I remember feeling like I wasn't "curing" any of my patients at the hospital, nor was I yet able to negotiate the foreign territory of my new neighborhood—for example, I couldn't even find a laundromat in which I felt safe washing my clothes. I just basically wasn't doing much right in my life and most things felt out of my control. What I came across as having been significant to me at the time, worthy enough of note to find its way into my journal, was the fact that I was able to unstop the clogged toilet in my run-down apartment. This un-clogged toilet served from then on to remind me somehow that I was still vital and still adequate in some way.

Clearly, I had not just spent five years in graduate school and then moved to a new town to prove to myself that I could unstop a clogged toilet. Nevertheless, in this situation it was my ability to fix the toilet—without having to call landlord or plumber—that seemed to help me survive all of the other destabilizing and disorganizing factors in my life. It provided a kind of "anchor" that helped me to withstand the overwhelming experiences I was undergoing as an inexperienced intern in an unfamiliar setting.

How does this story relate to the experiences of our young woman with schizophrenia? The challenge of beginning a clinical internship in an unfamiliar setting is surely not comparable to having schizophrenia. It is necessary, however, for us to begin to understand Betty's experiences by locating some clues in our own experiences as to the kinds of struggles and issues that may be involved in her, more extreme, situation. For this person, beginning internship was an event associated with disorientation and a sense of being overwhelmed and inadequate. This proved to be a temporary state of affairs, however, as he became more comfortable and self-assured and found that he could do much more than fix a clogged toilet. For Betty, on the other hand, we are talking rather about 10 years, at least, of being mostly disoriented and disorganized on a regular basis. We are talking about someone who is beseiged by voices and who believes that she is controlled by external forces; a woman who is, in fact, in control of very little in her life. While once she could play piano and paint, now she can barely control her ability to attend and concentrate for brief periods of time. With considerable cognitive interference, ideas of reference, and poor social skills, she remains a foreigner to most environments and feels unsafe a lot of the time.

Clearly, Betty's experiences are very different from our intern's. And yet, nonetheless, these two accounts do have something in common. In both of these situations, value has been placed on, and reassurance derived from, a discovery of the person's ability to do something, achieve something, in the midst of difficult and stressful circumstances. By fixing his toilet without help, the intern proved to himself that, while unable to cure his patients, he was able to be responsible for some things in his life. He was still able to be active and effective on perhaps a smaller, but more tangible, scale. For Betty, being able to regulate her own entertainment and artistic productivity seemed to provide her with a similarly positive sense of generativity. In finding that she could turn her radio on and off as she pleased, to whatever station she chose, and that she could produce a few drawings in the process, she seemed to be comforted in a similar fashion by this tangible proof of her own agency.

As captured in the heading for this section, when people are able to do something well, this helps them to feel good about themselves and about life, in general. It appears that in the case of prolonged psychosis, what people find that they can do well, that gives them a sense of being generative, becomes less important than the fact that whatever it is makes a positive contribution. It leaves, in Betty's words, "evidence" of the person's continued abilities to be productive. As described by Tom, a participant in the supported socialization study that used his stipends to buy cards and presents for relatives, it is this sense of having something to offer of benefit that restores and solidifies the person's sense of being a somebody somewhere:

> I could choose to be a nobody, a nothing, and just [say] "the hell with it, the hell with everything, I'm not going to deal with anything." And there are times when I feel like that. And yet, I'm part of the world, I'm a human being. And human beings usually kind of do things together to help each other out, that type of thing. And I want to be part of that. . . . If you're not part of the world, it's pretty miserable, pretty lonely. So I think degree of involvement is important . . . involvement in some kind of activity. Hopefully an activity which benefits somebody. [That gives me the sense that] I have something to offer . . . that's all I'm talking about. And I think the project made it a little bit easier for me to think in those terms, to not be afraid to give things to people, and not be afraid to take things from people in return.

"It's Hard to Get Up, It's Agony . . . Because I Don't Want to Face Consciousness"

In addition to the objectifying elements of the treatment system that have been described above, major barriers to defining and expanding on the self in relation to others described by people with schizophrenia are posed by stigma, the inertia and despair resulting from repeated experiences of failures and rejection, and the anergia (lack of energy), apathy (lack of interest), anhedonia (lack of pleasure), and avolition (lack of being goal directed or purposeful) characteristic of the negative symptoms of the disorder. We describe these below.

Much attention has been paid over the last several years to the stigma that continues to accrue to serious mental illness. The U.S. Surgeon General's (1999) report, referenced in the Introduction, for example, cited stigma as the number one barrier to access to care. Most often, however, research has treated stigma as a societal phenomenon measured by attitude surveys or, at its most sophisticated, by behaviors toward hypothetical strangers or by giving people artificial vignettes to rate on various indicators. Such research is useful, but it does not begin to touch upon stigma as it is experienced by people with mental illness. Like racism and other forms of discrimination, stigma is experienced in various forms at various levels and with various degrees of subtlety. In our interviews with people with schizophrenia, the most damaging forms of stigma appeared to be those forms of so-called internalized stigma that the person directs toward him- or herself and those experienced within the context of important interpersonal relationships.

Internalized stigma is expressed often in interviews, with participants describing themselves as "nuts," "crazy," or as a "mental patient." This is one of the factors that contributes to the loss of self to the illness described in more detail in the previous chapter. An example of the second kind of stigma was provided by a woman who describes the impact her psychosis and her son's continued perception of her as a mental patient has had on their relationship.

> *Participant:* He stigmatizes me. He thinks sometimes that I'm that same person at 26 now and that's not true. He doesn't give himself a chance to realize that I'm really in remission.
>
> *Interviewer:* How is it that he still treats you the same?
>
> *Participant:* Like there's a certain talk that people have when they are stigmatizing a mental person and he has that conversation, like he would say, for example, I know you don't feel well and I know your mental illness is why you're behaving a certain way. And that's not true. I have no signs of psychosis.

Interviewer: But he still thinks that it's your mental illness?

Participant: He thinks that once you're mentally ill, you're always mentally ill, and that's not the case.

Interviewer: Like you could be having problems that anyone has but somehow he sees it . . .

Participant: Yeah, say, for example, I'm upset. He puts it, he thinks it has something to do with mental illness that I'm upset and anybody can get upset.

Interviewer: Does he hear it when you tell him, you know, it's not that I'm mentally ill, it's that I just . . .

Participant: Yea, but in the back of his mind I'm mentally ill and I'm going to always be mentally ill.

Another example was provided by a woman who found a different, more subtle, form of stigma to impede her becoming more involved in her family's faith community once she began to feel better. At first she reported that "I used to stay home a lot but I'm more active now. After I joined the church I got more active." But then later in the interview she pointed to an unspoken form of stigma as limiting her opportunities to become a full member:

I notice in church sometimes they give you a form for three months of duties which you're going to do all the time, and I've been going to church for five years and only one time I've been asked to do something. I got up to read one of the scriptures in front of the church and I never asked nobody but they never put my name down again for doing nothing, and I wondered about that. I even asked my mom about it and she said sometimes they'll put you down for reading the scripture or presiding or they put you down for different things they're doing on Sunday morning.

It may be difficult in practice to differentiate between inertia brought about by demoralization and despair resulting from repetitive failures and losses, co-morbid depression, and the anergia, apathy, avolition, and anhedonia thought to be negative symptoms of the disorder. Regardless of the cause, the person is faced with an uphill battle of the will, the only solutions for which appear to be perseverance, pleasure, and learning to push back against the illness. Early in the course of illness, for example, people report being overcome by despair and powerlessness in face of the disorder. This sentiment was captured poignantly by one participant who responded to a question about his goals for the future by saying "I'm just dying slowly here in my mind, so how can you have a goal?" In this case, or in that of the heading for this section in which the person reported not wanting to "face consciousness," it appears to matter little where such a pervasive sense of hopelessness and helplessness comes from.

Later in the course of illness, participants report finding ways to counteract these barriers. In some cases, this is done both directly and simply by pushing on through, persevering with one's interests, goals, and activities despite not feeling up to it. In a representative statement, for example, one participant reported: "I've been having a lot of inertia and I feel like I have to just push myself to do every little thing." In some cases, such perseverance is facilitated by the person having come to identify the inertia, despair, or depression as being another of the more difficult and disruptive aspects of the illness. Identifying this barrier as one symptom of the illness then allows the person to call into play coping skills such as self-talk and coaching. Describes another participant:

> Every morning it's a hassle, you got to get up, ram yourself out of that bed, you know? You say now, I say to myself I gotta get out of here, I gotta get out of bed now and it has to be now.

A final strategy for overcoming the barriers of inertia, depression, and apathy is to counteract them by experiencing pleasure or a sense of being productive, as described above. The experiences of joie de vivre and generativity we described as facilitating recovery may build on themselves in the same way that experiences of failure or loss may; in this case producing an upward rather than downward spiral. Such a process may be initiated, if not sustained, by the shear novelty of new and interesting experiences. This was captured in the following passage by another participant in the horseback riding program. This gentleman found it hard to believe that he was actually going to ride horses rather than simply talk about riding horses or watch other people ride horses on television—things he apparently had become accustomed to in his social club. As he said: "It was very different than what I've seen on television, actually being there." He continued:

The first week I didn't know what to expect. I thought we would just get there and talk about riding. But seeing the horse in person really opened my eyes, you know, at that time. And getting on the horse was early, so that was the first day I had gotten on a horse. Just being in the barn, it smelled different. The surrounding was different. It wasn't noisy or anything. It was quiet. So my first week was pretty much nervousness. I wasn't too nervous, but I was, it was a good nervous, not like a paranoia kind of thing. . . . My mind was going wild. "Can I, are we gonna do that today? Are we gonna ride today? How would I get up on a horse?" And, sure enough, I was the first one.

For this man, the smell of the barn, the lack of noise, and the feel of being on a real horse provided a stark contrast to sitting on a couch in his social club, appearing to jolt him back into life.

A participant in the control condition of the supported socialization study similarly described the initiation of such a process as a "jump start" ignited by a particularly novel or enjoyable experience that propelled him out of his "'I can't' mode." Once the process is underway, it appears then to serve to counteract, and provide protection against, inertia, despair, or depression, leading this participant to label such experiences the "best anti-depressant" he could take:

Initially it started out as having the ability to do it because of a couple of extra bucks every month. But that's what I kind of needed to get my engines started and it got to the point where, then, it wasn't necessarily the money, it was just the desire to get out of the house and do something. . . . One day I said to myself "so, big deal, so you don't have a partner, does that mean that you just have to take the money . . . put it away somewhere and not do anything with it. Why don't you go out and gain some enjoyment from it?" . . . It's almost like opening up a little hole in a piece of paper that you kind of poke and it gets bigger and bigger and bigger. . . . To me, the project opened up, gave me that opening. Maybe I made it a little bit bigger, but I think without the project, it would have been tough for me to find another way to . . . see something other than that "I can't" mode. . . . I said to myself one day "you've got a couple of extra bucks, so why don't you just try at least to do something that maybe you normally wouldn't do." So I went and did something. . . . I actually did something different and I enjoyed it!

Then I found myself saying: "What can I do tomorrow?" And one [thing] led to another. . . . If you could bottle it, it [would be] the best anti-depressant I could take. . . . It's enabled me to go out looking for a job so now I can get some extra money. Getting used to having that $28 a month and learning . . . the things I could do with that, enabled me to want to go out again, to go out and make more money, so I could spend more time with my friends.

"I'm Afraid I'm Gonna Make a Mistake"

In addition to challenges specific to schizophrenia, people struggling to recover also have to deal with myriad issues that are more generic to making significant life changes of any kind. We mention only a couple of these to provide concrete examples, but there are many more ways in which overcoming a severe and prolonged illness requires Herculean efforts and persistence in breaking away from habits initially established for survival purposes once they are no longer required. In this respect, it is important to note that schizophrenia is a disease that often afflicts people at the very time they are being launched into the world to become contributing members of society. Prior to onset of the illness, many people with schizophrenia led ordinary lives with hopes and plans for the future not unlike their peers. Unfortunately, the illness then interrupts the life cycle at a time that should be filled with developmental milestones such as graduating high school, going to college, starting a career, or getting married. Watching peers proceed through these milestones often leaves people with schizophrenia feeling left behind and not sure how to catch up.

Among the issues presented by having fallen behind are the sense of being different, lacking an appropriate peer group with which to share the experiences of trial and error involved in learning new skills, fearing success because of the increased demands associated with it, and viewing any progress as fragile and especially vulnerable to falling apart. As described by one participant who was feeling out of place on returning to school:

It's hard for me to learn because when I was going to school we didn't have computers and them kids in the class they had it for five or six years. The things I'm still struggling to learn, they already know, so it kind of put me back half a step from most of the kids in my class. . . . It's a little uncomfortable when you're not used to that.

Finally, doing well after a period of prolonged disability raises the specter of relapse, and the fear of losing all that for which the person has fought so hard. Said one participant:

Sometimes doing stuff really well scares me because I'm afraid I'm gonna make a mistake . . . like I get such a good feeling when I'm doing something really well that sometimes I have to stop and wonder if I'm gonna mess up. . . . Like it won't last, like it's going really well right now but what's it going to be like tomorrow or in a few moments.

"I'm in a Contest of Will with the World"

We close this chapter with a brief discussion of the ways in which an enhanced sense of self in relation to others, what we also have called social agency, can be employed as a coping strategy for managing some of the symptoms of schizophrenia. We noted above how, once the person identifies inertia or apathy as a symptom of the illness, coping strategies can be called into play and become effective in overcoming these barriers to recovery. The same appears to be true of the positive symptoms of the disorder such as hallucinations, delusions, and disorganization. Although exactly how such a mechanism works is far from clear, participants reported that feeling better about themselves had the added, if unexpected, benefit of decreasing these symptoms or their disruptiveness. For example, the following interchange characterizes a common experience among people who have learned strategies for minimizing their voices:

Participant: Every night [I paint] and I get away from the voices.
Interviewer: How does that work? What happens when . . .
Participant: It rests me, and every time I seem to make a picture, it always comes out and turns out like a face and I don't know why [but] I feel good afterwards.

For those participants who are not successful in finding ways to actually decrease the voices, similar strategies may have the effect of allowing the person to ignore the voices instead, thereby diminishing their disruptiveness. As described in the following interchange with another participant, many people learn that listening or paying attention to voices only makes them worse, while ignoring them has the opposite effect:

> *Participant:* I learned a trick. The voice, once I ignore it . . . I stop listening
>   to the voices and they go away eventually but when I feed into it . . .
> *Interviewer:* Pay attention to it?
> *Participant:* Yeah, it gets more and more involved.

These coping strategies may be highly idiosyncratic, in that for other people ignoring certain voices may have yet a different effect, such as escalating their criticism or abusiveness toward the person. In such cases, talking with or negotiating with the voices may be more effective than attempting to ignore them. What appears consistent across all such experiences, however, is that they both require and are made possible by the person's having regained an effective sense of self apart from the illness. This self gives the person a place to stand, from which she or he can then learn, typically through a process of trial and error, ways to manage, compensate for, or contain the illness and its impact. As described by Betty, these experiences too can build on each other in an upward spiral, gradually diminishing the deleterious effects of the illness while simultaneously building up one of the person's most useful tools in combating the disease: a functional sense of self.

> I'm in a contest of will with the world . . . and I say to myself: "Well, damn it, you just calm down and drink your coffee." And I say to myself: "You'll just have to wait five minutes." So I wait. And then the roommate's still bugging me out [but] then I have the control, the self-esteem, the confidence, and it's manageable. Then I just proudly walk to my room and take space. I mean, it's successful.

Conclusion

The concept of recovery is rooted in the simple yet profound realization that people who have been diagnosed with a mental illness are [and remain] human beings.
—Patricia Deegan, Ph.D., psychologist, spokesperson,
advocate, and person diagnosed with schizophrenia

WHAT HAVE WE NOW LEARNED from our phenomenological analysis of first-person accounts of living with schizophrenia, and what implications do these findings hold for future research and for clinical and rehabilitative practice? We take up each of these issues in turn as we bring this volume to a close.

The Beginning of a Map of the Territory

Figure 7 depicts those elements of an emerging model of recovery from schizophrenia that we have been able to distill from over 100 open-ended, narrative interviews of people diagnosed with this disorder. Recalling our analogy from chapter 3, in which we suggested that phenomenological investigation is like becoming immersed in a foreign culture, we offer this figure as a broad-stroke map of psychosis, much as you would find in a

Figure 7

Some Paths to Life Outside Schizophrenia

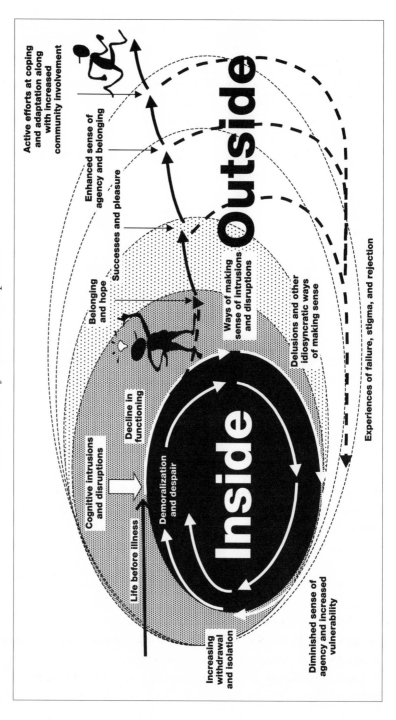

Fodor's guide to a land that has been only provisionally explored and charted. Implications for research and practice can both be derived from this map, and in doing so, we will have one last opportunity to elaborate on the elements of experience that have gone into creating paths into and out of severe mental illness. It is important to remember, however, that we offer this as the *beginning* of a map only and encourage you to take up exploration of this territory on your own. In doing so, we hope you will find these landmarks helpful in navigating this complex and variegated terrain.

At the end of chapter 4, we discussed the centrifugal force that can pull people further and further inside of the illness. Personal accounts suggested a path involving a downward spiral, initiated by the cognitive disruptions introduced by the illness followed by repeated experiences of failure, rejection, and stigma, which then led to a diminished sense of agency and increased vulnerability, leading in turn to increasing isolation and withdrawal. With heightened isolation and withdrawal, the person then becomes increasingly at risk for being subsumed by demoralization and despair, which in turn create new experiences of failure, rejection, and stigma, and so on. Rather than suggesting that we view this spiral as a predetermined fate for the person with schizophrenia, we offer this account as a basis for identifying potential junctures at which experiences or interventions may enable the person to escape the spiral and begin to stake out a life outside of the illness. The map depicted in Figure 7 offers several such points.

According to this map, the more severe and debilitating the cognitive intrusions and disruptions introduced by the illness, the more difficult it will be for the person to come to an adaptive understanding of these experiences and his or her subsequent decline in functioning. The more frequent, the louder, and the more insistent a person's voices are, the more likely she or he will be to become absorbed in these voices and in the delusional explanations he or she then has to develop in order to account for the voices (e.g., the CIA is using me to conduct thought experiments). Similarly, the more unusual and idiosyncratic the person's way of making sense of the intrusions introduced by the illness becomes, the more likely she or he will be to suffer failures and rejections in his or her attempts to connect to others, attend school, or hold down a job.

If the intrusions and disruptions are not so severe and the person is able to contain their damage, on the other hand, then even delusional accounts that the person keeps to him- or herself do not necessarily have to result in experiences of failure or rejection. Clinical accounts are replete with examples of people who learn to contain the symptoms of their illness and its debilitating effects enough so that they can work, live independently, and maintain satisfactory social relationships. Similarly, when people are able to develop or accept more adaptive accounts of their disorder that enlist rather than alienate others, even the most severe symptoms can be managed and accommodated to allow the person a decent, if not optimal, quality of life. The map offered above provides ways to understand numerous combinations and permutations of these various components, suggesting roles both for the person with the disorder and for supportive others.

Moving to the paths that lead outside of the illness clarifies and elaborates this point. For example, the map indicates that the first essential components required for the person to be able to move outside of the illness are a sense of belonging and hope. Most people do not lose their sense of belonging and hope altogether when they first become ill, so that it is possible for them to maintain one foot inside and one foot outside of the illness from the start. Recovery will be much more likely, in fact, if a person's sense of belonging and hope are not lost altogether, as it is easier to maintain such a sense than to have to regain it once it is lost. For those individuals who have lost both hope and a sense of belonging among a community of fellow human beings over a prolonged period of time, however, the map suggests that these basic components will have to be restored before any steps can be taken to address the illness or any other treatment- or rehabilitation-related issues.

Clinicians have acknowledged the difficulty of engaging people in active treatment without a foundation in belonging and hope by arguing for the importance of establishing trust or a therapeutic relationship with people with psychotic disorders before other interventions may be introduced. We are suggesting, in addition, that a sense of belonging and hope may be offered, and is more likely to be accepted, outside of the relationships people have with mental health providers. This is particularly true given the hierarchical and asymmetrical nature of traditional clinical relationships, in which the person with the disability has to accept being less than the other, and accept not being allowed to give back to the other, in order to gain any sense of hope or belonging.

What this map suggests overall, in fact, is that most of the work of recovery happens in the person's life outside of treatment relationships and settings. In addition to belonging and hope, the successes and pleasures the person needs to experience in order to regain a sense of agency are more likely to occur—and to be personally relevant and gratifying when they do occur—as part of intrinsically meaningful activities that take place in natural, community settings. Given the relative effectiveness of "place then train" models such as supported employment (Bond et al., 2001), supported housing (Carling, 1993), and supported education (Unger, 1991) over traditional "train then place" models such as skills training in clubhouses or other mental health settings, it may require less effort and expense to support people engaging in the activities of their choice in vivo, that is, in the natural community settings in which these activities typically take place, than to create artificial settings in which the challenge then becomes one of affording the person some semblance of a realistic experience that will generalize to other settings.

In addition to the failure of skills learned in one context to generalize to other contexts, this position is supported by the value our emerging map places on experiences of pleasure, success, and generativity. The mental health system has not been designed to offer such experiences, and even if it were to be redesigned to do so, such experiences are hard to manufacture. As we pointed out in chapter 5, these experiences rely somewhat on the elements of grace and reciprocity. The best that we can do is offer people access to opportunities to have such experiences and provide them with the supports needed for them to take full advantage of these opportunities when they present themselves. We will return to this issue below when we consider the implications of our findings for practice. Before doing so, however, we turn first to research.

Implications for Clinical Research

The phenomenological method of course enters just as little into competition with the experimental-psychological one as do the mathematical methods in physics with the physical ones. . . . Let it here be expressly added that the critical refutation of the opinion that one can obtain phenomenological results from natural-scientific experimental psychology . . . in no way implies that experimental arrangements cannot acquire phenomenological function in a good sense.

—Husserl (1983)

We begin with this quote from Husserl in anticipation of the criticism that empirical phenomenological methods cannot be reconciled with conventional quantitative approaches to the clinical investigation of schizophrenia. A typical reaction from a skeptical reader would be something like: "Well, fine, you found out some interesting things about the life experiences of people with schizophrenia, but so what?" The "so what" of this challenge can be taken to mean one of two things; either that (1) what we have discovered about schizophrenia is true of all of us and not specific to people with schizophrenia per se (a variant of the criticism we offered in chapter 1 in our review of existing qualitative research), or (2) what we have described about experiences of schizophrenia has been obvious from the start and, even if it weren't, it would remain to be tested and confirmed through experimental, quantitative methods (consigning phenomenology to the preparatory role described and critiqued in chapter 3). In either case, the skeptical reader remains convinced that empirical phenomenology cannot offer valid, scientific insights into the nature of schizophrenia.

The quote from Husserl above should silence both those critics who assume that qualitative and quantitative methods are contradictory or mutually exclusive and those practitioners of qualitative research who dismiss quantitative methods wholesale upon whom the first critics base their critiques. We have argued elsewhere (e.g., Davidson, Stayner, Lambert, et al., 1997; Davidson and Stayner, 1997; Davidson, Stayner, and Haglund, 1998), and reiterate here, that there is no compelling reason of which we are aware to assume that qualitative and quantitative methods cannot both yield empirical insights about psychological phenomena. As we mentioned above, Husserl devoted a good portion of his career to outlining how phenomenology provides a descriptive framework for the development of a natural science of human physiology. We conducted the interviews of participants in our supported socialization program within the context of a randomized, controlled experimental trial involving 260 people with mental illness. Our findings to date suggest that the relationship between quantitative and qualitative approaches is neither mutually exclusive nor competitive but rather is complementary.

When they are done well, qualitative and quantitative methods strengthen each other. Quantitative, experimental studies can be used to test and confirm or challenge qualitative findings without rendering qualitative research merely preparatory. This is so because qualitative methods can be used in the same fashion to test and confirm or challenge quantitative findings just as well. As both are independent approaches to generating scientific insights, neither one need be given priority over the other as long as they each remain within their appropriate parameters, utilizing their own respective criteria of validity (cf. Robinson, 1985).

The issues of whether or not our findings pertain only to people with schizophrenia and whether or not they are to be dismissed as merely obvious, we will leave to you to decide. From our perspective, these findings transcend the *merely* obvious, at least to the degree that they suggest new approaches to research and practice.

In terms of research, learning the importance for people with schizophrenia of being viewed by others as people capable of being more than sick has encouraged us to include research participants in all phases of the research enterprise (e.g., Davidson, 1997; Davidson, Stayner, Lambert, et al., 1997). Given the centrality of feeling like an object to living inside of the illness, and the importance of recovering a sense of oneself as a subject alongside other subjects in the recovery process, we consider it unethical, if not also damaging, to treat people with schizophrenia solely as objects of scientific scrutiny. In attempting to develop research methods that will foster, rather than impede, their recovery, we have become convinced that participants must be viewed as partners, as opposed to objects, in the investigation. Only then will our research cease feeding the illness and perhaps instead provide a bit of fuel for the process of recovery.

The possibility that methods selected for conducting research on a disorder might either exacerbate the illness or stimulate steps toward recovery is worth further consideration. We were alerted to this possibility by our study participants prior to coming to the conclusions described above related to the value of participatory methods. Our first indication of the potential impact of participation in qualitative interviews on the lives of people with schizophrenia came from a follow-along study led by

John Strauss, in which people were interviewed repeatedly following discharge from the hospital in an attempt to identify and articulate processes of disorder and recovery as they unfolded over time (e.g., Strauss et al., 1985b).

In addition to narrative interviews, this study included a few standard measures of symptoms and social and occupational functioning. One of the social functioning measures involved asking participants to place the names of significant people in their lives at varying distances from the center of a circle, based on how close they felt to each person. In his third interview with one of the investigators in this study, a young male participant placed the name of the investigator who was interviewing him as one of the few names to reside within his inner circle of social support. The genuine interest this investigator had shown in the young man on two previous occasions had earned him a place of honor as one of the few significant people in the young man's life.

In the supported socialization study described above, there was a similar finding among some of the people assigned to the control condition; the condition in which they did not receive a partner with whom they were meant to interact. In this case, it was not so much the role of the investig*ators* in the lives of the participants as much as the role of the investig*ation* itself, and what participation in the research enterprise meant for participants. Some people in the control condition, for example, were able to overcome their initial disappointment in not receiving a partner by reassuring themselves that they were doing something important that would benefit other people if not themselves. Said one participant: "I was glad that I was able to participate in it to maybe help out more with mental illness." A similar sentiment was expressed by another participant, who said: "I felt like I was a participant in something pretty important, you know, as far as helping people like me maybe find something or maybe have a little more of an advantage." We also heard from several participants how important and worthwhile it had been for them to be involved in an experiment conducted by "Yale doctors," and how much they enjoyed being associated with Yale Medical School, the source of their monthly stipends. For some, this was the first time in a long time they could recall feeling like something meaningful was being requested of them. They liked being asked and clearly had a lot to contribute.

Implications for Clinical and Rehabilitative Practice

If they could just say something, like if they could say we want you to do this
and this and this and we can let you perhaps be discharged in the future if
you do this and this and this, but they never say that.
—Man with schizophrenia speaking to interviewer

From among the various implications that can be derived from our findings for clinical and rehabilitative practice, the most important one—and
the one that underlies all others—is that recovery requires the active role
of the person with the disorder. Recovery, in other words, is something
that the person with schizophrenia *does,* not something that can be *done to*
him or her by others. Love, positive regard, and the support of others are
essential to providing a foundation for the person's efforts at recovery. In
addition, the dedication, technical skill, and talent of mental health professionals can be extremely useful in equipping the person for the journey,
in providing useful information about landmarks and other things the person may expect to encounter in his or her path, and in offering guidance,
encouragement, and even companionship along the way. The primary
focus of treatment and rehabilitative efforts, however, needs to be squarely
on what the person with the illness is doing currently, on the consequences
of those actions both for the illness and for the person's life in general, and
on what she or he could be doing instead in order to minimize the illness
and maximize his or her chances for establishing and expanding a life outside of the illness.

As a result of this principle, it becomes clear that simply demanding
compliance with providers' recommendations or, even worse, ignoring the
person's role altogether, will likely be counterproductive to the recovery
process. Basing the entire treatment and rehabilitation process on what the
person wants to be doing with his or her time and what she or he needs in
order to be able to do such things successfully, on the other hand, provides
much in the way of concrete direction for the efforts of mental health
providers and other caring people in the person's life. "But what if he says
he wants to be the next president of the United States?" asks the skeptical
reader, or "What if she says she wants to get pregnant and have children,
even when we know she won't be able to take care of them and will lose

custody the moment they are born?" These questions express the common concerns of professionals when encouraged to use the person's own desires, wants, and aspirations as the basis for treatment and rehabilitation. And some people will say these things at first.

Once a respectful and trusting relationship is formed, however, people are much more likely to say—as did participants in our research interviews—such things as: "I'd like to live in a better neighborhood" or I'd like to go "to the movies or out for pizza. Just try to enjoy life to the best." These represent more typical responses from people with schizophrenia when asked what recovery would look like for them. In many cases, answers reflect incremental steps along the path of increasing agency and generativity, as in the examples of: "To clean my own house, to do my own laundry, not to drink, to stay clean, and just try to make myself as happy as possible" and "I like living alone and I like things like taking care of myself and not having people watch me take my medicine 'cause I can take it on my own." In other cases, people identify a return to a previous way of life and level of functioning that they found meaningful and gratifying prior to their illness, as in the following examples:

> I don't have too good an answer to any of this but I like to stay productive, keep in touch with people, write letters and just like how it used to be, write letters, have a job, clean my room, do laundry, walk to the store.

> You know, like every Sunday we used to go to grandma's house for Sunday dinner before I became mentally ill and it hasn't been the same [since]. So I would like to do that.

Unlike becoming president, all of these examples involve people engaging in activities that are both realistic and potentially achievable within their current situation.

In addition to wanting to engage in meaningful, productive, and enjoyable activities, people express desires to establish or improve reciprocal and caring relationships. "I'd like to have friends that are not mentally ill," said one participant, whereas another described wanting "to stay married, to stay loyal to my wife and to get a relationship with all of my kids one day, that's very important to me." Even in cases in which the person is severely debilitated by the illness and does not yet see recovery as even the remotest possibility, it is still possible for him or her to identify activities that will improve his or her quality of life and begin to develop a foundation for future efforts toward recovery. We saw this earlier in this volume in examples of not having to eat alone, enjoying fried clams and iced tea on a hot summer day, and sending birthday cards to relatives. As described in the following passage from an interview with a young man who was living a life largely restricted to within his illness, the first step or two toward recovery also could involve such seemingly trivial actions as picking up the neighbor's trash:

> I'd probably come out and if I see the neighbor's trash out, trash can, I would put it in their back yard and I would pick up the garbage on the street and I would talk to the kids about different things, tell them you know you only got one mother just try to be good and have a family.

When the stepping-stones to recovery are broken down to this level of specificity and concrete detail, it becomes obvious that at least some opportunities for a life outside of the illness could be made available to everyone, no matter how severe their disability. The challenge is to provide access to, or to create, opportunities that they will find appealing and then not to stand in each person's way of taking whatever advantage of them he or she can at the time. Beyond creating access and providing support, we can lay a foundation for future recovery efforts by offering people hope and the sense that no matter how disabled they are or become, there will always be a place for them at the table. Once there, they no longer *have to* eat alone, and in this case, as in most cases, it is having the choice that is most important.

Epilogue

We began this investigation with the question: *"How do the person's experiences and activities affect processes of recovery in schizophrenia?"* Our qualitative analysis indicated that experiences of being stigmatized and/or rejected by others, as well as those of failing at efforts to accomplish normative life tasks, make recovery more difficult. Being accepted and valued by others, as well as experiences of success, pleasure, and being generative, play important roles in promoting recovery. In addition, withdrawal, isolation, and absorption in idiosyncratic ways of making sense of one's illness-related experiences make recovery a more remote possibility, while engagement in the world and with others, and struggling to make constructive sense of one's difficulties, make recovery possible.

What these findings suggest is that schizophrenia, in its more severe forms, may be more like a prolonged illness such as type 2 diabetes than an acute condition such as an infection. In this vein, recovery requires more than simply taking medication and waiting for the condition to abate. On the other hand, it appears that psychosis can abate over time, unlike type 1 diabetes and other chronic physical conditions. With appropriate self-care and adequate alterations in one's daily life, many people will be able to overcome the effects of schizophrenia altogether. To make this statement no more implies that it therefore is the person's fault that he or she has schizophrenia than it is to imply that people are at fault for having type 2 diabetes. Causation in both conditions is most likely the result of the convergence of numerous factors, many—if not most—of which lie outside of the person's control. To make this statement does imply, however, that regardless of the nature of the causation involved, for people with schizophrenia to recover they need to be at least one of the heroes of their own story.

It is this story, the one in which the person takes center stage as protagonist, that we have tried to elicit, encourage, and attend carefully to as it has unfolded through the words of our participants. It also is this story that we encourage you to join in bringing to light, like the water in Rilke's poem that reached into "the silence of stone" to recover its hidden gold. Inviting the person to tell his or her story and understanding this story in its own terms not only promise to shed light on processes of recovery in schizophrenia, after all, but also promise to promote recovery.

In becoming an autobiographer, the person with psychosis first has to assume the role of a somebody somewhere about whom a story may be told. By bringing his or her story into the public sphere—whether through research or practice—we invite the person to reassume this role as a member of a shared community here, alongside us. Given Husserl's insight with which we began this volume, namely, that I am treating a fellow human being as a "mere thing" unless I take him or her to be a person as a subject and a member of a shared community, this approach would seem to provide an important starting point for efforts to understand and promote recovery from this most dehumanized, and dehumanizing, of human conditions.

Works Cited

Allende, M. (2000). *Serious mental illness and the experience of being in psychiatric treatment: A phenomenological study.* Unpublished doctoral dissertation, Yale University, New Haven, CT.

Amador, X. (2000). *I am not sick I don't need help.* Peconic, NY: Vida Press.

Amador, X., Strauss, D.H., Yale, S.A., and Gorman, J.M. (1991). Awareness of illness in schizophrenia. *Schizophrenia Bulletin, 17*(1), 113–132.

American Psychiatric Association. (1980). *Diagnostic and statistical manual of mental disorders (3rd ed.).* Washington, DC: American Psychiatric Association.

Andreasen, N.C. (1984). *The broken brain: The biological revolution in psychiatry.* New York: Harper and Row.

Andreasen, N.C., and Flaum, M. (1991). Schizophrenia: The characteristic symptoms. *Schizophrenia Bulletin, 17*(1), 27–49.

Anonymous. (1986). "Can we talk?": The schizophrenic patient in psychotherapy. *American Journal of Psychiatry, 143,* 68–70.

Anthony, W. (1993). Recovery from mental illness: The guiding vision of the mental health service system in the 1990s. *Psychosocial Rehabilitation Journal, 16* (4), 11–23.

Baez, B. (2002). Confidentiality in qualitative research: Reflections on secrets, power, and agency. *Qualitative Research, 2*(1), 35–58.

Barham, P. (1984). *Schizophrenia and human value.* Oxford: Basil Blackwell.

Barham, P. (1992). *Schizophrenia and human value: Chronic schizophrenia, science, and society.* London: Blackwell Publishers.

Barham, P., and Hayward, R. (1998a). *From the mental patient to the person.* London: Routledge.

Barham, P., and Hayward, R. (1998b). In sickness and in health: Dilemmas of the person with severe mental illness. *Psychiatry, 61,* 163–170.

Barker, S., Lavender, T., and Morant, N. (2001). Client and family narratives on schizophrenia. *Journal of Mental Health, 10* (2), 199–212.

Baxter, E.A., and Diehl, S. (1998). Emotional stages: Consumers and family members recovering from the trauma of mental illness. *Psychiatric Rehabilitation Journal, 21* (4), 349–355.

Beers, C.W. (1935). *A mind that found itself; an autobiography* (25th anniversary ed.). New York: National Committee for Mental Hygiene.

Bell, M., Bryson, G., Greig, T., Corcoran, C.M., and Wexler, B. (2001). Neurocognitive enhancement therapy with work therapy. *Archives of General Psychiatry, 58.*

Binswanger, L. (1958). The case of Ellen West. In R. May, E. Angel, and H. Ellenberger (Eds.), *Existence* (pp. 237–364). New York: Basic Books.

Binswanger, L. (1963). Introduction to schizophrenia. In J. Needleman (Ed.), *Being-in-the-world* (pp. 249–265). New York: Basic Books.

Birchwood, M. (1995). Early intervention in psychotic relapse: Cognitive approaches to detection and management. *Behaviour Change, 12* (1), 2–19.

Birchwood, M., Smith, J., Macmillan, F., Hogg, B., Prasad, R., Harvey, C., et al. (1989). Predicting relapse in schizophrenia: The development and implementation of an early signs monitoring system using patients and families as observers: A preliminary investigation. *Psychological Medicine, 19* (3), 649–656.

Boman, J., and Jevne, R. (2000). Pearls, pith, and provocation: Ethical evaluation in qualitative research. *Qualitative Health Research, 10* (4), 547–554.

Bond, G.R., Becker, D.R., Drake, R.E., Rapp, C.A., Meisler, N., Lehman, A.F. (2001). Implementing supported employment as an evidence-based practice. *Psychiatric Services, 52* (3), 313–322.

Borgna, E. (1981). Delusion of schizophrenic time. *Rivista Sperimentale di Freniatria e Medicina Legale Delle Alienazioni Mentali, 105* (6), 1283–1291.

Borkin, J. (2000). Recovery attitudes questionnaire: Development and evaluation. *Psychiatric Rehabilitation Journal, 24* (2), 95–103.

Boss, M. (1963). *Psychoanalysis and daseinsanalysis.* New York: Basic Books.

Bruner, J. (1986). *Actual minds, possible worlds.* Cambridge, MA: Harvard University Press.

Buechner, F. (1973). *Wishful thinking: A theological ABC.* New York: Harper and Row.

Bullock, W., Ensing, D., Alloy, V., and Weddle, C. (2000). Leadership education: Evaluation of a program to promote recovery in persons with psychiatric disabilities. *Psychiatric Rehabilitation Journal, 24* (1), 3–13.

Camus, A. (1956). *The rebel: An essay on man in revolt* (A. Bower, Trans.). New York: Vintage Books.

Carling, P.J. (1993). Housing and supports for persons with mental illness: Emerging approaches to research and practice. *Hospital and Community Psychiatry, 44,* 439–449.

Carpenter, W., and Buchanan, R.W. (1994). Schizophrenia. *New England Journal of Medicine, 330* (10), 681–690.

Carpenter, W.T., and Kirkpatrick, B. (1988). The heterogeneity of the long-term course of schizophrenia. *Schizophrenia Bulletin, 14* (4), 645–652.

Carpenter, W.T., Strauss, J.S., and Bartko, J.J. (1974). Use of signs and symptoms for the identification of schizophrenic patients: I. *Schizophrenia Bulletin, 11,* 37–49.

Casement, P.J. (1991). *Learning from the patient.* London: British Psychoanalytic Society.

Charlton, J. (1998). *Nothing about us without us.* Berkeley, CA: University of California Press.

Cieurzo, C., and Keitel, M.A. (1999). Ethics in qualitative research. In M. Kopala and L. A. Suzuki (Eds.), *Using qualitative methods in psychology* (pp. 63–75). Thousand Oaks, CA: Sage Publications.

Ciompi, L. (1980). The natural history of schizophrenia in the long term. *British Journal of Psychiatry, 136,* 413–420.

Cohen, A. (1992). Prognosis for schizophrenia in the Third World: A reevaluation of cross-cultural research. *Culture, Medicine and Psychiatry, 16* (1), 53–75.

Cooke, A. (1997). The long journey back. *Psychiatric Rehabilitation Skills, 2* (1), 33–36.

Corin, E. (1998). The thickness of being: Intentional worlds, strategies of identity, and experience among schizophrenics. *Psychiatry: Interpersonal and Biological Processes, 61* (2), 133–146.

Corin, E.E. (1990). Facts and meaning in psychiatry: An anthropological approach to the lifeworld of schizophrenics. *Culture, Medicine and Psychiatry, 14* (2), 153–188.

Corin, E.E., and Lauzon, G. (1992). Positive withdrawal and the quest for meaning: The reconstruction of experience among schizophrenics. *Psychiatry: Journal for the Study of Interpersonal Processes, 55* (3), 266–278.

Corin, E.E., and Lauzon, G. (1994). From symptoms to phenomena: The articulation of experience in schizophrenia. *Journal of Phenomenological Psychology, 25* (1), 3–50.

Corrigan, P., and Penn, D. (1998). Disease and discrimination: Two paradigms that describe severe mental illness. *Journal of Mental Health, 6,* 355–366.

Csikszentmihalyi, M. (1991). *Flow.* New York: Harper Collins.

Davidson, L. (1987). What is the appropriate source for psychological explanation? *Humanistic Psychologist, 15* (3), 150–166.

Davidson, L. (1988). Husserl's refutation of psychologism and the possibility of a phenomenological psychology. *Journal of Phenomenological Psychology, 19* (1), 1–17.

Davidson, L. (1992). Philosophical foundations of humanistic psychology. *Humanistic Psychologist, 20* (2–3), 136–157.

Davidson, L. (1994). Phenomenological research in schizophrenia: From philosophical anthropology to empirical science. *Journal of Phenomenological Psychology, 25* (1), 104–130.

Davidson, L. (1997). Vulnérabilité et destin dans la schizophrénie: Prêter l'oreille à la voix de la personne. (Vulnerability and destiny in schizophrenia: Hearkening to the voice of the person). *L'Evolution Psychiatrique, 62,* 263–284.

Davidson, L. (2001). Us and them. *Psychiatric Services, 52* (12), 1579–1580.

Davidson, L., Chinman, M.J., Kloos, B., Weingarten, R., Stayner, D., and Tebes, J.K. (1999). Peer support among individuals with severe mental illness: A review of the evidence. *Clinical Psychology: Science and Practice, 6* (2), 165–187.

Davidson, L., and Cosgrove, L.A. (1991). Psychologism and phenomenological psychology revisited: I. The liberation from naturalism. *Journal of Phenomenological Psychology, 22* (2), 87–108.

Davidson, L., and Cosgrove, L.A. (in press). Psychologism and phenomenological psychology revisited: II. The return to positivity. *Journal of Phenomenological Psychology.*

Davidson, L., Haglund, K.E., Stayner, D.A., Rakfeldt, J., Chinman, M.J., and Kraemer Tebes, J. (2001). "It was just realizing . . . that life isn't one big horror": A qualitative study of supported socialization. *Psychiatric Rehabilitation Journal, 24* (3), 275–292.

Davidson, L., Hoge, M.A., Merrill, M.E., Rakfeldt, J., and Griffith, E.E.H. (1995). The experiences of long-stay inpatients returning to the community. *Psychiatry: Interpersonal and Biological Processes, 58* (2) 122–132.

Davidson, L., and McGlashan, T.H. (1997). The varied outcomes of schizophrenia. *Canadian Journal of Psychiatry, 42* (1), 34–43.

Davidson, L., and Stayner, D. (1997). Loss, loneliness, and the desire for love: Perspectives on the social lives of people with schizophrenia. *Psychiatric Rehabilitation Journal, 20* (3), 3–12.

Davidson, L., Stayner, D.A., and Haglund, K.E. (1998). Phenomenological perspectives on the social functioning of people with schizophrenia. In K.T. Mueser and N. Tarrier (Eds.), *Handbook of social functioning in schizophrenia.* (pp. 97–120). Needham Heights, MA: Allyn and Bacon.

Davidson, L., Stayner, D., Lambert, M.T., Smith, B., and Sledge, W.H. (1997). Phenomenological and participatory research on schizophrenia: Recovering the person in theory and practice. *Journal of Social Issues, 53,* 767–784.

Davidson, L., Stayner, D.A., Nickou, C., Styron, T.H., Rowe, M., and Chinman, M.J. (2001). "Simply to be let in": Inclusion as a basis for recovery. *Psychiatric Rehabilitation Journal, 24* (4), 375–388.

Davidson, L., and Strauss, J.S. (1992). Sense of self in recovery from severe mental illness. *British Journal of Medical Psychology, 65* (2), 131–145.

Davidson, L., and Strauss, J.S. (1995). Beyond the biopsychosocial model: Integrating disorder, health, and recovery. *Psychiatry: Interpersonal and Biological Processes, 58* (1) 44–55.

Deegan, P.E. (1988). Recovery: The lived experience of rehabilitation. *Psychosocial Rehabilitation Journal, 11* (4), 11–19.

Deegan, P.E. (1992). The Independent Living Movement and people with psychiatric disabilities: Taking back control over our own lives. *Psychosocial Rehabilitation Journal, 15* (3), 3–19.

Deegan, P.E. (1993). Recovering our sense of value after being labeled. *Journal of Psychosocial Nursing, 31* (4), 7–11.

Deegan, P.E. (1994). "A letter to my friend who is giving up." *Journal of the California Alliance for the Mentally Ill, 5,* 18–20.

Deegan, P.E. (1996a). Recovery and the conspiracy of hope. Paper presented at the Sixth Annual Mental Health Services Conference of Australia and New Zealand, Brisbane, Australia. retrieved March 1, 2001, from Intentional Care web site: http://www.intentionalcare.org/articles/articles_hope.pdf.

Deegan, P.E. (1996b). Recovery as a journey of the heart. *Psychiatric Rehabilitation Journal, 19,* 91–97.

Deegan, P.E. (2001). Recovery as a self-directed process of healing and transformation. Retrieved March 1, 2001, from Intentional Care web site: http://www.intentionalcare.org/articles/articles_trans.pdf.

Dennett, D.C. (1991). *Consciousness explained.* Boston: Little, Brown, and Company.

de Waelhens, A. (1978). *Schizophrenia* (W. Ver Eecke, Trans.). Pittsburgh: Duquesne University Press.

Dixon, L. (2000). Reflections on recovery. *Community Mental Health Journal, 26* (4), 443–447.

Drake, R.E. (2000). Introduction to a special series on recovery. *Community Mental Health Journal, 36* (2), 207–208.

Drüe, H. (1963). *Edmund Husserl's System der Phanomenologischen Psychologie.* Berlin: De Gruyter.

Edelson, M. (1993). Telling and enacting stories in psychoanalysis and psychotherapy: Implications for teaching psychotherapy. *Psychoanalytic Study of the Child, 48,* 293–325.

Estroff, S.E. (1989). Self, identity, and subjective experiences of schizophrenia: In search of the subject. *Schizophrenia Bulletin, 15* (2), 189–196.

Estroff, S.E. (1994). Keeping things complicated: Undiscovered countries and the lives of persons with serious mental illness. *Journal of the California Alliance for the Mentally Ill, 5* (3), 40–46.

Estroff, S.E. (1995). Brokenhearted lifetimes: Ethnography, subjectivity, and psychosocial rehabilitation. *International Journal of Mental Health, 24* (1), 82–92.

Ferguson, P.M., Hibbard, M., Leinen, J., and Schaff, S. (1990). Supported community life: Disability policy and the renewal of mediating structures. *Journal of Disability Policy Studies, 1,* 9–35.

Fisher, D.V. (1984). A conceptual analysis of self-disclosure. *Journal for the Theory of Social Behaviour, 14* (3), 277–296.

Fisher, D.V. (1994). Health care reform based on an empowerment model of recovery by people with psychiatric disabilities. *Hospital and Community Psychiatry, 45* (9), 913–915.

Foucault, M. (1965). *Madness and civilization: A history of insanity in the age of reason* (R. Howard, Trans. 1961 ed.). New York: Vintage Books.

Frank, R., and Elliott, T. (2000). *Handbook of rehabilitation psychology.* Washington, DC: American Psychological Association.

Frese, F.J. (2000). Psychology practitioners and schizophrenia: A view from both sides. *Journal of Clinical Psychology, 56* (11), 1413–1426.

Frese, F.J., and Davis, W.W. (1997). The consumer-survivor movement, recovery, and consumer professionals. *Professional Psychology: Research and Practice, 28* (3), 243–245.

Frese, F.J., Stanley, J., Kress, K., and Vogel-Scibilia, S. (2001). Integrating evidence-based practices and the recovery model. *Psychiatric Services, 52* (11), 1462–1468.

Freud, S. (1949). *An outline of psychoanalysis* (J. Strachey, Trans.). New York: W.W. Norton and Company.

Gardner, M. (Ed.). (1971). *The Wolfman by the Wolfman.* New York: Basic Books.

Giorgi, A. (1970). *Psychology as a human science: A phenomenologically-based approach.* New York: Harper and Row.

Giorgi, A. (Ed.). (1985). *Sketch of a psychological phenomenological method.* Pittsburgh: Duquesne University Press.

Green, M. (1993). Cognitive remediation in schizophrenia: Is it time yet? *American Journal of Psychiatry, 150,* 178–187.

Green, M., Satz, P., Ganzell, S., and Vaclav, F. (1992). Wisconsin Card Sorting Test performance in schizophrenia: Remediation of a stubborn deficit. *American Journal of Psychiatry, 149,* 62–67.

Hadjistavropoulos, T., and Smythe, W.E. (2001). Elements of risk in qualitative research. *Ethics and Behavior, 11* (2), 163–174.

Harding, C.M., Strauss, J.S., Hafez, H., and Lieberman, P.B. (1987). Work and mental illness: I. Toward an integration of the rehabilitation process. *Journal of Nervous and Mental Disease, 175* (6), 317–326.

Harding, C.M., Zubin, J., and Strauss, J.S. (1987). Chronicity in schizophrenia: Fact, partial fact, or artifact? *Hospital and Community Psychiatry, 38* (5), 477–486.

Hatfield, A.B. (1994). Recovery from mental illness. *Journal of the California Alliance for the Mentally Ill, 5* (3), 6–7.

Hatfield, A.B., and Lefley, H.P. (1993). *Surviving mental illness: Stress, coping, and adaptation.* New York: Guilford Press.

Hemingway, E. (1964). *A moveable feast.* London: Jonathan Cape.

Herman, N.J., and Smith, C.M. (1989). Mental hospital depopulation in Canada: Patient perspectives. *Canadian Journal of Psychiatry, 34,* 386–391.

Husserl, E. (1965). *Phenomenology and the crisis of philosophy, Philosophy as rigorous science,* and *Philosophy and the crisis of European man.* (Q. Lauer, Trans.). New York: Harper and Row.

Husserl, E. (1970a). *The crisis of European science and transcendental phenomenology* (D. Carr, Trans.). Evanston, IL: Northwestern University Press.

Husserl, E. (1970b). *Logical investigations* (J. Findlay, Trans.). Atlantic Highlands, NJ: Humanities Press.

Husserl, E. (1977). *Phenomenological psychology* (J. Scanlon, Trans.). The Hague: Martinus Nijhoff.

Husserl, E. (1981). Philosophy as rigorous science (Q. Lauer, Trans.). In P. McCormick and F. Elliston (Eds.), *Husserl: Shorter works* (pp. 166–202). Notre Dame: University of Notre Dame Press and the Harvester Press.

Husserl, E. (1983). *Ideas pertaining to a pure phenomenology and to a phenomenological philosophy.* (F. Kersten, Trans. *First book: General introduction to a pure phenomenology*). The Hague: Martinus Nijhoff.

Husserl, E. (1989). *Ideas pertaining to a pure phenomenology and to a phenomenological philosophy. Second book: Studies in the phenomenology of constitution* (R. Rojcewicz and A. Schuwer, Trans. original work published in 1952). Boston: Kluwer Academic Publishers.

Jacobson, N. (2001). Experiencing recovery: A dimensional analysis of recovery narratives. *Psychiatric Rehabilitation Journal, 24* (3), 248–256.

Jacobson, N., and Curtis, L. (2000). Recovery as policy in mental health services: Strategies emerging from the states. *Psychiatric Rehabilitation Journal, 23* (4), 333.

Jacobson, N., and Greenley, J.R. (2001). What is recovery? A conceptual model and explication. *Psychiatric Services, 52* (4), 482–485.

Jaeger, J., and Douglas, E. (1992). Neuropsychiatric rehabilitation for persistent mental illness. *Psychiatric Quarterly, 63,* 71–94.

Jaspers, K. (1964). *General psychopathology.* Chicago: University of Chicago Press.

Jaspers, K. (1968). The phenomenological approach in psychopathology. *British Journal of Psychiatry, 114* (516), 1313–1323.

Kierkegaard, S.A. (1983). *Fear and trembling* (H. Hong, Trans.). Princeton, NJ: Princeton University Press.

Kimura, B. (1982). The phenomenology of the between: On the problem of the basic disturbance in schizophrenia. In A. de Koning and A. Jenner (Eds.), *Phenomenology and pscyhiatry* (pp. 173–186). London: Academic Press.

Kockelmans, J. (1967). *Edmund Husserl's phenomenological psychology: A historico-critical study.* Pittsburgh: Duquesne University Press.

Kockelmans, J. (1972). Phenomenologico-psychological and transcendental reductions in Husserl's crisis. In A. Tymieniecka (Ed.), *Analecta Husserliana, vol. 2* (pp. 78–89). Dordrecht: D. Reidel.

Kockelmans, J. (1973). Theoretical problems in phenomenological psychology. In M. Natanson (Ed.), *Phenomenology and the social sciences* (pp. 225–280). Evanston, IL: Northwestern University Press.

Kohák, E. (1978). *Idea and experience: Edmund Husserl's project of phenomenology in "Ideas I."* Chicago: University of Chicago Press.

Kraepelin, E. ([1904] 1987). Dementia praecox. In J. Cutting and M. Shepherd (Eds.), *The clinical roots of the schizophrenia concept: Translations of seminal European contributions on schizophrenia* (pp. 13–24). New York: Cambridge University Press.

Laing, R.D. (1960). *The divided self.* London: Tavistock Publications.

Laing, R.D. (1961). *Self and others.* London: Tavistock Publications.

Leete, E. (1993). The interpersonal environment: A consumer's personal recollection. In A.B. Hatfield and H.P. Lefley (Eds.), *Surviving mental illness: Stress, coping, and adaptation* (pp. 114–128). New York: Guilford Press.

Leete, E. (1994). Stressor, symptom, or sequelae? Remission, recovery, or cure? *Journal of the California Alliance for the Mentally Ill, 5* (3), 16–17.

Liberman, R., and Green, M. (1992). Wither cognitive behavioral therapy for schizophrenia? *Schizophrenia Bulletin, 18,* 27–35.

Lin, K.M., and Kleinman, A.M. (1988). Psychopathology and clinical course of schizophrenia: A cross-cultural perspective. *Schizophrenia Bulletin, 14* (4), 555–567.

Lord, J., Schnarr, A., and Hutchison, P. (1987). The voice of the people: Qualitative research and the needs of consumers. *Canadian Journal of Community Mental Health, 6,* 25–36.

Lovejoy, M. (1982). Expectations and the recovery process. *Schizophrenia Bulletin, 8,* 605–609.

Lovell, A. (1997). "The city is my mother": Narratives of schizophrenia and homelessness. *American Anthropologist, 99,* 355–368.

Lunt, A. (2000). Recovery: Moving from concept toward a theory. *Psychiatric Rehabilitation Journal, 23* (4), 401–405.

MacLeod, R. (1964). Phenomenology: A challenge to experimental psychology. In T. Wann (Ed.), *Behaviorism and phenomenology* (pp. 47–78). Chicago: University of Chicago Press.

MacLeod, R.B. (1947). Can psychological research be planned on a national scale? *Canadian Journal of Psychology, 1,* 177–191.

Macnab, F. (1966). *Estrangement and relationship: Experience with schizophrenics.* Bloomington, IN: Indiana University Press.

Mayer-Gross, W. (1924). Selbstschilderungen der verwirrheit. In *Die oneiroide erlebnisform.* Berlin: Springer.

McGhie, A., and Chapman, J. (1961). Disorders of attention and perception in early schizophrenia. *British Journal of Medical Psychology, 34,* 103–116.

McGlashan, T.H. (1988). A selective review of recent North American long-term follow-up studies of schizophrenia. *Schizophrenia Bulletin, 14* (4), 515–542.

McGlashan, T.H., Carpenter, W.T., and Bartko, J.J. (1988). Issues of design and methodology in long-term follow-up studies. *Schizophrenia Bulletin, 14* (4), 569–574.

McNally, S.E. (1997). *Conversations of the mind: A qualitative analysis of schizophrenic consciousness.* Toronto, Ontario: York University Press.

Mead, S., and Copeland, M. (2000). What recovery means to us: Consumers' perspectives. *Community Mental Health Journal, 36* (3), 315–328.

Merleau-Ponty, M. (1962). *The phenomenology of perception* (C. Smith, Trans.). New York: Humanities Press.

Minkowski, E. (1927). *La schizophrenie: Psychopathologie des schizoids et des schizophrenes.* Paris: Payot.

Minkowski, E. (1970). *Lived time: Phenomenological and psychopathological studies* (N. Metzel, Trans.). Evanston, IL: Northwestern University Press.

Monahan, J. (1992). "A terror to their neighbors": Beliefs about mental disorder and violence in historical and cultural perspective. *Bulletin of the American Academy of Psychiatry and the Law, 20* (2), 191–195.

Monahan, J., and Arnold, J. (1996). Violence by people with mental illness: A consensus statement by advocates and researchers. *Psychiatric Rehabilitation Journal, 19* (4), 67–70.

Mulvey, E.P. (1994). Assessing the evidence of a link between mental illness and violence. *Hospital and Community Psychiatry, 45* (7), 663–668.

Munetz, M.R., and Frese, F.J. (2001). Getting ready for recovery: Reconciling mandatory treatment with the recovery vision. *Psychiatric Rehabilitation Journal, 25* (1), 35–42.

Munetz, M.R., Geller, J.L., and Frese, F.J. (2001). Commentary: Capacity-based involuntary outpatient treatment. *Journal of the American Academy of Psychiatry and the Law, 28* (2), 145–148.

Nasar, S. (1998). *A beautiful mind: The life of mathematical genius and Nobel laureate John Nash.* New York: Touchstone.

North, C. (1987). *Welcome, Silence.* New York: Simon and Schuster.

Orb, A., Eisenhauer, L., and Wynaden, D. (2001). Ethics in qualitative research. *Journal of Nursing Scholarship, 33* (1), 93–96.

Perlick, D. (2001). Special section on stigma as a barrier to recovery: Introduction. *Psychiatric Services, 52* (12), 1613–1614.

Pettie, D., and Triolo, A. (1999). Illness as evolution: The search for identity and meaning in the recovery process. *Psychiatric Rehabilitation Journal, 22* (3), 255–263.

Piercy, F.P., and Fontes, L.A. (2001). Teaching ethcial decision-making in qualitative research: A learning activity. *Journal of Systemic Therapies, 20* (4), 37–46.

Politzer, G. (1974). *Critique des fondements de la psychologie.* Paris: Presses Universitaires de France.

Price, J. (1996). Snakes in the swamp: Ethical issues in qualitative research. In R.

Josselson (Ed.), *Ethics and process in the narrative study of lives* (Vol. 4, p. 293). Thousand Oaks, CA: Sage Publications.

Punch, M. (1994). Politics and ethics in qualitative research. In N. Denzin and Y. Lincoln (Eds.), *Handbook of qualitative research* (pp. 83–97). Thousand Oaks, CA: Sage Publications.

Raudonis, B.M. (1992). Ethical considerations in qualitative research with hospice patients. *Qualitative Health Research, 2* (2), 238–249.

Ricoeur, P. (1966). *Freedom and nature: The voluntary and the involuntary* (E. Kohak, Trans.). Evanston, IL: Northwestern University Press.

Ridgway, P. (2001). Re-storying psychiatric disability: Learning from first-person narrative accounts of recovery. *Psychiatric Rehabilitation Journal, 24* (4), 335–343.

Rilke, R.M. (1903). *Das Stundenbuch* (R. Bly, Trans.). New York: Harper and Row.

Robinson, D.N. (1985). *Philosophy of psychology*. New York: Columbia University Press.

Rogers, J. (1995). Work is a key to recovery. *Psychosocial Rehabilitation Journal, 18* (4), 5–10.

Rowe, M. (1999). *Crossing the border: Encounters between homeless people and outreach workers*. Berkeley: University of California Press.

Rümke, H.C. (1990). The nuclear symptom of schizophrenia and the praecox feeling. *History of Psychiatry, 1,* 331–341.

Salinger, J.D. (1951). *The catcher in the rye*. Boston: Little, Brown and Company.

Sartre, J.P. (1956). *Being and nothingness* (H. Barnes, Trans.). New York: Washington Square Press.

Sass, L.A. (1987). Schreber's panopticism: Psychosis and the modern soul. *Social Research, 54,* 101–147.

Sass, L.A. (1988). The land of unreality: On the phenomenology of the schizophrenic break. *New Ideas in Psychology, 6* (2), 223–242.

Sass, L.A. (1990). The truth-taking-stare: A Heideggerian interpretation of a schizophrenic world. *Journal of Phenomenological Psychology, 21* (2), 121–149.

Scanlon, J. (1982). Empirio-criticism, descriptive psychology, and the experiential world. In J. Sallis (Ed.), *Philosophy and archaic experience* (pp. 185–192). Pittsburgh: Duquesne University Press.

Schank, R. (1982). *Dynamic memory*. New York: Cambridge University Press.

Schank, R. (1990). *Tell me a story: A new look at real and artificial memory*. New York: C. Schribner and Sons.

Schofield, W. (1964). *Psychotherapy: The purchase of friendship*. Englewood Cliffs, NJ: Prentice Hall.

Schreber, D.P. (1955). *Memoirs of my nervous illness*. London: William Dawson.

Schwartz, M., and Wiggins, O. (1987). Typifications: The first step for clinical diagnosis in psychiatry. *Journal of Nervous and Mental Disease, 175,* 65–77.

Sechehaye, M. (1951). *Autobiography of a schizophrenic girl*. New York: Grune and Stratton.

Skirboll, B.W., and Pavelsky, P.K. (1984). The Compeer Program: Volunteers as friends of the mentally ill. *Hospital and Community Psychiatry, 35* (9), 938–939.

Smith, M. (2000). Recovery from a severe psychiatric disability: Findings of a qualitative study. *Psychiatric Rehabilitation Journal, 24* (2), 149–159.

Spaniol, L., and Koehler, M. (1994). *The experience of recovery*. Boston: Center for Psychiatric Rehabilitation.

Spring, B., and Ravin, L. (1992). Cognitive remediation in schizophrenia: Should we attempt it? *Schizophrenia Bulletin, 18,* 15–20.

Stayner, D.A., Davidson, L., and Tebes, J.K. (1996). Supported partnerships: A pathway to community life for persons with serious psychiatric disabilities. *The Community Psychologist, 29,* 14–17.

Stewart, E. (2000). Thinking through others: Qualitative research and community psychology. In J. Rappaport and E. Seidman (Eds.), *Handbook of community psychology* (pp. 725–736). Dordrecht, Netherlands: Kluwer Academic Publishers.

Strauss, J.S. (1969). Hallucinations and delusions as points on continua function: Rating scale evidence. *Archives of General Psychiatry, 21* (5), 581–586.

Strauss, J.S. (1989a). Mediating processes in schizophrenia: I. Towards a new dynamic psychiatry. *British Journal of Psychiatry, 155* (Suppl 5), 22–28.

Strauss, J.S. (1989b). Subjective experiences of schizophrenia: Toward a new dynamic psychiatry: II. *Schizophrenia Bulletin, 15* (2), 179–187.

Strauss, J.S. (1992). The person—key to understanding mental illness: Towards a new dynamic psychiatry: III. *British Journal of Psychiatry, 161* (Suppl 18), 19–26.

Strauss, J.S. (1994). The person with schizophrenia as a person: II. Approaches to the subjective and complex. *British Journal of Psychiatry, 164* (Suppl 23), 103–107.

Strauss, J.S. (1996). Subjectivity. *Journal of Nervous and Mental Disease, 184* (4), 205–212.

Strauss, J.S., and Carpenter, W.T. (1974). The prediction of outcome in schizophrenia: II. Relationships between predictor and outcome variables: A report from the WHO International Pilot Study of Schizophrenia. *Archives of General Psychiatry, 31* (1), 37–42.

Strauss, J.S., and Carpenter, W.T. (1977). Prediction of outcome in schizophrenia: III. Five-year outcome and its predictors. *Archives of General Psychiatry, 34* (2), 159–163.

Strauss, J.S., and Estroff, S. (1989). Introduction. *Schizophrenic Bulletin, 15* (2).

Strauss, J.S., Hafez, H., Lieberman, P., and Harding, C.M. (1985a). "Do longitudinal principles exist?": Dr. Strauss and associates reply. *American Journal of Psychiatry, 142* (11), 1387.

Strauss, J.S., Hafez, H., Lieberman, P., and Harding, C.M. (1985b). The course of psychiatric disorder: III. Longitudinal principles. *American Journal of Psychiatry, 142* (3), 289–296.

Sullivan, W. (1994). A long and winding road: The process of recovery from severe mental illness. *Innovations and Research, 3,* 19–27.

Swick Perry, H. (1953). *Psychiatrist of America: The life of Harry Stack Sullivan.* New York: Belknap.

Tebes, J.K., and Kraemer, D.T. (1991). Quantitative and qualitative knowing in mutual support research: Some lessons from the recent history of scientific psychology. *American Journal of Community Psychology, 19* (5), 739–756.

Thornicroft, G., and Bebbington, P. (1989). Deinstitutionalisation: From hospital closure to service development. *British Journal of Psychiatry, 155,* 739–753.

Torrey, E.F., and Hafner, H. (1983). *Surviving schizophrenia: A family manual.* New York: Harper and Row.

Unger, K. (1991). Serving students with psychiatric disabilities on campus. *Journal of Postsecondary Education and Disability, 9* (4).

U.S. Surgeon General. (1999). *Mental Health: A Report of the Surgeon General.* Rockville, MD: U.S. Department of Health and Human Services, Substance Abuse and Mental Health Services Administration, Center for Mental Health Services, and National Institutes of Health, National Institute of Mental Health.

Van den Berg, J. (1982). The schizophrenic patient: Anthropological considerations. In A. de Koning and F. Jenner (Eds.), *Phenomenology and psychiatry* (pp. 155–164). London: Academic Press.

Walsh, D. (1996). A journey toward recovery: From the inside out. *Psychiatric Rehabilitation Journal, 20* (2), 85–90.

Weingarten, R. (1994). The ongoing process of recovery. *Psychiatry, 57,* 369–374.

White, W. (2000). *Toward a new recovery movement: Historical reflections on recovery, treatment, and advocacy.* www.treatment.org.

Whitwell, D. (2001). Recovery as a medical myth. *Psychiatric Bulletin, 25* (2), 75.

World Health Organization (WHO). (1973). *The international pilot study of schizophrenia.* Geneva: World Health Organization.

Wiley, J. (1989). *Precarious haven: An ethnography of a holistic therapeutic community for schizophrenics.* San Diego: University of California Press.

Williams, T. (1947). *A Streetcar Named Desire.* New York: Signet.

Wrysch, J. (1940). Uber die psychopathologie einfacher schizophrenien. *Monatsschrift fur Psychiatrie und Neurologie, 102,* 75–106.

Wrysch, J. (1942). Zur theorie und clinik der paranoiden schizophrenie. *Monatsschrift fur Psychiatrie und Neurologie, 106,* 57–101.

Young, S., and Ensing, D. (1999). Exploring recovery from the perspective of people with psychiatric disabilities. *Psychiatric Rehabilitation Journal, 22,* 219–231.

Index

About the Author

Larry Davidson, Ph.D., is Associate Professor of Psychology in the Department of Psychiatry of the Yale University School of Medicine, where he serves as Director of Behavioral Health Policy and Research; Director of the Program on Poverty, Disability, and Urban Health of the Connecticut Mental Health Center and Yale University Institution for Social and Policy Studies; and Senior Clinical Officer and Mental Health Policy Director for the Connecticut Department of Mental Health and Addiction Services.